RACE-RELATIONS IN ANCIENT EGPYT

RACE-RELATIONS
IN ANCIENT EGYPT
GREEK, EGYPTIAN, HEBREW, ROMAN

by

S. DAVIS

M.A.(Witwatersrand and Cantab.), D.Litt.(Witwatersrand)
Senior Lecturer in Classics, Hofmeyr Fellow in Classical Archaeology,
University of the Witwatersrand, Johannesburg

METHUEN & CO. LTD., LONDON
36 Essex Street, Strand, W.C.2

First published August 2nd, 1951
Reprinted 1953

1.2
CATALOGUE NO. 5325/U

PRINTED IN GREAT BRITAIN

ACKNOWLEDGEMENT

Grateful acknowledgement is made to the University of the Witwatersrand for undertaking most of the cost of publication of this book, also to the National Council of Social Research for financial assistance. Opinions expressed and conclusions reached by the writer are his sole responsibility and can in no way be regarded as representing the views of the National Council.

τὸ τῶν Ἑλλήνων ὄνομα πεποίηκε μηκέτι τοῦ γένους
ἀλλὰ τῆς διανοίας δοκεῖν εἶναι, καὶ μᾶλλον Ἕλληνας
καλεῖσθαι τοὺς τῆς ἡμετέρας ἢ τοὺς τῆς κοινῆς φύσεως
μετέχοντας.

' She (Athens) has brought it about that the name
" Hellenes " suggests no longer a race but a mental
outlook, and that the title " Hellenes " is applied
rather to those who share our culture than to those
who share a common blood.'

Isocrates, *Panegyricus*, 50.

Ἕλληνες καλοῦνται οἱ τῆς παιδεύσεως τῆς ἡμετέρας
μετέχοντες.

Inscription on the Gennadeion in Athens.

' Duas res publicas animo complectamur, alteram
magnam et vere publicam, qua dii atque homines
continentur, in qua non ad hunc angulum respicimus
aut ad illum, sed terminos civitatis nostrae cum sole
metimur; alteram, cui nos adscripsit condicio
nascendi.'

Seneca, *De Otio*, IV, 1.

CONTENTS

INTRODUCTION

THE problem of race-relationships brought about by the inter-action of races possessing different cultures and often different ideals and the possibility of a fusion of the different elements into one organic whole has long exercised the minds not only of philosophers but also of statesmen and of absolute monarchs. Since history began mankind has always shown diversity of types, peoples, races, cultures, and ideals, and probably always will do so. Yet the possibility of reconciling the aims and ideals of the different elements of human society and of obtaining some sort of unity amid a diversity that cannot be banished, however much we may try, has always existed in the minds of men. The best minds have not been content with presupposing a superior racial type or *herren-volk* to which all must bow. Such an ideal is simply a figment in the minds of a few dangerous idealists who by the vagaries of an unkind fate have gained control over powerful peoples. History proves that this ideal of racial superiority is nothing new: it has existed from time immemorial. Mankind has always had its idealists who have envisaged Utopias of different kinds, but the Utopia that has found most favour with thinking men is not that of a Utopia based on race superiority, which can never solve the problem of the diversity of man, but the Utopia which seeks to find a Unity amid the Diversity. The former may be carried into practice for a period, but is bound to be shattered on the rocks of reality—we have had countless examples of this in the past—the latter seems to be the only solution, and is the way of civilization. The problem of race-relationships is the most outstanding and interesting one confronting the world of today, and on its solution depends the fate of our civilization.

During the 19th century ' race ' was conceived by some on the basis of hastily formed biological theories, and certain qualities and characteristics were regarded as the fixed attributes of particular races. Some were regarded on this basis as superior with a promising destiny before them and others as inferior, and so doomed to servitude. Coudenhove-Kalergi,[1] for example, mentions the extremes to which racial fanaticism rose in the 19th century by the invidious contrast it made between the so-called Aryan and Semitic races. He quotes, and incidentally disproves, an anti-Semitic catechism to this effect :

> Almost all the European nations belong to the Aryan or Indo-Germanic race, while the Jews are a branch of the Semitic

[1] Count Heinrich Coudenhove-Kalergi, *Anti-Semitism through the Ages.* Hutchinson & Co., London, 1935, pp. 26 seq.

race. The Aryans are of a more settled nature; they cultivate the land, and engage in trade, cultivate art and science; they found States, are courageous and brave; the fundamental traits of their character are straightforwardness, honesty, faithfulness and devotion. They alone are the really civilized nations. The genuine Semites, on the contrary, are nomads by nature; they have neither a really lasting residence nor a proper national home. They move and march whither the best booty lures them. They neither build nor do they cultivate the land themselves, but they seek out the civilized countries created by the industry of others, exploit the existing favourable conditions, graze, so to say, the pasture places, leaving them behind waste and desolate. Agriculture, handicraft and art are alien unto them, just as is every kind of honest creative work. They pretend to despise labour, while in truth they are lacking the capacity for it."

Coudenhove-Kalergi proves beyond dispute, as many authorities have done, that the Aryans as well as the Semites are *not* a group of nations related among themselves by blood,[1] but a group of nations speaking kindred tongues. The fact of their speaking cognate languages is no proof whatever of the kinship and community of race of the nations speaking these languages. Nor do the so-called Semites differ from the so-called Aryans anthropologically,[2] for science is anything but unanimous, both on the classification and the principle of classification of the different races of humanity. The Semites themselves, as well as the Aryans, comprise a wide variety of types. The attempt to establish the differences between Semites and Aryans stigmatizing the former as an inferior race has failed lamentably. The progress of Assyriology has shown that the Semites were capable of founding large states and empires. A wider knowledge of ancient history has ' proved that the most civilized and cultured of the oldest Semitic nations were polytheistic Semitic nations who possessed a rich mythology and an Epic, namely the Nimrod Epic, that they have bequeathed to us the oldest literary

---

[1] Count Heinrich Coudenhove-Kalergi, *Anti-Semitism through the Ages*. Hutchinson & Co., London, 1935, p. 51: The grouping of nations into Aryans and Semites is based on a linguistic and philological distinction, and it is absurd to arrive at the conclusion that linguistic and philological boundaries of the two groups must also coincide anatomically. Max Müller begins his article ' Aryan ' in the *Encyclopaedia Britannica* with the words: ' Aryan is a *terminus technicus* describing one of the great language-groups extending from India to Europe.' He then goes on to say that it was Frederich Schlegel who was the first to discover the family affinity between these tongues, which he designated by the name of ' Indo-Germanic ' languages. Just as the term ' Semitic ' used by Eichorn is a purely philological one, so the term ' Indo-Germanic ' employed by Schlegel is exclusively philological. These terms had not been invented before Eichorn (1780) and Schlegel (1808)—about a century ago the world as yet knew nothing of the difference supposed to exist between Semites and Indo-Germans—and if these two scholars were to contemplate the devastations caused by their respective inventions, they would surely turn in their graves.

[2] Ibid., p. 35, cf. also pp. 55–61.

monuments, that they were capable of founding great and mighty military empires with discipline that lasted for centuries, and that they were devoted to science, while the excavations in Mesopotamia have yielded the proof that art, too, had flourished among them '.[1]

The pseudo-scientific,[2] pseudo-rationalist theories of the racialists were not in evidence before the 19th century, when the term race denoted a sum of national and social traits difficult to acquire in one generation. There were recognized differences between peoples but no impassable chasm that good-will on either side could not bridge. It was the latter point of view, and not the modern one, that classical antiquity knew. Yet, if there was no scientific jargon in ancient times on which to base and justify race superiorities and hatreds, if there was nothing like the complex racial feeling that there is today, there were nevertheless two contrasting attitudes of mind that form to some extent a parallel with modern times—the policy of race-exclusiveness and the policy of co-operation which saw in all mankind, in spite of racial differences, one vast family. It is our duty to examine both attitudes, but in doing so we must beware of transporting modern attitudes of mind to ancient times.

Among the peoples of the Ancient World that have done most to shape the basis of Western civilization as it is today we find several important contacts that were clearly defined and of far-reaching importance, which were established in Egypt, the meeting-place since the earliest times of the most diverse of peoples with their different cultures and religions. These were the contact between Greek, Egyptian, Hebrew, and Roman.

It is above all in the cosmopolitan atmosphere of the Egypt of the Hellenistic and Roman periods, in a state which provided us with the first highly centralized and bureaucratic system of administration, that we see the culmination of these various contacts, when these peoples met, were influenced by each other's culture and even came into conflict.

---

[1] Coudenhove-Kalergi, op. cit., p. 39 ; cf. pp. 249–54.
[2] Coudenhove-Kalergi, op. cit., pp. 249 seq. : ' The Aryan myth of race is untenable as a scientific thesis, because there are great civilizations, like the Japanese and the Chinese, which have neither been created nor carried on by Aryans, and which have nevertheless produced geniuses, heroes and saints of the highest degree.' Further : ' There is no proof for the superiority of the Northern Europeans over the Mediterranean peoples, of the blond over the dark-haired Europeans.'

INTRODUCTION TO SECOND EDITION

*R*ACE is used in this work in a sense different from that of the Anthropologists and more in conformity with popular opinion.

The ancient Egyptians were the first in recorded history to attempt a classification of races. On the reliefs of the Royal Tombs of the XIXth Dynasty (1314–1194 B.C.) are depicted types of mankind as they conceived them according to differences in skin-colour : red for the Egyptians, yellow for the inhabitants of Asia, black for the negroes of Africa, white for Northerners, who are shown with blue eyes and fair beards. ' Here ', says Casson, ' is the germ of racial discrimination in art. But it remains in the hands of artists only. . . . No non-artist at this time in Egypt was ever prompted to write a pamphlet on " Ye Beastlie devices of ye heathen " or on the " Dark Races of Mankind "! ' [1] Yet the Egyptians did refer to themselves as ' Rot ' or ' The Men ', and to other peoples as coloured imitations of them, but this was not necessarily a ' racial ' attitude in the anthropological sense of the word. It was an ' in-group ' attitude of mind which can be paralleled in other parts of the world, both in ancient and modern times. Throughout the world it is a common phenomenon for a tribal unit, however small it might be, to call itself ' The Men ', as, for example, ' Zuñi ' in California and ' Bantu ' or ' Kung ' (Bushmen) in South Africa. [2] Others outside the tribe are ' the not-human ' with whom the tribe has no common cause and who may be hunted like animals. ' Such a primitive in-group is not a race, not even a small local sub-race or breed. The smallest racial unit is usually split up into many mutually death-dealing in-groups. Their antagonism is not " racial " but cultural.' [3]

According to some authorities there is only one race, the Human race.

> ' I would prefer to say that our study of man and his diffusion first over the Old and later over the New World clearly indicates that all living men belong to one race, the human race, and that whatever physical or cultural differences may have arisen during the long process of diffusion, and in whatever sense biologists may use the term *race*, the essential one-ness of the human race cannot be disputed.' [4]

[1] S. Casson, *The Discovery of Man*, Hamish Hamilton, London, 1939, p. 17.

[2] M. D. W. Jeffreys, in *S. African Journal of Science*, vol. 49, nos. 3–4, 1952, and in ' The Peoples of S. Africa', *Annual of S. Africa*, 1950–1, p. 8.

[3] R. Benedict, *Race and Racism*, Routledge and Kegan Paul, London, 1951, p. 100.

[4] C. van Riet Lowe, Prehistory and the Humanities, *South African Journal of Science*, vol. 47 (1950), p. 6.

Mankind in fact does not 'include a series of fully developed species the proper criterion for which was, according to Darwin, sterility or the production of sterile offspring if they were crossed.' [1] Others have defined *race* biologically as a term descriptive of a group who have certain physical characteristics in common, thus following the example set by the ancient Egyptians. Such characteristics today are listed as : Skin colour, Eye colour and Eye form, Hair colour and Hair form, Shape of the Nose, Stature, Cephalic Index, and Blood grouping. Yet several of these characteristics are held in common by, and some do not even distinguish between, the Caucasian (white), Mongoloid (yellow), and Negroid (black) varieties of mankind into which as *races* they classify man today.

> ' No one doubts that the groups called Caucasoid, Mongoloid, and Negroid each represent a long history of anatomical special-ization in different areas of the world ; but great numbers of individuals cannot be assigned to one or another of these races on the basis even of several of the above criteria.' [2]

Furthermore

> ' Racial heredity in Western Civilization is a myth which sets up, in place of true heredity in family lines, an absurd picture of heredity from a race. *Race* is an abstraction even as it is defined by a geneticist ; as it is defined statistically by a physical anthropologist it is even more of an abstraction.' [3]

A great deal of confusion about race comes from confusing hereditary traits, especially colour, with traits that are socially acquired. Language, for example, is not hereditary, but learned behaviour and the sociological term for man's learned behaviour is culture. [4] That learned behaviour or culture is restricted to any one section of humanity because they are white or yellow, tall or short, long-headed or short-headed is a myth that has constantly been exploded. [5] Again, the mere isolation or measurement of racial differences in the biological sense does not indicate either superior or inferior mental qualities. That outward or even internal physical qualities go hand in hand with intelligence is not proven. The natural differences between such biological races are actually in-significant as compared with the natural differences between in-dividuals, without regard to race or colour as intelligence tests have shown. [6] Race, as interpreted biologically by the anthropologists, may be a satisfactory term from the point of view of measuring

[1] Benedict, op. cit., p. 22.
[2] Idem, op. cit., p. 28.
[3] Idem, op. cit., p. 50.
[4] A. L. Krober, *Anthropology*, Harrap, London, 1948, p. 8.
[5] S. Davis, Planning from a Multi-Racial Aspect, *S. African Journal of Science*, vol. 47, 1951, p. 334.
[6] O. Klineberg, *Race Differences*, Harper and Bros., New York, 1935, p. 342. Benedict, op. cit., p. 78. R. Firth, *Human Types*, Nelson and Sons, London, 1943, p. 37.

physical differences, but such a view is not the whole matter—it does not of itself explain antagonisms and repulsions between one people and another. An adequate explanation of these can be found in impulses and motives that are independent of race as so interpreted. Antagonisms have arisen between peoples of the same biological race and between classes of the same race without any thought of such a connotation of ' race '. In modern times such antagonisms, which in the past may have been actuated by religious, political, commercial, or other motives, have been disguised under the form of, or accentuated by a realization of colour difference, and false pseudo-scientific doctrines which will not stand the test of close examination have been based thereon. Ultimately most antagonisms, if not all, can be attributed to cultural differences. Thus, since an interpretation which covers a vaster field and gives more adequate reasons for conflicts between different peoples is desirable, the term ' race ' is used in this book as applicable to a group with common cultural features, not in a biological sense, and in a much more general way than the anthropologist's division of mankind into three ' biological groups '.

The concept of *race*, as a biologically inbred group possessing physical traits that tend to breed true from generation to generation, was unknown to the ancients. Hatred, ideas of superiority or inferiority, prejudice against mixed marriages or against colour, and exclusiveness were not in the ancient world based on *race* in the anthropologist's sense of the word, but on its general sense as connoting differences in origin, culture, and ideology.

The history of inter-relations between one people or group and another is, however, not merely one of friction. *Acculturation*, the effect exercised on cultures by contact with others, is always at work. Examples of it can be quoted in the Hellenization of the Romans in Italy during the two or three centuries following 270 B.C.[1] and in the Romanization of the barbarian hinterland to the north-west of the Mediterranean area from the 1st century B.C. onwards. It is a process that has influenced the course of our civilization, and is still at work in the more backward societies of today.[2]

It has been the aim of this work not only to describe the intensification of antagonisms and antipathies and their interplay but also to stress this process of acculturation in the cultural contacts in Ancient Egypt between Greek, Egyptian, Hebrew, and Roman. This has influenced the course of our development no less than the better-known Romanization of a large part of Europe in ancient times.

[1] Krober, A. L., op. cit., p. 427.
[2] Cf. Lowie, R. H., *Primitive Society*, Routledge, 1921, p. 427. ' Cultures develop mainly through the borrowings due to chance contact. Our own civilization is even more largely than the rest a complex of borrowed traits . . . the specious plea that a given people must pass through such or such a stage in *our* history before attaining this or that destination can no longer be sustained.'

CORRECTIONS AND ADDITIONS

p. 27, line 33   *for* ' such figure ' *read* ' such a figure '.

p. 30, line 1   *for* ' battle ' *read* ' battles '.

p. 35, line 12   *for* ' Darius ' *read* ' Artaxerxes III '.

p. 43, line 24   *for* ' Ptolemias ' *read* ' Ptolemais '.

p. 81   At end of note 4 *add* : W. F. Albright, *Archaeology of Palestine* (Penguin Books), London, 1949, p. 109.

p. 83   Note 13, *add* : For Egyptian influence on the Bible, e.g. The Teaching of Amen-em-ope' on Proverbs, Psalms, and Deuteronomy, cf. *Legacy of Egypt*, ed. S. R. K. Glanville, Oxford, 1947, pp. 67–79, 240–8. It may also be detected in Psalm civ (cf. Hymn of Akhenaton to the Sun), Job, Ecclesiastes, Wisdom of Ben Sirach, Tobit, Esdras III, Song of Songs, Jeremiah, Story of Achikar. Cf. *Legacy of Egypt*, p. 70, A. Erman, *The Literature of the Ancient Egyptians*, Methuen, London, 1927, p. xxvii and J. H. Breasted, *The Dawn of Conscience*, Scribner's, New York, 1944, pp. 345–88.

p. 169   *Add to* IV. Periodicals, *South African Journal of Science*.

pp. 169–70   *Add, under* VI. Modern Works :

Albright, W. F.   *The Archaeology of Palestine*, Penguin Books, London, 1949.

Benedict, R.   *Race and Racism*, Routledge and Kegan Paul, London, 1951.

Breasted, J. H.   *The Dawn of Conscience*, C. Scribner's Sons, New York, 1944.

Casson, S.   *The Discovery of Man*, Hamish Hamilton, London, 1939.

Erman, A.   *The Literature of the Ancient Egyptians*, trans. A. M. Blackman, Methuen, London, 1927.

Firth, R.   *Human Types*, Nelson and Sons, London, 1943.

Klineberg, O.   *Race Differences*, Harper and Bros., New York, 1935.

Krober, A. L.   *Anthropology*, Harcourt, Brace and Co., New York, 1948.

Glanville, S. R. K.   *Legacy of Egypt, Essays*, Oxford, 1947.

Lowie, R. H.   *Primitive Society*, Routledge, London, 1921.

Schofield, J. N.   *The Historical Background of the Bible*, Nelson and Sons, London, 1938.

PART I

CHAPTER I

GREEK EXCLUSIVENESS AND THE POLITICAL IDEALS OF ALEXANDER THE GREAT

IN Greek literature of the Classical Age it is a commonplace to find a distinction made between Greek and Barbarian. Yet this primary Greek distinction had not been fully formed in Homer's time. The Trojans were not felt to be fundamentally different from the Achaeans.[1] A Greek was one whose speech was intelligible to other Greeks—all others were barbarians,[2] 'jabberers'. The term βαρβαρόφωνος [3] could be applied to them. The sense of national unity among the different Greek tribes may to some extent have arisen in the great movement against the common foe that the *Iliad* tells of, but there is nothing to show that any real feeling of common origin and responsibility existed at that time.[4] The first realization of national unity came with the first real, great national danger, the Persian invasions, and thus it was in the 5th and 4th centuries B.C. that the concept of a Greek race first received a real outline and the feeling of a common race-pride became highly developed.[5]

The Greeks were not indifferent to the races about them—no

[1] Archaeological investigations have proved that as regards civilization Troy was in no way behind that of mainland Greece. On the contrary, there are striking resemblances. The architecture, for example, of Troy II, c. 2200 B.C. resembles that of Mycenae and Tiryns. The early μέγαρον type of building is found at Troy as well as at Mycenae and Tiryns, and was the predecessor of the Greek Doric temple. The Achaeans, whatever the date of their entrance into Greece, must have enjoyed a type of civilization similar to that of the Trojans and felt themselves much less apart from them than the Greeks of the Classical Age from the Persians. The general impression to-day seems to be that the Trojans were northerners, just as the Achaeans were.

[2] Cf. Herod. ii. 158 : βαρβάρους δὲ πάντας οἱ Αἰγύπτιοι καλέουσι μὴ σφίσι ὁμογλώσσους. For ' barbaros ' generally see Haarhoff, *The Stranger at the Gate*, Longmans, Green & Co., 1938, pp. 6 and 7. Stages in the Greek attitude to non-Greeks can be traced. The word βάρβαρος originally meant one who speaks an unintelligible language, and, as such, it had no derogatory implication. The word was next used undisparagingly to mean ' foreign ', and then later it acquired a contemptuous meaning.

[3] Homer, *Iliad*, ii. 867.

[4] Cf. Thuc. i. 3, who adduces Homer to prove the name Ἕλληνες is late : πολλῷ γὰρ ὕστερον ἔτι καὶ τῶν Τρωικῶν γενόμενος οὐδαμοῦ τοὺς ξύμπαντας ὠνόμασεν οὐδ' ἄλλους ἢ τοὺς μετὰ Ἀχιλλέως ἐκ τῆς Φθιώτιδος, οἵπερ καὶ πρῶτοι Ἕλληνες ἦσαν, Δαναοὺς δὲ ἐν τοῖς ἔπεσι καὶ Ἀργείους καὶ Ἀχαιοὺς ἀνακαλεῖ. οὐ μὴν οὐδὲ βαρβάρους εἴρηκε διὰ τὸ μηδὲ Ἕλληνάς πω, ὡς ἐμοὶ δοκεῖ, ἀντίπαλον ἐς ἓν ὄνομα ἀποκεκρίσθαι.

[5] Herod. viii. 144 : τὸ Ἑλληνικὸν ἐὸν ὅμαιμόν τε καὶ ὁμόγλωσσον καὶ θεῶν ἱδρύματά τε κοινὰ καὶ θυσίαι ἤθεά τε ὁμότροπα, τῶν προδότας γενέσθαι Ἀθηναίους οὐκ ἂν ἔχοι.

people were more eager for curious tales of out-of-the-way peoples. But it was natural that in beating back the greatest empire then known they should believe they were the superiors of other peoples, and from this many other corollaries followed.[1] Moreover, the contrast between their own comparatively liberal forms of government and the despotic, illiberal domination of the peoples they came into contact with could not be ignored.   In Euripides we meet the declaration : ' It accords with the fitness of things that barbarians should be subject to Greeks, for Greeks are free men and barbarians are slaves by nature '.[2] We find this idea of the inferiority of non-Greeks also in Herodotus where ' barbaros ' is occasionally used with a derogatory implication,[3] and often as a synonym for Persian,[4] and not always in the neutral sense of non-Greek.   The theory of the inferiority of the barbarians became accentuated during and after the Persian Wars.   In the 4th century it was a dogma that was accepted throughout the Greek world and one which was firmly held by men like Aristotle and Isocrates.   In the eyes of the Greeks the barbarians were not only foreigners, but inferior beings :   between Greek and barbarian, says Isocrates, there is no less difference than between man and beast.[5]

The superiority of the Greeks gave them rights :   it was natural and just that Barbarians should obey them as slaves obeyed freemen.[6] Between them no friendship was possible, but there must be eternal war.[7] Passages illustrative of this view of the Greeks from the 5th century onwards could be multiplied, but a few examples are sufficient to point out the general attitude of the Greeks to other races before Alexander.

The term ' barbaros ' is sometimes used and sometimes carefully avoided by Greeks in reference to Macedonians.   In antiquity one party held that they were Hellenes, as did the Macedonians them-

---

[1] It is to be noted that the Ionians of the coastlands of Asia Minor were less inclined to erect racial or national barriers, being, as they were, more in contact with other races and civilizations and more open to influence.   Moreover, they had greater opportunities for travel all over the East.   The Sophists, too, with their tendency to upset by their teachings traditional doctrines and ideas, developed a more liberal attitude.

[2] Eur. Iph. In Aulide, 1400–1 : βαρβάρων δ' ῞Ελληνας ἄρχειν εἰκὸς, ἀλλ' οὐ βαρβάρους . . . ῾Ελλήνων· τὸ μὲν γὰρ δοῦλον, οἱ δ' ἐλεύθερον.   In Euripides these are the views of average Greeks of the time, not necessarily of the poet himself or of other enlightened minds.   Cf. Eur. Troades, 764 : ὢ βάρβαρ' ἐξευρόντες ῞Ελληνες κακά.   Apparently Greeks are no better than barbarians, and are painted in a bad light in this play.   Cf. Aristotle, Pol. i. ii.

[3] Herod. vii. 35 : Ξέρξης . . . τὸν ῾Ελλήσποντον . . . ἐνετέλλετο ῥαπίζοντας λέγειν βάρβαρά τε καὶ ἀτασθάλα.   Cf. viii. 142 : ὡς βαρβάροισι ἐστι οὔτε πιστὸν οὔτε ἀληθὲς οὐδέν.   Herodotus too gives the view of the average Greek.   He has been blamed for being philo-barbarian (Plutarch, De malignitate Herodoti, 12) owing to the impartiality of his history.

[4] In relation to the Hellenes he speaks of the Persians as Barbarians, in relation to other nations as Persae.

[5] Isocr. xv. 293.

[6] Eur. Androm. 665–7 ; Aristotle, Pol. I. i. 5 ; Isocr. Pan. 181 ; Dem. In Mid. 48 (xx. 530).

[7] Eur. Hec. 1199–1201 ; Livy xxxi. 29.

selves. The alternative view that they were ' barbaroi ' was for the most part a product of 4th century Athenian politics.[1] It is likely that the political opponents of Macedon accused the Macedonians of being ' barbaroi ', owing to the relatively backward state of their culture as compared with their own.

Certainly, in the 5th century both Herodotus and Thucydides regarded the ruling element among them as racially Greeks. Herodotus, moreover, classes Persians, Lydians, Scythians, and Thracians together as barbarians,[2] but nowhere does he call the Macedonians barbarians, nor does Thucydides, though he does not openly call them Hellenes.

According to tradition, the population of Macedonia had neither one source nor one history ; for one element in it was ' barbarian ', another Hellene. The first element was called Pelasgic,[3] a term applied to any early people of doubtful origin who had lived where in later times Hellenes were found. The other element was held to be Hellenic—a belief which is encountered in the legends of the migrations of ' Macedonian ' peoples from Greece, such as Bottiaeans from Crete,[4] and Dorians from Histiaeotis in Thessaly [5] or Argos.[6] Indeed, it was on the strength of the belief that the last-named city was the earliest home of the Macedonian kings and their immediate followers that the Macedonian kings obtained admission to the common festivals of Greece.[7]

Thus to the second element the dominant race in Macedonia, the Macedonians properly so called, belonged. They were, in Greek opinion, an immigrant people from the south whose ' leader conquered land for his subjects and became king '.[8] They settled in the fertile plains on the lower courses of the Haliakmon and Vardar (Pieria and Emathia) and pushed the older peoples (Orestians, Lyncestians, Elimiotes, and Paeonians) into the western and northern highlands.[9] The belief that the ' Macedonians ' of the coast-plains and the men of the hills were distinct peoples with distinct traditions

---

[1] Hogarth, *Philip and Alexander*, p. 5, note 4 ; Casson, *Macedonia, Thrace, and Illyria*, p. 158.
[2] Herod. ix. 75.
[3] Cf. e.g. Justin, vii. 1. Cf. How and Wells, *A Commentary on Herodotus*, Appendix XV, where a clear distinction is drawn between the actual Pelasgi and the theoretic extension of the name to denote a stage in Greek civilization. The Pelasgi in Macedonia were probably composed largely of an Aryan race, to which the Bryges and many other European tribes belonged, whose final home was Phrygia. They were, nevertheless, in the eyes of the Greeks ' barbarians '. In Bk. ii. 56 of his history Herodotus even calls the Athenians a Pelasgian nation, but the Spartans he terms a Dorian and Hellenic nation. Yet the main distinction between Greek and barbarian must have been one of culture.
[4] Place-names like Gortynia, Idomenaea, are found in historical times in the Vardar valley. Cf. Strabo, pp. 279, 282, 330 ; Plut. *Thes.* 16 (quoting Aristotle).
[5] Herod. in i. 56, calls this race Μακεδνόν.
[6] Ibid. v. 22 ; viii. 137 ; Thuc. ii. 99 ; Isocr. *Phil.* 32 ; Theopomp., fr. 30 ; Justin, vii. 1 ; Strabo, p. 239 ; Paus. vii. 8, 9 ; Appian, *Syr.* 63 ; Diod. xvii. 1. Plut. *Alex.* 2.
[7] Cf. Herod. v. 22.   [8] Cf. Thuc. ii. 89.
[9] Strabo, p. 330 ; cf. also Justin, vii. 1.

was held not only in Greece, but in Macedonia as well.[1] Under Alexander I, and later under Philip II, the process of conquest was completed and the two elements were combined into one strong nation.

In the 5th century both Herodotus and Thucydides agree in tracing the descent of the Macedonian kings from Temenos of Argos. In Herodotus, Alexander, son of Amyntas king of the Macedonians at the time of the Persian Wars, bids the Persian envoys ' report to the king who sent you that a Greek, the prince of the Macedonians, gave you a good reception '.[2]

On the eve of Plataea, Alexander, who is now king, tells the Greek generals : ' I myself am by ancient descent a Greek, and I would not willingly see Hellas change her freedom for slavery.' [3] Herodotus, who exaggerates the phil-Hellenism of Alexander, insists on his Hellenic lineage :

' That these princes, who are sprung from Perdiocas, are Greeks, as they themselves affirm, I myself happen to know : and in a future part of my history I will prove that they are Greeks.' [4]

His proofs depend on the family legend,[5] and the verdict of the judges at Olympia when this same Alexander claimed admission as a Greek, a verdict probably based on the legend.[6] Thucydides, too, says :

' The country on the sea-coast now called Macedonia, was first acquired by Alexander, the father of Perdiccas, and his ancestors, originally Temenids from Argos.' [7]

Most of the later authors also accept the legendary origin of the Macedonian kings, though with some variations.[8] Whether the legendary story is true or not is not so important ; what really matters

---

[1] Cf. e.g. Arrian, iii. 18, 20, 23, with vii. 4; & Plut. *Eum.* 4. The clearest distinction is always drawn between ' Macedonians ' and all other components of the national phalanx in the Asiatic army of Alexander, Cf. also J. B. Bury, *A History of Greece*, Macmillan, London, 1902, p. 683.

[2] Herod. v. 20.

[3] Ibid. ix. 45 : αὐτός τε γὰρ Ἕλλην γένος εἰμὶ τωρχαῖον καὶ ἀντ᾽ ἐλευθέρης δεδουλω- μένην οὐκ ἂν ἐθέλοιμι ὁρᾶν τὴν Ἑλλάδα.

[4] Ibid. v. 22 : Ἕλληνας δὲ εἶναι τούτους τοὺς ἀπὸ Περδίκκεω γεγονότας, κατά περ αὐτοὶ λέγουσι, αὐτός τε οὕτω τυγχάνω ἐπιστάμενος καὶ δὴ καὶ ἐν τοῖς ὄπισθε λόγοισι ἀποδέξω ὡς ἐισὶ Ἕλληνες.

[5] Ibid. viii. 137.

[6] Ibid. v. 22 : πρὸς δὲ καὶ οἱ τὸν ἐν Ὀλυμπίῃ διέποντες ἀγῶνα Ἑλληνοδίκαι οὕτω ἔγνωσαν εἶναι. Ἀλεξάνδρον γὰρ ἀεθλεύειν ἑλομένου καὶ καταβάντος ἐπ᾽ αὐτὸ τοῦτο ἐξείργον μιν, φάμενοι οὐ βαρβάρων ἀγωνιστέον εἶναι τὸν ἀγῶνα ἀλλὰ Ἑλλήνων· Ἀλέξανδρος δὲ ἐπειδὴ ἀπέδειξε ὡς εἴη Ἀργεῖος, ἐκρίθη τε εἶναι Ἕλλην καὶ ἀγωνιζόμενος στάδιον συνεξέπιπτε τῷ πρώτῳ.

[7] Thuc. ii. 99 ; cf. v. 80.

[8] In the 4th century another account was current, probably derived from Theopompus (fr. 30, *F.H.G.* i. p. 283 ; cf. Justin, vii. 1 ; Diod. vii. fr. 17 ; Euphor- ion, fr. 24 ; Vell. *Paterculus*, i. 65), that Caranus, son or brother of the Argive king, Pheidon, was the founder of the Macedonian dynasty.

is that it was a generally accepted account among the Greeks of the 5th century, and even later, of the origins of the Macedonians, and, as such, must have influenced the Greek attitude towards them.[1] It is significant too that during the conquests of Alexander the Great and later both Greek and Macedonian found little difference between one another's culture, outlook, and language.[2]

In the 5th century the belief in the Hellenic origin of one element of the Macedonian people was not seriously questioned.   The kings of Macedon, too, made a bid for Greek support.   Alexander I, as has been mentioned, was a competitor in the stadium of Olympia,

[1] S. Casson, in *Macedonia, Thrace,* and *Illyria,* Oxford, 1926, pp. 159 seq., discusses the philological and archaeological evidence that seems to confirm the main outlines of the traditional story. Hoffman (*Die Makedonen,* 1906, p. 259) and Hatzidakis (*Zur Abstammung der alten Makedonen* 1897) both maintain on philological grounds that the Macedonians were Hellenic in stock and origin. Hoffman says, ' The last word on the subject is preserved in the remains of the Macedonian dialect ' (preface).   He remarks that the famous letters of Alexander the Great, whether false or not, contain not one trace of a Macedonian language ; that all extant inscriptions of Alexander are in pure Greek, and that the strata of the dialect which preserve domestic words contain a preponderance of pure Greek. The names of true-born Macedonians, above all those of princes and nobles, are pure Greek.   They show a colouring of dialect, however, and are related to Thessalian names.   Macedonian was a Greek dialect.   Casson himself deduces from the archaeological evidence that suddenly about the 11th century a new and more vigorous people, not necessarily of a different stock, but essentially of a different type of culture, displaced, but did not quite exterminate, the so-called Phrygians of the Bronze Age in north-west and central Greece (cf. the double-pottery tradition in the cemetery of Chauchitsa), and brought with them the Iron Age.   After this people had passed on southwards some of the same stock returned to Macedonia from Thessaly.   This event coincides with the first recorded fact in Macedonian history—the arrival from the south of their dynasty, who pushed back the tribes of the Haliakmon and Vardar valleys and took over control of these areas.   This took place between the first arrival from the north of the Iron Age people and the appearance of the first historical monarch Alexander I.   Later the invaders—the Macedonians or Argeadai, as they were called (who perhaps called themselves Makednoi, Strabo, 329, fr. ii ; Herod. i 56 ; vii. 43), extended their domination in two moves recorded in history.   The three advances of the ruling tribe were :—

1. From Thessaly and Pindos into the plains at the foot of Olympus of the Haliakmon valley *c.* 850–750 B.C. (a century being allowed for the sojourn of the original Iron Age people in Macedonia and their subsequent passage south).
2. From the Haliakmon to the Vardar valley and west of it—a move attributed by Thucydides (ii. 99) to ' Alexander I and his ancestors ' : *c.* 600–500 B.C.
3. From the Vardar to the Struma valley, representing an extension by Alexander I of his domain, enabling him to seize and work the silver-mines of Dysoron (Herod. v, 17) after 480.

Thus, according to Casson, history and archaeology are not at variance.   Another view which Casson's theory seems wholly to refute is that given in How and Wells' *Commentary to Herodotus on Herod,* viii. 37, that the likeness of the name Argos (Argos Oresticum near the source of the Haliakmon, cf. Strabo 326, *Steph. Byz.*) led the Macedonian kings from the time of Alexander I to claim descent from the Heraclid kings of Peloponnesian Argos.

[2] Cf. Bevan, *A History of Egypt under the Ptolemaic Dynasty,* Methuen, London, 1927, p. 83.   Men of Macedonian origin in Ptolemaic Egypt were to all intents and purposes Greeks, and though many papyri were written by people calling themselves Macedonians ' no one has ever found a papyrus in the Macedonian language '.

and earned the epithet ' Philhellene ', like Amasis of Egypt later, and on the night before Plataea actually proclaimed himself to the generals their friend and a Greek.

Archelaus patronized Athenian poets and Athenian drama, and commissioned Euripides to dramatize the deeds of his Argive ancestor, and it was in Macedonia that Euripides drew inspiration for his Bacchae.[1] Even the later kings maintained alliances with Greek states and made efforts to introduce Greek civilization into their land. In the 4th century Greek opinion seens to have hardened, and this Demosthenes seems largely to reflect, if he is not himself to blame for it. He stigmatizes Philip as ' not only no Greek and no way akin to Greeks, but not even a barbarian of a place honourable to mention ; in fact a vile fellow of Macedon ' (ὀλέθρου Μακεδόνος).[2]

The reasons for such taunts from a hostile orator like Demosthenes were most probably the danger to the independence of the free Greek city-states that the ominous advance of Macedon represented, and moreover the fact that Philip actually did exercise rule over many barbarians.

Yet even in the 4th century men like Isocrates,[3] and those belonging to the Pro-Macedonian party, adopted an outlook that, in contrast to that of Demosthenes, appears to some authorities to have been the saner.

Isocrates seems to have aimed at freeing the Greeks from the narrow circle of the city-state and at forming a wider pan-Hellenic world. He had no thought of merging the individuality or the independence of the Greek states in the sovereignty of a Greek empire, but had rather in mind the Delian League in its early days before Athens had turned it into an empire maintained by force ; and what he dreamed of was a great confederacy of free states voluntarily united under a single leadership, in the cause of a final and decisive war against their common enemy, the Persian Empire.[4] Others had held the idea before Isocrates—for instance, Gorgias at the Olympic festival in 408, and Lysias in 384 [5]—but with Isocrates it was more like a religious principle than an idea. In his *Panegyricus* of 384 he turned to Athens, as the mother of civilization and free institutions, to take the lead in the campaign against the barbarians. Yet in his *Address to Philip*, c. 346, he calls upon the King of Macedon, an absolute ruler of an uncultivated race, whom Demosthenes, as we have seen, denounced as a barbarian, and an

[1] The plays of Euripides called ' Archelaos ' and ' Alexander ' had certainly a didactic and propagandist purpose. Moreover, the appearance of the head of Heracles on Archelaus' coins is most probably a reference to the mythical ancestor of the Macedonian kings, who traced their descent back, as has been seen, to the Heraclid Temenos (Herod. viii. 138, Thuc. ii. 99). Isocrates bases his great appeal to Philip on this fact (Philippus 109 ff.) Seltman, however (*Greek Coins*, Methuen, 1933, p. 198), ascribes the introduction of the Head of Heracles to Amyntas III (389–369 B.C.).
[2] Dem. Phil. iii. 31 ; Cf. Phil. i. 10 ; Olynth. iii. 24 ; F. L. 327.
[3] Isocr. *Philip.*, 109, seq. ; cf. 32.   [4] Isocr. *Paneg.* 80, 81.
[5] Philostratus, *Vit. Soph.* i. 9. 4.

enemy of Greece, to undertake what he now conceives that neither Athens nor any other Greek state can do—to reconcile the quarrels of Greece and lead her against the common enemy.[1] Philip had announced his ambition to be ' captain-general of Hellas in a war against the Persians ' ; [2] he had by this time proved those qualities of leadership which made him one of the great figures of history. Shortly after the publication of Isocrates' address to him, he was elected a member of the Amphicytonic Council and given the presidency of the Pythian Games—a signal recognition of his paramount influence in Greek affairs.

Isocrates had a great admiration for him, and believed that he was friendly to Athens. He regarded him as a pure Hellene of the line of Heracles,[3] as a man of education and culture,[4] and as a lover of Hellas with high ideals and a broad vision [5]—a judgement which is supported by historians who do not echo the views of Demosthenes.[6] To Isocrates Philip was to be the leader of a confederacy of free states only. There was, indeed, no thought of surrendering the independence of Greek states to an imperial Power, any more in the *Letter to Philip* than previously there had been in the *Panegyricus*. But matters turned out differently. Demosthenes and the war party in Athens prevailed and forced the issue : the result was the battle of Chaeronea and the subjection by force of the Greek states to the overlordship of the Macedonian king.

Bury [7] puts it well when he locates the reason why, in spite of Isocrates' sane and practical view of the situation, co-operation with Macedon was doomed to failure—it was the old feeling of exclusiveness reviving.

> ' Macedon was regarded in Hellas as an outsider. This was a feeling which the southern Greeks entertained even in regard to Thessaly when Jason threatened them with a Thessalian hegemony ; and Macedonia, politically and historically and as well as geographically, was some steps further away than Thessaly. If Thessaly was hardly inside the inner circle of Hellenic politics, Macedonia was distinctly outside it. To Athens and Sparta, to Corinth and Argos and Thebes, the old powers, who, as we might say, had known each other all their lives as foes or friends, and had a common international history, the Supremacy of Macedonia seemed the supremacy of an upstart. And, in the second place, this supremacy was the triumph of an absolute monarchy over free commonwealths, so that the submission of the Greek states to Macedon's king might be rhetorically branded as an enslavement to a tyrant in

---

[1] Isocr. Philip. 41.
[2] Holm, *History of Greece*, iii. 245 ; Hogarth, *Philip and Alexander of Macedon*, p. 97; Diodorus, XVI. 60.
[3] Isocr. *Philip*, 76, 32–4 ; 105.   [4] Ibid. 29.   [5] Ibid. 132.
[6] Holm, *History of Greece*, iii. ch. 19 ; Bury, *History of Greece*, ii. chap. 6; Hogarth, *Philip and Alexander of Macedon*.
[7] Bury, *A History of Greece*, Macmillan, 1902, p. 731.

a sense in which subjection to a sovereign Athens or a sovereign Sparta could not be so described.' [1]

The Greek attitude of exclusiveness to other peoples has been described—an attitude which as regards the half-Greek Macedonians underwent some limitations, but did not differ in its essentials. Just as a Xerxes could make the Greeks realize the gulf that separated Greek and Persian, so Philip could make Demosthenes emphasize what difference there was culturally, if not racially, between Greek and Macedonian—a difference, however, that was destined to be bridged by Philip's son Alexander.

An attitude of mind totally different from the exclusiveness just described was brought about by the conquests of Alexander the Great and the inauguration of the Hellenistic Age. The situation created by Alexander's conquest of the East has frequently been compared with that which resulted in the discovery of America, a new world being opened up to the economic enterprise of the old. [2] Rostovtzeff points out how misleading this statement can be. [3] The East was well known to Greece at least as early as the 5th and 4th centuries, and was a world of long-established civilization and of highly developed economic activity.

'Alexander did not discover a new, hitherto unknown world; nor did he throw open to the Greeks a no-man's land, or conquer a country whose barbarian inhabitants were then gradually exterminated in spite of a hopeless resistance.'

The conquest of the East was quite different in its political, social, and economic results from the discovery of America. Alexander's achievements were quite different from those of Columbus. He created a Greco-Oriental empire, and thus succeeded in carrying out a plan which for centuries had been the dream of the Persian kings—that of unifying under a single rule the whole of the eastern part of the Mediterranean world. Political unification was his principal achievement, if not his principal aim. It is true to say with Tarn that

'Alexander was one of the supreme fertilising forces of history. He lifted the civilized world out of one groove and

---

[1] Cf. Dem. *Phil.* iii. 30: καὶ μὴν κἀκεῖνο γ᾽ ἴστε, ὅτι ὅσα μὲν ὑπὸ Λακεδαιμονίων ἢ ὑφ᾽ ἡμῶν ἔπασχον οἱ Ἕλληνες, ἀλλ᾽ οὖν ὑπὸ γνησίων γ᾽ ὄντων τῆς Ἑλλάδος ἠδικοῦντο, καὶ τὸν αὐτὸν τρόπον ἄν τις ὑπέλαβε τοῦθ᾽ ὥσπερ ἂν εἰ υἱὸς ἐν οὐσίᾳ πολλῇ γεγονὼς γνήσιος διώκει τι μὴ καλῶς μηδ᾽ ὀρθῶς, κατ᾽ αὐτὸ μὲν τοῦτ᾽ ἄξιον μέμψεως εἶναι καὶ κατηγορίας, ὡς δ᾽ οὐ προσήκων ἢ ὡς οὐ κληρονόμος τούτων ὢν ταῦτ᾽ ἐποίει, οὐκ ἐνεῖναι λέγειν.

[2] U. Wilcken, *Alexander der Grosse und die hellenistische Wirtschaft*, p. 50. J. B. Bury in article 'The Hellenistic Age and the History of Civilization', in *The Hellenistic Age*, Cambridge, 1923, p. 4, and Tarn in *C.A.H.* vi. 432, seem to have been influenced by Wilcken's parallel.

[3] M. Rostovtzeff, *The Social and Economic History of the Hellenistic World*, Oxford, 1941, i. 127. The only resemblance Rostovtzeff can see between the discovery of America and Alexander's conquest of the East is the increased amount of gold and silver subsequently put into circulation in western Europe and Greece, respectively.

set it in another : he started a new epoch ; nothing could again be as it had been '.[1]

It is the political ideals, however, of Alexander and their effect on the new world of the Hellenistic era that to-day possess for us a far greater appeal than the long list of his conquests which brought about that new phase in the history of mankind. The contrast between the ideas of Aristotle and those of Alexander has often been pointed out. Although, as his tutor, Aristotle must have inspired him with a passionate love of Greek culture and ideals, in the political sphere the two men later pursued completely different paths. Aristotle represented the old attitude of mind. Aristotle's defence of slavery [2] and his justification of war against the barbarian as natural [3] are well known. He even advised his pupil to treat the Greeks as friends and relations, but the barbarians as plants and animals.[4] Furthermore, he is in agreement with Plato that in war Greeks should not be subject to enslavement : that is the natural lot of the barbarian.[5] Wilcken [6] assumes that Alexander was more in agreement with the advice with which Isocrates concludes his *Philip*, that Philip should free the barbarians from barbarian despotism and entrust them to Hellenic care and protection. It seems clear, however, from Alexander's consolidation of his empire, that in his treatment of the peoples who came under his rule he gave expression to a policy that was diametrically opposed to that of Aristotle and other philosophers—and one which has secured him the admiration of subsequent generations to a much greater extent than all his territorial conquests.

It was Alexander's desire to fuse the peoples under his rule in a common polity and culture which were to be Hellenic. Wilcken claims that he aimed only at a fusion of Macedonians and Persians. At the great feast of reconciliation at Opis,[7] after quelling a mutiny of his troops, Macedonians sat next to the King ; after them the Persians and some leading men of other nationalities. The feast began with the libations which Alexander and his guests poured to the gods out of the same mixing-bowl, the conduct of the ceremony being in the hands of Greek soothsayers and Persian Magians. In the sacrificial prayers Alexander uttered the wish that besides all other good things concord (ὁμόνοια) and partnership in rule might be granted to Macedonians and Persians.[8] Wilcken says [9] : ' He could not have revealed his political aims more clearly : the two nations, conquerors and conquered, were to live in harmony with one another and rule conjointly '. Tarn [10] disagrees, and the probability seems to lie with him. He holds that when Alexander prayed

---

[1] Tarn in *C.A.H.* vi. 436.   [2] *Politics*, 1253b.   [3] Ibid. 1256b. 23.
[4] Plut. *Mor.* 329a.   [5] *Politics*, 1255a ; Plato, *Rep.* 5, 470b.
[6] Wilcken, *Alexander the Great*, Chatto & Windus, London, 1932, p. 57 (Eng. Trans.). Isocr. *Philip.* 154.
[7] Arrian, *Anabasis* vii. 8–11.   [8] Idem, ibid., p. 11.
[9] Wilcken, *Alexander the Great*, p. 22.   [10] *C.A.H.* vi. 437.

for a union of hearts and a joint commonwealth of Macedonians and Persians, he proclaimed for the first time,[1] through a brotherhood of peoples, the brotherhood of man.   He first of all men was ready to transcend national differences and to declare, as Paul was to declare, that there was neither Greek nor barbarian.   Wilcken [2] holds that the actual prayer makes it most plain that the ideal before him was simply the fraternization of Macedonians and Persians and that there is no trace of Alexander's treating all mankind as one brotherhood.[3] But all that Alexander ever did in the consolidation of his empire seems to be a complete refutation of Wilcken's thesis.   The states-man-like treatment of his subjects and the founding of Greek cities of mixed population like Alexandria, which Alexander intended to play a special part in his empire, where the different nationalities were to have practically equal, if not citizen, rights—a phenomenon that rarely occurred or was not widespread before his time—seem to disprove Wilcken's thesis.   It seems improbable, in view of what is known of his general policy, that Alexander intended the barbarians to be permanently excluded from citizenship in the new cities he founded, although at Alexandria in Roman times the citizen body was exclusively Greek, and the Egyptians had no political rights.[4] This rule may well date from the foundation, but it is less certain that Alexander intended such a state of affairs to be permanent.   The barbarians needed to be trained for their responsibilities, but after the first generation they were not unfitted for citizenship.   Nor did Alexander intend the Greeks to remain racially segregated from their fellow townsmen, as they were later by strict laws prohibiting that intermarriage which Alexander did his best to encourage.[5]   It is interesting to notice the political development of Alexander.   He first appears as leader of a war of revenge against the barbarian [6]—

[1] In *The Stranger at the Gate* Haarhoff makes an interesting contribution to this question.   He claims (p. 179) that Alexander is not the first man known to us who contemplated the brotherhood of man or the unity of mankind.   The idea may have existed from the time of the Ionian philosophers onwards, but Alexander was the first to carry it into practice.   In any case, the idea could not have sprung suddenly from the brain of Alexander, like Athena from the head of Zeus !   We cannot afford to ignore the training in Greek literature and philosophy that went to build up the character of Alexander.

[2] Wilcken, *Alexander the Great*, p. 221.

[3] ' It looks as if Alexander, while he entertained the large idea of the ultimate unity of mankind, aimed as *an immediate step* at an Empire under the joint rule of Greeks and Persians.'   Haarhoff, op. cit., p. 80.

[4] A. H. M. Jones, *The Greek City from Alexander to Justinian*, Oxford, 1940, p. 5.

[5] Alexander's colonies were still in an experimental stage when he died, and when his guiding hand was removed the normal Greek attitude of exclusiveness prevailed ;   cf. the strict marriage laws of Alexandria and Naucratis, later in Ptolemaic times.

[6] The Panhellenic idea is evidenced in Alexander's coinage.   Cf. Seltman, *Greek Coins*, Methuen, 1933, p. 204.   It was probably with his headship of the League of Corinth, to which he had succeeded on his father's death, and his benevolence to Athens in mind that he adopted new types for his gold coins.   The Head of Athena, wearing a triple-crested Corinthian helmet and with archaic locks on the obverse of his gold staters, appears to be a free copy of the bronze Athena

the devastation of Attica and Athens in 480 had not been forgotten—
but once the Persian Empire was conquered and Darius dead,
Alexander became the inheritor of a vast empire, and his outlook
suffered a great change.[1] To give his empire a secure foundation,
he had to base it inevitably on wider and more generous lines than
the narrow ones Athens or Sparta had made the Greeks acquainted
with. Alexander's object was not that defined by the limited aims
of Isocrates,[2] simply to extend his power over the greatest possible
number of barbarians, for the victory of the Macedonian territorial
state over the city-state, with its exclusive nationalism, had rendered
the old conception of empire by the city-state obsolete. Alexander
did not expect Hellenism by itself to make the unity of his empire :
neither Greece nor Macedonia could supply enough colonists to
maintain a racial supremacy everywhere, apart from the fact that
the Greeks, if left to themselves were, as their history proved, incapable of achieving unity. His aim therefore was to weld together
the various races of his empire and to place them on the same footing,
for the blending of races and nations was the only way to achieve
unity.[3]

As successor to an Empire composed of heterogeneous elements
Alexander's constitutional position was peculiar. The many aspects
of his government have been thus defined :

> ' In Egypt Alexander was an autocrat and a god. In Iran
> he was an autocrat but not a god. In the Greek cities he was a
> god not but an autocrat. In Macedonia he was neither autocrat
> nor god but a quasi-constitutional king . . . in the Amphi-
> ctyonic League a man who owned two votes.' [4]

A coin issued at Babylon on Alexander's return from India throws
further light on his position, for there is the thunderbolt of Zeus to
link him with Ammon and Egypt, the royal Persian headdress for
Iran ; Nike Stephanephoros links him with the Greek cities, from
the greatest of which he had borrowed her for his first staters ; and
for Macedon he figures as the cavalry leader, on horseback, like the

---

Promachos by Pheidias, while the reverse type was a forecast of victory to come,
Nike holding a wreath and a ship's stylis, or naval standard, the name ΑΛΕΞΑΝΔΡΟΥ
in the field (Seltman, Pl. XLVIII, 1, 2.) The ship's standard was a sop to Athens,
whose fleet Alexander needed against Persia.

The types on his silver coinage can also be interpreted as having a Panhellenic
significance : Heracles, the greatest of the Greek heroes, on the obverse, and Zeus
Olympios enthroned, the greatest of gods, on the reverse. Moreover, Alexander
gave up the Thracian standard which Philip had employed for his silver, and coined
both gold and silver on the Attic standard, and thus linked up his coinage with
Attic commerce—the most important in Greece.

[1] Cf. Arrian, ii. 14.

[2] Isoc. *Philip.* 9 ; *Paneg.* 17 ; *Philip.* 154 gives Isocrates advice to Philip : φημὶ
γὰρ χρῆναι σε τοὺς μὲν Ἕλληνας εὐεργετεῖν, Μακεδόνων δὲ βασιλεύειν, τῶν δὲ βαρβάρων ὡς
πλείστων ἄρχειν.

[3] P. Jouguet, *Macedonian Imperialism and the Hellenization of the East*, London,
Kegan Paul, 1928, p. 474.

[4] W. W. Tarn, *C.A.H.* vi. 432.

king on the coins of his ancestor, the first Alexander, and of his father
Philip.[1] This coin is clear evidence that Alexander regarded himself not merely as the protector and ruler of a Macedonian and
Persian aristocracy, but of all men who had become subject to his
imperial rule. It was struck in the very heart of his empire, a few
months before he died of fever in Babylon at the age of thirty-three.

As the apostle of Hellenism, Alexander felt it his mission to carry
culture over the barbarian world, and his foundations or colonies
must be taken in conjunction with this social and cultural policy.[2]
He is said to have founded seventy cities, some absolutely new, like
Alexandria in Egypt and Chodjend, others royal residences turned
into cities, like Candahar and Herat. These cities formed a vast
scheme of colonization in Asia, differing from the old Greek colonies
in that the settlers were not all Greeks, but mixed.

Alexander's aim, furthermore, was to obliterate the line which
separated Greek and barbarian, and the most obvious way to do so
was to encourage intermarriage. He himself married a Persian
princess, and at the great marriage-feast of Susa [3] he allotted wives
drawn from the Persian nobility to eighty of his Companions. The
Macedonian and Persian aristocracies were thus to be blended, and
the common soldiers were encouraged by this example and by
Treasury grants to marry Asiatic wives of lower degrees.

The Greek cities formed a separate world in Alexander's empire.
The greater number of the Greek cities of Asia and Europe (outside
Italy and Sicily) were his free and independent allies, in respect of
whom his rights and duties were formulated and limited by the
League of Corinth; but many Greek cities both in Europe and Asia
had no relations with him at all. The Phoenician kings were subject
allies; the Cyprian kings were free allies, who coined gold, the token
of independence; the High-Priests still governed Judaea. With
the peoples of the Punjab Alexander had no point of contact, and
he was merely the suzerain of certain rajahs who ruled groups of
villages.[4]

In the Greek cities of the Persian Empire the Persian satraps had
favoured oligarchy and still more tyranny, but Alexander showed

---

[1] C. T. Seltman, *Greek Coins*, Methuen, 1933, pp. 213–14. AR. Decadrachm.
Obverse, artist's version of Battle of the Jhelum River; Alexander on horseback
attacking with his lance the Rajah Porus riding upon an elephant, the driver of
which turns to throw a javelin at the attacker. Reverse, Alexander as a god; he
wears Greek cuirass and sword, a Macedonian cloak, and on his head a composite
helmet composed of Greek and Persian elements; in his right hand is a thunderbolt, in his left a spear; a Nike flies towards him with a wreath for his head; below
is BAB in monogram for Babylon. The only two extant specimens of this coin are
in the British Museum.

[2] Many other motives, which do not, however, exclude the primary one mentioned above, have been suggested for Alexander's policy of colonization: Isocrates' scheme for thus relieving the over-population of Greece and disembarrassing
it of hordes of homeless adventurers; military motives—the colonies would serve
as fortresses to hold down rebellious districts; commercial motives—Alexander
was keenly interested in the development of trade, especially in the backward
regions.

[3] Arrian, *Anabasis*, vii. 4.   [4] Tarn *C.A.H.* vi. 432–3.

himself implacably hostile to tyrants and restored democracy everywhere. From this time on democracy and freedom became closely allied concepts.[1]

It was a somewhat difficult problem to reconcile the autonomy of these little states with the sovereignty of the King. As we shall see in the case of the Greek cities in Egypt, though they kept their laws, assemblies, and magistrates, their position tended eventually in practice to become subservient to that of the King. In theory, of course, the cities of the Hellenistic world made alliances with the kings on a footing of equality; in practice there must have been various degrees of independence or subjection. The royal power could be exerted more directly on the cities Alexander himself founded. Here he frankly applied the policy of the fusion of races and accustomed his subjects to political life in the Greek sense. Isocrates[2] could proclaim that what made the Greek, in contrast with the citizen of the narrow polis, was ‘education’, not ‘origin’; so every cultivated man, πεπαιδευμένος, was a Hellene. It was his policy, then, to set up on all sides new Greek cities whose manners and laws would attract men and civilize them.

We cannot be certain about the constitution of these cities, nor do we know definitely whether all races had the same rights in them. Yet we seem to see the idea of a world empire based on municipal self-government taking place when we consider the policy of Alexander towards the Greek cities themselves, both the most ancient and those which he created.[3]

Alexander's intention was that the cities should tend to lose their character as states, and become municipalities managing only their internal affairs. In this respect his work paved the way for the Roman Empire, although his conception was not quite that of the Romans. Hellenism was not the only important aspect of his empire—he did not desire to sacrifice all the authority with which Asiatic tradition endowed the sovereign, and which fascinated him, as it did his successors.

But divergent forces, conflicting interests, heterogeneous manners, and cultures were soon at work breaking up what the will of one man had sought to unify. How far his policy would have succeeded had he not died, it is hard to say. It is true to say, however, that owing to his early death his policy never had a fair trial, and that even while he lived there was much opposition to his policy.

Haarhoff[4] describes his policy as a reaction against previous exclusiveness and, like most reactions, as going too far.

‘ A sudden fusion of different racial elements is hardly ever a success; it is safer to let them grow together, in such a way that what deserves to survive on either side preserves its identity.

[1] Jones, *The Greek City*, p. 157.   [2] Isocr. *Paneg.* 50.
[3] Jouguet, *Macedonian Imperialism and the Hellenization of the East*, p. 89.
[4] Haarhoff, *Stranger at the Gate*, p. 72.

If that identity is prematurely smothered, it struggles back to rebellion or its ghost rises up to avenge it; and forthwith the way is paved for another reaction.'

The feeling which his mercenaries displayed at Opis shows us why Alexander, like Caesar, failed—because his policy was too rapid a one to be understood by the ordinary run of men.   Arrian [1] states the Macedonians were annoyed during the whole campaign, frequently by his Persian dress, the Macedonian equipment of the Oriental ' Successors ', and the importation of cavalry of foreign tribes into the ranks of the Companions—all of which deeply touched Macedonian pride.   They even ' bade him carry on war with the help of his sire (by which they hinted slightingly at Ammon !) '. In his attempt to introduce ' proskynesis ' [2]—though Wilcken [3] says the attempt concerned only those Macedonians and Greeks who were with him in Asia—he deeply affronted Macedonian sentiment, and was forced by the passive resistance of the Macedonians to give it up.

[1] Arrian vii. 8.   [2] Plutarch, *Life of Alexander*, p. 54.
[3] *Alexander the Great*, p. 251.

CHAPTER II

THE HELLENISTIC AGE

THE habit of treating the Hellenistic Age—i.e., the three centuries after Alexander the Great—as though it were nothing more than an annexe to the Golden Age of Greek history no longer exists. The enormous mass of new material relating to this age recently discovered and dealt with at great length by scholars like Rostovtzeff, Tarn, and others has done much to emphasize its essential modernity and to do away with the false impression long prevalent in the minds of some critics that this age was ' decadent ' as compared with the foregoing periods and was interesting merely as the link uniting Greek and Roman history. Indeed, in some important particulars this age was even superior to the previous periods of Greek history.

Any picture of the Greek world based exclusively on a knowledge of Athens and Greece of the 6th to the 4th centuries B.C. must necessarily be incomplete and fail to represent the universalism of the Greek genius that is so characteristic of the Hellenistic Age. It was in this Age that the κοινή, the Greek language as an international instrument, and the idea of a ' cultured world ' first gained world-wide currency. It was only through the great creative forces of the Hellenistic period that the language, literature, habit of thought, and culture of the Greeks succeeded in spreading over a far wider area than the Greek motherland. Furthermore, without an understanding of what the Hellenistic age achieved in the realm of politics, economics, and law it is almost impossible to realize adequately how the world-empire of Rome herself developed.

There are two aspects of the Hellenistic Age that merit consideration owing to the light they throw on the political life of the period.

It was the Hellenistic Age that was the first to attempt to solve a fundamental problem of ancient political life.[1]

The ancient world produced two types of state—the great monarchical and bureaucratic organization of the Orient, and the free autonomous and democratic organization of the Greek city-state. The Greek πόλις was powerless to unite the whole Greek nation into one concrete state. It therefore had to submit to the old monarchical state system of the East, and to adapt the fundamental principles of its life to the bureaucratic organization of the Orient. The corner-stone of this system was the submission of the individual to the State in all spheres of his activity. Such was the case in Ptolemaic Egypt, with which we are directly concerned. In other

---

[1] Rostovtzeff, in *J.E.A.* 1920, pp. 162 seq.

15

countries, such as Macedonia, Asia Minor, and Syria, Greek genius tried to create a compromise between the Eastern monarchy and Greek polity by building up monarchic states from a conglomeration of Greek states which lost their economic self-sufficiency (αὐτάρκεια) and their political autonomy (αὐτονομία).

Rome, too, in the long run, was obliged to follow the example of the Hellenistic monarchies, and to continue the work of combining the principles of the Greek city-state and the Eastern bureaucratic monarchy.

In the second place, in the generation after Alexander's death we find taking shape the idea of mankind as one great community, the idea of a state embracing the whole world. To Zeno, a hellenized Semite born in Cyprus and the founder of Stoicism, who established a school of philosophy at Athens in 301 B.C.[1] some authorities have attributed the introduction of the idea of cosmopolitanism, transcending patriotism ; of the whole world as a man's true fatherland without distinction of Greek and barbarian, or of freeman and slave. The philosopher thus feels himself citizen of a state to which all human beings belong.[2] The effect of this philosophy on Roman Stoicism was incalculable.[3]

It was the changed political situation, however, due to the conquests of Alexander, which broke down the self-sufficiency and security of the old city-state, that was the immediate cause of both the new philosophies of the age, Stoicism and Epicureanism. New Comedy, too, was profoundly influenced by the course of events. There appear now both in the new philosophies [4] and in New Comedy [5] two qualities almost unknown in earlier literature— cosmopolitanism and individualism.

[1] Diogenes Laertius, vii. 1 : Ζήνων Μνασέου ἢ Δημέου Κιτιεὺς ἀπὸ Κύπρου, πολίσματος Ἑλληνικοῦ, Φοίνικας ἐποίκους ἐσχηκότος. 5. ἀνακάμπτων δὴ ἐν τῇ ποικίλῃ στοᾷ τῇ καὶ Πεισιανακτείῳ καλουμένῃ, ἀπὸ τῆς γραφῆς τῆς Πολυγνώτου ποικίλῃ, διετίθετο τοὺς λόγους . . . . προσήεσαν δὴ πολλοὶ ἀκούοντες αὐτοῦ καὶ διὰ τοῦτο Στωικοὶ ἐκλήθησαν.
[2] Plutarch, de Alexandri virtute, i. 329 A : καὶ μὴν ἡ πολὺ θαυμαζομένη πολιτεία τοῦ τὴν Στωικῶν αἵρεσιν καταβαλομένου Ζήνωνος εἰς ἓν τοῦτο συντείνει κεφάλαιον, ἵνα μὴ κατὰ πόλεις μηδὲ κατὰ δήμους οἰκῶμεν, ἰδίοις ἕκαστοι διωρισμένοι δικαίοις, ἀλλὰ πάντας ἀνθρώπους ἡγώμεθα δημότας καὶ πολίτας, εἰς δὲ βίος ᾖ καὶ κόσμος ὥσπερ ἀγέλης συννόμου κοινῷ συντρεφομένης.
[3] Cf. Seneca, de otio, iv, 1. Duas republicas animo complectamur, alteram magnam et vere publicam, qua dii atque homines continentur, in qua non ad hunc angulum respicimus aut ad illum, sed terminos civitatis nostrae cum sole metimur ; alteram, cui nos adscripsit condicio nascendi. Cf. also Marcus Aurelius, vi. 44 : Cicero, de fin. iii. 63 seq.
[4] There are other interesting points of agreement and difference between the two schools of philosophy—for example, on the question of free-will and their attitudes to the State and to religion. In general, the two philosophies tend to supplement each other ; and although their morality is too self-centred, they both helped to break down the exclusiveness of the ancient world and to open the way for a more cosmopolitan outlook and more humanitarian ideals. For Stoicism and Epicureanism generally, see R. D. Hicks, Stoic and Epicurean, London, 1910, and C. Bailey, Epicurus, Oxford, 1926.
[5] Terence's famous line, ' homo sum, humani nihil a me alienum puto ', seems to be an echo of Menander's (Frag. 60) Οὐδείς ἐστί μοι

ἀλλότριος, ἂν ᾖ χρηστός· ἡ φύσις μία
πάντων, τὸ δ' οἰκεῖον συνίστησιν τρόπος.

Thus, although the Stoics did most to spread the ideal of cosmopolitanism, they only gave current expression in philosophical parlance to the great revolutionary feature in the policy of Alexander which aimed at breaking down racial antagonisms and distinctions. The theory had been preached as early as the Sophists and, as Haarhoff claims,[1] may have existed from the time of the Ionian philosophers onwards. Plutarch states that the cause which made it practicable was not philosophy : ' While Zeno sketched his philosopher's Utopia on paper, it was Alexander who gave the theory realization.'[2]

' Zeno's inspiration was Alexander's idea of the unity of mankind ; and what Zeno himself did was to carry this idea to one of its two logical conclusions. Zeno abolished all distinctions of race, all the apparatus of national groups and particular states, and made his world-state a theoretic whole.'[3]

His scheme, in spite of its inspiring effect, remained unrealizable. It was Alexander's way, however—that of working through national groups, inevitable in an empire like his, comprising many different states and subject peoples—which led eventually to the Roman Empire being called one people. Only a partial realization, however, of the ideas of Alexander took place, when Marcus Aurelius, the Stoic emperor, could say about himself, ' As a man I am a citizen of the world-state, but as the particular man Marcus Aurelius, I am a citizen of Rome.'[4] His statement implies he had made terms with the national state. It was only when Caracalla gave the citizenship to all, that Rome came nearest to the realization of Alexander's ideal.

As regards the whole of the Hellenistic world, a consideration of the development of the ideas put into practice for the first time by Alexander would merit far larger treatment than is possible in a work of short compass. It is therefore the aim of the present work, after the broad outlines of Greek exclusiveness and the new tendency to break down the barriers between race and race have been mentioned, to review what effects the new spirit, the sudden awakening to man's unity, had on the development of race-relations in one particular corner of the ancient world. For other parts of that world the means to discuss this question are not so abundant : yet we can hope to learn something of what happened in these regions, too, by considering the parallel of Egypt.

---

[1] Haarhoff, *The Stranger at the Gate*, Longmans, Green & Co., 1938, p. 179.
[2] Plutarch, *de Alex. virtute, Moral*, p. 329A : τοῦτο Ζήνων μὲν ἔγραψεν ὥσπερ ὄναρ ἢ εἴδωλον εὐνομίας φιλοσόφου καὶ πολιτείας ἀνατυπωσάμενος, Ἀλέξανδρος δὲ τῷ λόγῳ τὸ ἔργον παρέσχεν.
[3] W. W. Tarn, ' Alexander the Great and the Unity of Mankind ', Raleigh Lecture, 1933, p. 26. (*Proceedings of the British Academy*, vol. xix.)
[4] Marcus Aurelius vi. 44 : πόλις καὶ πατρίς, ὡς μὲν Ἀντωνίνῳ, μοι ἡ Ῥώμη, ὡς δὲ ἀνθρώπῳ, ὁ κόσμος.

C

CHAPTER III

THE EARLIEST GREEK CONTACT WITH EGYPT

HERODOTUS [1] claims that the Greeks were the first people of a different language who settled in Egypt, but this view is untenable, since the Hebrews had settled there before them— if only in the land of Goshen—centuries before. Egypt must have long been accustomed to the presence of strangers in her midst. The Hyksos (c. 1680–c. 1580), who were certainly of a different language and race from the Egyptians, remained in Egypt for about a century before the kings of the 18th dynasty (c. 1580–c. 1350 B.C.) expelled them. These invaders adopted Egyptian usages and even Egyptian names : but to the natives they were ' the accursed ', and Herodotus heard nothing of their rule in Egypt.

There had been very active intercourse between the Egyptian and Aegean worlds before the Greeks clearly emerged into history. With Crete Egypt had always been in a close relationship which may have involved some community of blood. Egyptian objects are found in the Cretan palaces, and Cretan objects in the Egyptian tombs. [2] It is, however, with the period after the resurrection of Egypt from the Hyksos oppression—with the advent of the 18th Dynasty (L.M. I Period in Crete, c. 1600 B.C.) that relations between the two countries became very close indeed. But towards the end of the 15th century B.C. Crete suffered an overwhelming catastrophe before most of the island had reached the L.M. II stage of culture. [3] Until this catastrophe Egypt and Crete had the closest relations. [4] It seems clear that the opening of relations between Egypt and the mainland and islands of Greece coincides with the fall of the Minoan State and the

---

[1] Herod. ii. 154.

[2] C.A.H. Vol. of Plates, i. 104–5. Vases of Camares type have been found in Egypt. Further excavations in the Delta will probably throw light on relations between the two countries in the Early Minoan period.

[3] This, too, explains why no L.M. II pottery has as yet appeared in Egypt. It had no chance to filter through the Cretan provinces or to Egypt. L.M. I and II were the most flourishing periods that Crete had known or was to know before Roman times. A number of sites, deserted after the final catastrophe at the end of L.M. I and II. were not reinhabited until the 1st century B.C. This catastrophe occurs at practically every site at the end of L.M. I, but at Cnossos at the end of L.M. II. Cf. J. D. S. Pendlebury, *The Archaeology of Crete*, Methuen, 1939, p. 180.

[4] The last mention of Keftiu (Crete) occurs in the reign of Amenophis III, and the circular seal of his queen Ty from Agia Triada is the latest datable object found in Crete before the catastrophe (found with L.M. Ib. pottery, contemporary with L.M. II of Cnossos) ; cf. Pendlebury in *J.E.A.* xvi. (1930), 85, and in the *Archaeology of Crete*, Methuen, 1939, p. 222. ' There is a moral certainty that the destruction of the Minoan cities took place in the reign of Amenhotep III, i.e. between 1414 and 1378 B.C.,' says Pendlebury.

destruction of its political and commercial importance. The Egyptians called both the inhabitants of the Aegean and those of the mainland ' the Peoples of the Isles in the midst of the Sea ', for they knew little of the Greek mainland, and thought that all the peoples in this neighbourhood came from some island or other and were subject to Crete.[1]

The disaster which overtook the Cretan cities has been generally attributed to the men of the mainland who sacked and burned the cities in a raiding expedition. Sir Arthur Evans attributes the overthrow of Cnossos, at least, to an earthquake.[2] Pendlebury, however, shows that it was due to a great organized effort,[3] since at the time of its downfall Crete shows no weakness : ' no scattered shiploads of vikings could have laid her low '.

The Peoples of the Sea, of whose existence somewhere on the far side of Crete the Egyptians had been vaguely aware, came direct to Egypt with their wares, exactly as if Crete had never existed, and relations were peacefully maintained for a century and a half. But in the reign of Merenptah, Egypt was threatened by a desperate attack, not only from her neighbours, the Libyans, but also by a confederacy of the Peoples of the Sea. There were two of these invasions ; [4] both were smashed, and Egypt was troubled no more.

These invasions left an effect on Egyptian sentiment and attitude

[1] It is after the reign of Amenophis IH (c. 1411–1375 B.C.) from the Amarna letters and from the accounts of the battles of Merenptah and Rameses III that Danauna, Zakaray and Shakalasha, Shardana and Lukki and Pulesatha appear (see Hall, B.S.A. VIII, 175 ff.), showing that the Isles included some of the coastland of Asia Minor while a body of Danauna had appeared in Syria as early as the Amarna letters (Letter 151, in Winckler's edition).

The archaeological finds, too, prove that it was not till the late Mycenaean or L.H. III period, beginning c. 1400 B.C., that something occurred to throw Egypt and ' the Peoples of the Isles ' together. Dating from this period, numerous Egyptian objects have been found in the Aegean area, notably at Mycenae, and enormous quantities of late Helladic III pottery have been discovered in Egypt. (Pendlebury in J.E.A. xvi. (1930), 86–9).

[2] Evans, Palace of Minos, vol. ii. 1, p. 320.

[3] In J.E.A. xvi. (1930), 90 and Cretan Archaeology, pp. 230–1, Pendlebury holds that in L.M. I and II. (c. 1600-c. 1400 B.C.) Crete possessed an empire which extended over a large part of the Southern mainland of Greece as well as the islands. This empire had probably become to a large extent independent, though subject to tribute, and, increasing in prosperity, desired an outlet. Crete herself held the monopoly of the most profitable trade in the eastern Mediterranean at that time— the Egyptian trade. The subjects of Minos banded themselves together, perhaps under Theseus (the one man whom ancient tradition connected, if not with the fall of Cnossos, at least with the liberation of her subjects), and, the enormity of the tribute of youths and maidens arousing national enthusiasm, they collected their fleets and set out deliberately to destroy the power of Crete and to open up the way to Egypt. Wainwright criticizes this view on the ground that it is presupposing too much to suggest that the Achaeans destroyed Crete in order to open up the Egyptian trade for the men of the mainland (J.E.A. xvii. (1931), 260). The destruction of Crete did open the Egyptian trade, but it may well have been an extra and quite fortuitous benefit accruing to the conqueror.

[4] The first raid took place in 1232 B.C. Cf. Cretan Archaeology, p. 260.

The leadership of the second invasion has been attributed with great probability to Agamemnon, the son of Atreus, c. 1184 B.C. Cf. Myers and Frost, KL10, 1914, 446 seq. This not only fits in with the accepted date of the Trojan war, but goes far to explaining it. (See note 1 on next page).

towards foreigners that cannot be estimated and does much to explain their exclusiveness made famous by classical writers.

The Peoples of the Sea and Egypt had traded peacefully with one another for nearly two centuries. Thus the sudden hostility of the Aegean peoples is inexplicable, and the result was utterly disastrous to them, since they had benefited most from this intercourse.

After her escape from this latent danger, Egypt shuts herself up. There is no more commercial intercourse. Egyptian ports are closed and the appearance of a sail on the horizon is a call to arms.[1]

These raids mark the end of a period in the history of the Mediterranean world, but though Egypt escaped conquest for a time, the war-like energy of the native Egyptians was exhausted and her forces were becoming largely mercenary. The strength of Egypt rapidly declined: she was overrun by the Ethiopians from the south and by the Assyrians from the north under Esarhaddon (670 B.C.) and Assurbanipal who took Thebes (661 B.C.). The policy of the Assyrian conquerors was to encourage the native Egyptian princes of the Delta against the Ethiopian rulers of the South; the result of this policy was the rise of the XXVIth or Saite Dynasty (663–525 B.C.).

The Saite dynasty drove the Ethiopian invaders from Egypt and vindicated her independence from the declining power of Assyria. It was at this period, when the land enjoyed a century and a half of prosperity under native kings, that the country was brought into connexion with the western world, with the Greeks in particular.

The changing attitude of the Egyptians to the Greeks down to the time of Herodotus has been well summarized.[2] The successive stages were :—

(i) Hostility to all foreigners [3] and avoidance of foreign customs,[4] some of the reasons for which have already been noticed ;

(ii) the need of foreign help [5] under the Saite kings of the XXVIth Dynasty ; leading to

(iii) the attempt to impress the Greeks with the superiority of Egyptian culture ;

---

[1] Cf. *Od.* xiv. 245 ff. Pendlebury, in *J.E.A.* xvi. (1930), 92, suggests that this rupture was the direct cause of the Trojan War. As they failed to gain access to Egypt, the Achaean chiefs turned to the Black Sea, attacking Troy, which kept the Black Sea trade as her pet preserve as two centuries earlier Crete had kept the Egyptian. This time it was the rape of Helen, as previously it may have been the human tribute for the bull-ring, that united the scattered tribes.

[2] *J.E.A.* xvi. (1930), 266.

[3] Cf. Strabo 17, 1, 6, p. 792, ' The early prejudice against all who sailed the sea and especially against the Greek '. Cf. Strabo, 17, 1,19, p. 802, where mention is made of the ξενηλασία, ἀξενία of King Busiris. Strabo says: ' According to Eratosthenes, the expulsion of foreigners is a custom common to all barbarians (cf. the Carthaginians and Persians), yet the Egyptians are condemned for this fault because of the myths which have been circulated about Busiris in connection with the Busirite name.' Cf. Herod. ii. 45, who denies that the Egyptians sacrificed human beings.

[4] Herod. ii. 41, 7; 91, 1.   [5] Ibid. 152.

(iv) political co-operation of Egyptians and Greeks arising from their common hostility to Persia ; and

(v) the attempt to prove ancient connexions between Greece and Egypt—e.g., Greek borrowings from Egypt.

We shall notice how these themes run throughout our account of Graeco-Egyptian relations, and it may be interesting to discuss them in the order given.

(i) It is on the question of the exclusiveness of the Egyptians that we owe one of our greatest debts to Herodotus for the information he gives us.

There were striking contrasts between the Egyptians and Greeks. Herodotus gives us the famous paradox that everything in Egypt is the reverse of what it is elsewhere.[1]   In this respect we may compare the usual European view of the customs of and manners of, say, China and Japan.   Herodotus says :

' The Egyptians have at once a climate peculiar to themselves, and in their river one that is different in nature from all other rivers ; and even so have they made themselves customs and laws contrary to those of all other men.   Among them the women buy and sell, the men abide at home and weave ; [2] and whereas in weaving all others push the woof upwards, the Egyptians push it down.   As for burdens, men carry them on their heads, and women on their shoulders.   They do their easement within doors and eat abroad in the streets and they give the reason that things unseemly but necessary should be done in secret, things not unseemly openly.   No woman is dedicated to the service of any god or goddess : men are dedicated to all gods and all goddesses : Sons are not compelled against their will to support their parents, but daughters must do so of necessity even against their will.   Everywhere else the priests of the gods wear their hair long ; in Egypt they are shaven.   Among other men, when the dead are mourned, it is the custom for those most concerned to have their heads shaven ; Egyptians are shaven at other times, but after a death they let their hair and beard grow.   Other men have their daily living separate from their animals, the Egyptians live with theirs. Other men live on wheat and barley ; to an Egyptian, who lives on these, it is the greatest reproach, but they make food from a coarse grain which some call spelt.   They knead dough with

---

[1] Herod. vi. 35, 2 seq.   The translation is the version given in Glover, *Sather Lectures*, Univ. of Calif. Press, 1924, p. 132.

[2] Sophocles followed his friend Herodotus when he made Oedipus contrast his daughters and his sons :   *Oedipus Coloneus*, 337–41 :

ὦ πάντ' ἐκείνω τοῖς ἐν Αἰγύπτῳ νόμοις
φύσιν κατεικασθέντε καὶ βίου τροφάς·
ἐκεῖ γὰρ οἱ μὲν ἄρσενες κατὰ στέγας
θακοῦσιν ἱστουργοῦντες, αἱ δὲ σύννομοι
τἄξω βίου τροφεῖα πορσύνουσ' ἀεί.

their feet and clay with their hands, and they will use their hands to pick up dung. The Egyptians, and those who have learnt it from them, are the only people who practise circumcision. Every man of them has two garments, every woman one. The rings and sheets of sails are made fast elsewhere outside the boat, but inside it in Egypt. The Greeks write characters and reckon with pebbles, moving the hand toward the right, but Egyptians from right to left; yet all the same they say their way of writing is towards the right and the Greek way to the left. They use two kinds of letters; one is called sacred and the other common. They are beyond measure religious, far more than any other nation '.

Herodotus furthermore observed the actual religious antipathy which hampered relations between native and Greek,[1] the refusal to kiss on the mouth, the need for purifying crockery after a foreign guest had used it,[2] the avoidance of the use of Greek customs and, generally speaking, of the customs of any men whatever.[3]

It is worth while remarking here that Herodotus, struck by the contrasts to Greece, sometimes presses the matter too far: for instance, women marketing and men weaving are indeed figured on the monuments, but these are the exceptions. Herodotus wishes to make the contrast with Greece more striking. Nevertheless, there seems to have been as much difference between Greek and Egyptian in his day as there is to-day between, say, Christian and Mohammedan or European and Asiatic.[4]

---

[1] Anaxandrides, a poet of the Middle Comedy (c. 340 B.C.) represented Athens as refusing alliance with Egypt because of the dissimilarity of the customs and laws of the two lands: Kock C.A.F. ii., 150, No. 39. (Pickard-Cambridge, Sel. Frag., 55), one of the characters in the comedy called Πόλεις addresses the Egyptians thus (references are to chapters in Herod. ii.) :—

οὐκ ἂν δυναίμην συμμαχεῖν ὑμῖν ἐγώ·
οὔθ' οἱ τρόποι γὰρ ὁμονοοῦσ' οὔθ' οἱ νόμοι
ἡμῶν, ἀπ' ἀλλήλων δὲ διέχουσιν πολύ.
βοῦν προσκυνεῖς (41.2), ἐγὼ δὲ θύω τοῖς θεοῖς·
τὴν ἔγχελυν μέγιστον ἡγεῖ δαίμονα (72.3)
ἡμεῖς δὲ τῶν ὄψων μέγιστον παρὰ πολύ.
οὐκ ἐσθίεις ὕει' (47.1), ἐγὼ δ' ἥδομαι
μάλιστα τούτοις· κύνα σέβεις (67.3), τύπτω δ' ἐγώ,
τοὔψον κατεσθίουσαν ἡνίκ' ἂν λάβω . . . .
τὸν αἰέλουρον κακὸν ἔχοντ' ἐὰν ἴδῃς,
κλάεις (66.10 ff.), ἐγὼ δ' ἥδιστ' ἀποκτείνας δέρω.
δύναται παρ' ὑμῖν μυγαλῆ (67.5), παρ' ἐμοὶ δὲ γ' οὔ.

[2] Herod. ii. 41, 7.   [3] Ibid. 91.

[4] There are naturally contradictions and discrepancies of all kinds in Herodotus, especially in chaps. 35–6. These are frequently to be accounted for by the difference of place and date, most of the monuments belonging to a period long anterior to Herodotus, and also mainly coming from Upper, and not from Lower Egypt, which Herodotus had primarily in view and of which he had seen far more than of Upper Egypt in his travels. Often, as a result of his comparatively short sojourn in Egypt, he rashly made use of isolated observations as though they were of universal application. Cf. Spiegelberg, *The Credibility of Herodotus' Account of Egypt*, Blackwell, Oxford, 1927, pp. 34–5. Yet Herodotus is on the right track when he attempts to explain national characteristics by the nature of the country.

(ii) The need of foreign help by the Saite kings has been referred to as a phase in Graeco-Egyptian relations.   It is true that Egypt had been closed to Greek curiosity for several centuries, since the threatened invasion of the Peoples of the Sea, yet the Delta at least had been well known to the Hellenic world.   The Pharos of the future Alexandria is mentioned by Homer ; [1] it was there, ' in front of Egypt ', that Menelaos moored his ships and forced ' Egyptian Proteus ' to declare to him his homeward road.   Even ' Egyptian Thebes ', with its hundred temple gates, is known both to the *Iliad* [2] and to the *Odyssey* [3] and the Pharaoh Polybos dwelt there when Alkandra, his wife, loaded Menelaos with gifts.

In more historical times, the Milesian Greeks, in spite of the vast differences in the Egyptian way of life and their dislike of strangers, succeeded in the *second half* of the 7th century B.C. ' in the time of Psammetichus I (who lived in the time of Cyaxares the Mede '), in obtaining a footing in the country and establishing a trading-station there, the ' Milesian Wall '.   ' In time they sailed up into the Saite nome and founded Naucratis ' on one of the western arms of the Nile.[4]   Circumstances—Assyrian expeditions and civil wars— made Greeks indispensable as mercenaries.   Herodotus relates how Psammetichus I, one of twelve princelings in the Delta and the founder of the XXVIth or Saite Dynasty, took into his service, in order to make himself master of Egypt and throw off the Assyrian yoke, certain Ionians and Carians who, voyaging for plunder, were forced to put in on the coast of Egypt, where they disembarked in their mail of bronze.[5]   He established his Greek mercenaries in ' The Camps ' at *Daphnae*, this time on the east side of the Delta on the Pelusiac arm of the Nile, commanding the eastern frontier.[6]   The Daphnae Camps were two in number ; one was occupied by Carian mercenaries, the other by Ionians, and the Nile flowed between them.   It was from this camp that the Greeks marched out under Necho, Psammetichus' son, on the expedition which overthrew Josiah,[7] and it was here that Jeremiah and many of his fellow-country-men sought refuge from the Nebuchadnezzar [8] and found it till that monarch fell upon Egypt and led them away captive to Babylon. Daphnae was thus the scene of the first intercourse in Egypt between the Jews and the Greeks—an intercourse that was to have such notable developments four centuries later at Alexandria.   According to Herodotus [9] the Camps at Daphnae continued to flourish till a civil war in the time of Apries (Hophra of the Old Testament), who

---

[1] *Od.* iv. 355.   [2] *Iliad.* ix. 381.   [3] *Od.* iv. 126.
[4] Strabo xvii. 1, 18.   [5] Herod. ii. 152.
[6] Diod. i. 67 ; Herod. ii. 145 : Στρατόπεδα : the position of these camps is defined as being on the Pelusiac branch of the Nile, below Bubastis.   This double encampment is usually identified, on no good grounds, with Daphnae (Herod. ii. 30, 10) : it may have been a suburb or appendage of Daphnae, but it seems more probable that the camps (with their reserve of veterans) lay at a little distance south of Daphnae (the frontier post).   See R. M. Cook, *J.H.S.*, 1937, pp. 233 ff.
[7] Cf. Jer. ii. 16.   [8] Jer. xliii. 5 seq.   Tahpanhes = Daphnae.
[9] Herod. ii. 163, 169.

had a bodyguard of 30,000 Ionians and Carians, put Amasis on the throne (566 B.C.). It was then that Amasis decided to transfer the Ionian and Carian mercenaries from Daphnae to Memphis, ostensibly to have them under his control, but in reality, owing to latent phil-hellenism, to be his trusted bodyguard against the Egyptians.[1]

The merchants were removed to Naucratis,[2] which was reorganized at this time, and Greeks were permitted access to Egypt only by the Canopic or westernmost branch of the Nile.[3]   In the days of Herodotus their old homes at Daphnae and the slips for their ships there were already in ruins.

Naucratis was open to all Greeks : among the Hellenic colonies it is the only instance of an international town.   Round a common sanctuary significantly named the Hellenion nine cities of Asiatic Greece were grouped, belonging to the three great racial divisions. Chios, Teos, Phocaea, and Clazomenae represented the Ionians, Mytilene the Aeolians, and Rhodes, Halicarnassos, Cnidos, and Phaselis the Dorians.   The Milesians, Samians, and Aeginetans formed separate groups, with their own temples.   Each people occupied a certain quarter, and had its magistrates and law-courts, from which, if necessary, appeal could be made to the jurisdiction of the mother-city.

Cook [4] has some interesting remarks to make on the date of the foundation of Naucratis and the traditional reconstruction of the Hellenic policy of Amasis.   He holds that the foundation of Naucratis has wrongly been put back to the middle of the 7th century B.C. and that in the past too much reliance has been placed on Herodotus' statement that Amasis removed the Greek mercenaries from Daphnae to Memphis—a statement that does not fit in with the archaeological evidence.

Herodotus' history, as far as regards Egypt, was not a history of Greek contact with Egypt, therefore his allusions to Greeks can only be casual.   Herodotus, Cook says, represents Amasis as a half-legendary figure and deliberately or from ignorance fails to mention,[5]

---

[1] Herod. ii. 154, 178.

[2] Ibid. 178 (This town on the Canopic branch of the Nile, 53 miles S.E. of Alexandria, was founded c. 615–610 B.C., more than forty years before Amasis came to the throne. For a link with Herodotus (potsherds bearing the name ΗΡΟΔΟΤΟΣ found in the Hellenium at Naucratis) see *J.H.S.* xxv. 116.

[3] Glotz, *Hist. Grecque*, i. 204; Hall, *C.A.H.* iii. 292, 303–4; Meyer, *Gesch. d. Altertums*, iii.[2] 623–4; How and Wells, *Commentary on Herodotus*, on ii. 30, 2, 154, 3, 178–9, attribute a double policy to Amasis.

[4] *J.H.S.* 1937, pp. 227–30.

[5] Cf. W. Spiegelberg, *The Credibility of Herodotus' Account of Egypt*, Blackwell, Oxford, 1927, pp. 28–31.   Yet Herodotus is our most prolific source for the Saite period of Egyptian history, for a period when native records and monuments, located as they were in the exposed Delta, have almost entirely perished (Breasted, p. 579).   As he himself states in ii. 155.   ' It comes of our intercourse with these settlers in Egypt that we Greeks have exact knowledge of the history of Egypt from the reign of Psammetichus onwards.'   Archaeology nevertheless provides a useful supplement to Herodotus.   For the earlier periods of Egyptian history, it is generally agreed, Herodotus is unreliable, since he records not history, but stories—historical romances, and legends—as opposed to chronicles and annals.   It was among the populace, including ' priests ' and dragomans, as guardians of popular tradition that Herodotus collected his stories.

as the Egyptian records do,[1] that he rose to power as the head of an anti-Greek movement, being the nominee of a fervid nationalist party. Furthermore, although they conflict with the conventional interpretation of Herodotus, the evidences from archaeology are better than the records of one who visited Egypt a century later.

From the archaeological evidence we see that Naucratis was probably founded about 615–610 B.C. as a very important East Greek settlement.

The proportion of East Greek pottery proves this, as well as the nationalities of the dedicators (the most prominent being Chiots indicating that the pottery was most probably manufactured in Chios and that there was close connexion between Naucratis and Chios—a fact Herodotus does not suggest.) The literary tradition, too, seems to be in favour of this view.

According to the traditional view, Amasis severely circumscribed the activities of the Greeks and their settlement, but the archaeological evidence disproves this. Actually the Egypt of Amasis seems to have been more open to the Greeks than before, for Naucratis was not the only settlement of Greeks during the reign of Amasis, the Golden Age of the Greeks in Egypt. In the East of the Delta, Daphnae (Tell Defenneh), and perhaps other Greek outposts, had a more or less independent life. The pottery suggests even closer East Greek connexions for this area than for Naucratis (Attic Black Figure, Fikellura, Clazomenian, and the Situlae). It ranges from c. 570 to 530, or even later to the end of the century—hence the common belief that Amasis recalled his Greek mercenaries from the eastern frontier at Daphnae about 565 is clearly wrong, and the contact between Greeks and Egyptians was probably greater than is usually thought to have been the case. There was some infiltration beyond Naucratis and Daphnae of Greek settlers or sentiments. In the Delta, round Memphis, and in the Thebaid, sherds of the late 7th and of the 6th centuries have been found—most being East Greek imports and belonging chiefly to the reign of Amasis. Cook inclines to the belief that Greek settlements were widespread— there were most probably other Greek settlements besides Naucratis and Tell Defenneh, and it remains for further progress in the archaeological investigation of the Delta to throw more light on a most interesting chapter in Graeco-Egyptian history before the coming of Alexander.

(iii) We come next to the attempt of the Egyptians to impress the Greeks with the superiority of their culture. Naucratis and Daphnae were the centres from which Egyptian influence reached Greece. Their existence meant that Egypt was known at first hand not merely to occasional enterprising travellers, but to a large body of Greeks

---

[1] 'The Stele of the Death of Apries' (*Recueil de Travaux Relat. Philol. Égypt.* xxii. (1900). 1 ff. recording his deposition by Amasis (in a damaged condition) and a demotic papyrus (*Rev. Eg.* i. 59) are relevant.

from various cities. During the long reign of Amasis (569–526) many of the Greeks were constantly passing to and fro between Naucratis and their native cities.[1] The wise men of Greece like Pythagoras and Solon visited the land, and tradition connected these visits with their search for wisdom. The pages of Herodotus, and the fragments of his predecessor Hecataeus (born at Miletus c. 550 B.C.), who travelled through the valley of the Nile before the Ionian revolt, show how much the Greeks were impressed when they discovered the extreme antiquity of Egyptian civilization.[2] The Persian Wars put an end to all this peaceful intercourse between Greece and the old land of the Pharaohs for a while. But once they had ended and the revolt of native princes had been suppressed, the country was once more opened up to Greek curiosity. Anaxagoras, the philosopher, investigated the rise and fall of the Nile; Hellanikos the historian, the older contemporary of Herodotus, seems to have travelled in Egypt [3] but it is to Herodotus (484–c. 430 B.C.) that we owe most of our information on the literary side for the Greek connexion with Egypt.

In the case of Herodotus, who visited Egypt about 450 B.C.,[4] the efforts of the Egyptians to impress the Greeks with the superiority of the Egyptian culture were successful.

[1] The effect of this intercourse must have been considerable, yet cases of direct Egyptian influence are surprisingly few. (a) Cf. C.A.H. iv. 108. Among the pre-Persian remains on the Athenian Acropolis (G. Dickins, Catalogue of the Acropolis Museum, i. 167, on Nos. 144, 146) the figures of two scribes are dressed in a Greek imitation of Egyptian Garb. (b) Cf. Breasted, A History of Egypt, 'the archaic (so-called), Apollos reproduce the standing posture prevalent in Egypt in every detail, including the characteristic thrusting forward of the left foot . . . there is a grain of truth in the Greek tradition that they received their philosophy from Egypt '. Periander of Corinth named his nephew and successor Psammetichus. (c) Cf. C.A.H. iv. 109. The Greeks received from Egypt, probably by way of Naucratis, a particularly precious gift, the papyrus which gave them a light and cheap material for book-making.
[2] For Hecataeus see Pearson, Early Ionian Historians, Oxford, 1939, pp. 25 seq., especially pp. 81 seq., on Egypt. He is mentioned by Herodotus in v. 36, 124–6, ii. 143, v. 49. ' There is no doubt that Herodotus did consult Hecataeus' " Periegesis " in writing about Egypt ', but the evidence does not enable us to decide the extent of his debt ' (Pearson, pp. 82 seq.). The phrase Egypt is the ' gift of the river ' originated with Hecataeus apparently. ' The fragments reveal neither the extent of his knowledge nor his method of description . . . about Egyptian customs he had something to say, possibly more than about other countries, since he did actually visit Egypt ' (Pearson, p. 90).
[3] For Hellanikos, see Pearson, Early Ionian Historians, Oxford, 1939, pp. 152 seq., and especially pp. 199 seq. for his work Aegyptiaca, a work in many respects comparable to Bk. II of Herodotus. ' There is nothing to show whether it was published before or after the history of Herodotus and no such close connexion can be shown between the two authors as between Herodotus and Hecataeus ' (ibid., p. 201).
[4] A terminus post quem is the Battle of Papremis (459 B.C.) which is mentioned by Herodotus (iii. 20). He saw the skeletons of the fallen Egyptians and Persians still lying there, and ascertained the difference in the hardness of the Persian and Egyptian skulls by throwing stones at them—thus indicating his thirst for knowledge. Spiegelberg, op. cit., pp. 3, 4. Also it may be fairly assumed from his account that the nationalist risings, which had seriously threatened the Persian rule between 460 and 450 B.C., had long been over, and that Egypt was now in undisturbed Persian possession.

' Yet though willing for the most part to accept the Egyptian estimate he remained a thorough Greek in his interpretation of Egypt in terms of the Greek mentality. Though ready to acknowledge the priority of other cultures and to regard Greek institutions as borrowed, he did so from no self-depreciatory motive, but by interpreting the foreign in the Greek spirit which he treated as the norm of common humanity.' [1]

The Egyptians of Herodotus' day, says Spiegelberg, manifested the same feeling towards the Greek spirit, which had so much to give them, that most modern Orientals, except the thin upper strata, manifest towards Western civilization—a feeling of superiority and even contempt. This is bound to be the attitude of a civilization whose forms and conventions are deeply rooted in the past towards one that is recent and insecure, and still striving after a settled mode of expression. It is only to be expected that this age should wish to seek refuge from a disagreeable present in the happier days of the past. Men dreamt of a fabulous antiquity for Egyptian history— 11,340 years were mentioned to Herodotus—and it was the boast of the Egyptians that during all this time no change had taken place in the nature, manners, or customs of the people.[2] Herodotus here uses the phrase, which occurs once again in another connexion [3] ' No change has taken place either in the products of the land or in the products of the river.' (οὔτε τὰ ἐκ τῆς γῆς οὔτε τὰ ἐκ τοῦ ποταμοῦ σφι γενόμενα).

Herodotus became acquainted with this pride in ancestry during the course of a talk with the priests of Amun of Thebes in the temple of Karnak.[4] He tells how when the Greek Hecataeus, a previous visitor there, had traced back his ancestry to a god in the sixteenth generation, the priests led him, as they did Herodotus, into the interior of the temple and showed him three hundred and forty-five statues erected there. The one was the son of the other in unbroken descent, without reaching back to a god, despite the three hundred and forty-five generations and such figure was a ' Piromis ', which Herodotus translates as a καλὸς κἀγαθός, a man of noble birth. Herodotus here has a dig at Hecataeus' pride in his ancestry.

Thus Herodotus had some inkling of this pride in the past, this overweening sense of racial superiority. Another instance is the famous conversation of Solon with the aged Egyptian priest [5] who spoke of the Greeks as children, since they had no immemorial past : ' Ye ever remain children, in Greece there is no old man '. (Ὦ Σόλων, Σόλων, Ἕλληνες ἀεὶ παῖδές ἐστε, γέρων δὲ οὐκ ἔστιν.)

The mark of this period, when Herodotus was in Egypt, was a rigid adherence to what was old, overweening pride in the past, a hostile

---

[1] Cf. *J.E.A.* 1930, p. 366. Bell's remarks on concluding section of Vogt's *Herodot in Aegypten : Ein Kapitel Zum griechischen Kulturbewusstein*, Stuttgart, 1929.
[2] Herod. ii. 142.   [3] Ibid. 177.   [4] Ibid. 143.
[5] Plato, *Tim.* 226 ; cf. *Joseph. cont. Ap.* i. 7.

attitude to what was new and foreign. Herodotus regarded this attitude as a distinguishing mark of Egyptian civilization in general, but was unaware that it was only characteristic of a period of stagnation and decay, in contrast with his own growing civilization. The great epoch of birth and development of Egyptian civilization, when Egypt had been drawn into close, permanent relationship with foreign civilizations, e.g. (c. 1450 B.C.), the Babylonian civilization of Mesopotamia and the Cretan (Minoan) civilization of the Mediterranean, was long before his day.

Spiegelberg [1] puts it well when he says:

> 'We ought not to regard the Egyptians of Herodotus' day as representatives of the Ancient Egyptian civilization, but as the puny offshoots of a mighty growth that had been in full foliage hundreds and thousands of years before. Herodotus was the representative of a people still in the full ferment of youthful development, and so Egypt, with its age-long civilization, and its by that time stereotyped culture, created in him the impression that here was the original home of all, even of the Greek civilization. Thus he fell an easy victim of the belief fostered by the Egyptian priests—that Greek religion, for example, with its gods and sacred observations, originated for the most part in the Nile Valley.'

'He thus tended to over-estimate a very ancient civilization in contrast to Tacitus who, as the product of an outworn decadent age, saw the virtues of the youthful Germans in far too rosy a light—the one valued age too highly, the other youth.' [2]

(iv) The next phase in Graeco-Egyptian relations marks a decided change for the better. Political co-operation between the two peoples arose from a common hostility to Persia, and this does much to explain the welcome later extended by the Egyptians to Alexander and his Macedonians.

The XXVIth or Saite Dynasty was but the first of a number of interruptions in the series of foreign rulers who beginning about 700 B.C. have controlled the destiny of Egypt till the present day. For a short period this dynasty, with the help of Greek mercenaries, brought Egypt again under native rulers—Psammetichus I, Necho, Psammetichus II, Apries, Amasis, Psammetichus III. It was a period of national rebirth, when the high standards of civilization of the ancient Pharaonic Age were revived, an Egyptian renaissance, which created life again from the best tradition of the past.

The most outstanding ruler of this dynasty, Amasis the Philhellene, [3] constantly maintained a good understanding with the

---

[1] Spiegelberg, *The Credibility of Herodotus' Account of Egypt*, Blackwell, Oxford, 1927.
[2] Idem, ibid. pp. 38–9.
[3] Herod. ii. 178, 1.

Greeks. His friendliness to the Greeks is seen in his granting
Naucratis to them,[1] his keeping a bodyguard of Ionians and Carians,[2]
and his marrying a Greek lady of Cyrene.[3] He had, moreover, a
treaty of friendship with Polycrates, the powerful Greek tyrant of
Samos.[4] Amasis' naval strength, too, was the foundation of the
sea-power, which under the Ptolemies later made Egypt the dominant
State on the Mediterranean.

The conquest of Egypt by Cambyses (525 B.C.) brought this
period to an abrupt end. The Greek mercenaries, however, were
still found playing a prominent, but by this time unavailing, part in
the struggle between Psammetichus III, the last king of the dynasty,
and Cambyses. Egypt became a Persian province, and the event
was disastrous not only to the Greek military settlement in the
country, but also to the prosperous trading settlement of Naucratis.
The Persian conquest indirectly dealt a blow to the Asiatic Greek
cities which had the principal share in Naucratic trade.

' There is little evidence that the Persian kings ever injured
Greek trade of set purpose, or gave preferential treatment to
the rival commerce of Phoenicia. Yet, part at least of Ionia's
losses was plainly the result of Persian interference, and when
the Greek trade felt the shoe pinching it was but natural that
they should throw the entire blame on Persia as being the most
obvious cause of the pressure.' [5]

The Ionic Revolt and the Persian Wars with Greece added fuel to
the flames, and from this time onwards Greek and Egyptian made
common cause against the enemy. Thus we find that whenever the
Egyptians decided to raise the standard of revolt there were not
wanting Greek States to aid and abet them. In religious affairs the
Persian conquerors of Egypt interfered but little, if we may except
the outrages against Egyptian feeling attributed by Herodotus to the
mad Cambyses.[6] Yet Herodotus' story is significant of the great
animosity aroused if Egyptian feelings—for example, in the sphere of
religion—were trampled upon. The Persians seem to have shown
the same disregard for the religious scruples of the Athenians.[7] It
was a mistake the Greeks never committed, and perhaps it was
compatibility in religious matters—the willingness, as we notice in
Herodotus, to see Greek gods in Egyptian—that did much to explain
later the great success of the Greeks in their intercourse with the
Egyptians.

The first Egyptian revolt occurred in 485 B.C., but was suppressed
the following year by Xerxes himself, and it was under him that the
Egyptians, who were now placed under a still harder yoke, sent an

---

[1] Herod. ii. 178, 3.   [2] Ibid. xi. 154, 14.   [3] Ibid. 181, 2.
[4] Ibid. 39-40.   [5] Dr. M. Cary, in *C.A.H.* vii. 218–19.
[6] Herod. iii. 1, 14, 16, 27, 29, 30. Cf. Diod. Sic. i. 44, 3. τὴν εἰς τοὺς ἐγχωρίους
θεοὺς ἀσέβειαν.
[7] Ibid. viii. 53–4 Burning of whole of the Acropolis, 143–4.

Egyptian contingent of two hundred ships to take part in the battle of Artemisium and Salamis during his invasion of Greece. Under Artaxerxes I, Inaros, a delta dynast, instigated a revolt and secured the help of an Athenian fleet of two hundred ships which was then operating against Persia in Cypriote waters.[1] But all these efforts were in vain, and the Athenian attempt to establish themselves in Egypt ended in disaster in 454 B.C.[2] The Peace of Callias, 448 B.C., which reconciled Greece and Persia, and the Peloponnesian War 431–404, left Persia a free hand in Egypt, and it was not till 404 that a fresh revolt under Amyrtaeus broke out, and was only put down six years afterwards. Various successive revolts broke out, which go to prove the weak hold Persia had on Egypt. We find national uprisings in the time of the Ptolemies, but, as we shall see in connexion with that period, Hellenism had made such great strides in Egypt that even if Greek influence was regarded by some ultra-nationalist elements as foreign to Egypt, it had won such wide acceptance that the Ptolemaic king himself, who was first and foremost regarded as ruler of Egypt, and not as a foreign monarch ruling a distant dominion, was by no means unpopular.

The most serious revolt of the native Egyptians—that led by Nectanebo—was put down by the Persians with Greek help in 343 B.C., and thenceforward we know little of the history of Egypt till 332 B.C., when she exchanged a Persian master for a Macedonian and welcomed Alexander.

(v) The attempt to prove ancient connexions between Egypt and Geece was simply a result of the great impression made by the Egyptian culture and civilization on minds like that of Herodotus, who saw in Egypt the early age of the world, and also a result of the close contact between Greek and Egyptian that had begun in the Saite period.

Characteristic of his lack of bias [3] towards foreigners was Herodotus' belief in manifold borrowings from Egypt. The Egyptians were the first men, he says, who reckoned by years and made the year to consist of twelve divisions.

In the sphere of religion, ' the Egyptians first used the appellations of twelve gods (which the Greeks afterwards borrowed from them); and it was they who first assigned to the several gods their altars and images and temples, and first carved figures on stone '.[4]

Herodotus holds that the name of Heracles came from Egypt to Hellas, as he is a very ancient god in Egypt and was made one of the twelve gods seventeen thousand years before the reigning of Amasis ! [5]

---

[1] Thuc. i. 104.   [2] Ibid. 109.

[3] Plutarch, in disgust, called him φιλοβάρβαρος as being pro-Persian (*De Maligni- tate Herodoti*, par. 12), while admitting that ' the man can write ' (γραφικὸς ἀνήρ) (ibid. par. 43).

[4] Herod. ii. 4.   There were twelve great gods of Greece, but they did not corre- spond exactly to those of Egypt, e.g. Poseidon was unknown in Egypt (cf. Herod. ii. 43, 11).

[5] Ibid. 43.

The teaching of the worship of Dionysos came indirectly from Egypt, for Herodotus ' will not admit that it is a chance agreement between the Egyptian ritual of Dionysos and the Greek '.[1] ' Indeed, well-nigh all the names of the Gods came to Hellas from Egypt, except the names of Poseidon, the Dioscuri, Hera, and Hestia, Themis, the Graces and the Nereids.'[2] Not only did the Greeks learn the practice of divining from the sacrificed victim from Egypt (the fashions of divination at Thebes in Egypt and Dodona being alike), but also the establishment of solemn assemblies, processions, and services. This, he says, is proved because the Egyptian cere- monies are manifestly very ancient, and the Greek are of late origin.[3] Further, the doctrine that the human soul is immortal and the trans- migration of souls were first taught by the Egyptians and taken over by ' some Greeks early and late '.[4]

The Greeks learnt the art of measuring land from Egypt, but the sun-clock, sun-dial, and twelve divisions of the day came not from Egypt, but from Babylonia.[5]

According to Herodotus, Solon of Athens adopted a law of Amasis from Egypt that every Egyptian should yearly declare his means of livelihood to the ruler of his province, and, failing to do so or to prove that he had a just way of life, be punished with death. Hero- dotus calls it a perfect law.[6]

Herodotus' belief was that Greek civilization was due to foreign influences; religion came to a great extent from Egypt,[7] and the alphabet from Phoenicia.[8] He attributed little to Greece itself. It is for reasons such as these that some authorities (e.g., Bauer) find an anti-Hellenic attitude in Book II of his work (his digression on Egypt) for the dependence of Greek religion on Egypt is emphasized, and even the management of the Olympic Games is treated with scarcely veiled irony.[9] The general tone of Book II seems to be one of extreme diffidence as regards Greek achievements in the face

[1] Herod. ii. 49.   [2] Ibid. 50.   [3] Ibid. 58.
[4] Ibid. 123. The Egyptians believed that man's soul (his *ba*, or the ' Ka ', his double) was immortal, hence the elaborate rites that were paid to the dead ; in regard to metempsychosis, although no evidence can be found in Egyptian literature, Spiegelberg (*Credibility*, p. 32) holds that it was a popular belief which failed to gain admittance into the official religion. Cf. Diod. Sic., i. 98, 2 (Pythagoras learned in Egypt, among other things, the transmigration of the soul into every creature).
[5] Ibid. 109. Practical surveying of land was regularly ascribed to the Egyptians by the Greeks (cf. Diod. Sic., i. 81, 2 ; Strabo, 17, 1, 3, p. 787), but it was the Greeks who developed geometry as a science. See Henry Lyons in *J.E.A.* xii. 1926, 242 f.
[6] Ibid. 177. Actually Solon cannot have borrowed his ἀργίας δίκη from the law of Amasis, who became king in 569 B.C., whereas Solon's archonship was probably in 594–593 B.C. ; cf. i. 29. 1.
[7] Ibid. 52. T. R. Glover, *Sather Lectures*, Univ. of Calif. Press, 1924, p. 274. ' He missed the importance of some Gods, e.g. Ra (The Sun), Hâpi (The Nile) Thoth (ii. 67). He hellenized his data, as Greeks were apt to do, and did it too much ; and partly so, and partly from defective information, he generalized too much. He ignored the large place that magic held in Egyptian religion.' (For a useful summary on Herodotus' view of Egyptian religion see How and Wells on Book ii. Ch. 35.)
[8] Ibid. v. 58.   [9] Ibid. ii. 160, 1.

of the age-old story of Egypt. The one Greek who seems to have been unimpressed by that ' wisdom of Egypt ' which was almost a by-word in the mouths of his fellow-countrymen was Plato.[1] Herodotus' views on Egypt have thus laid him open to a good deal of criticism.

Yet it is Glover who makes the most generous critical remark on Herodotus' wholesale charge of derivation from Egypt:

> ' A stranger in a strange land without the strange language and a researcher into religion at any time in that millennium, would be equally at a loss.[2] . . . Like many of the ancients, both Greek and Roman, he assumes that gods worshipped by one race may be identified in gods worshipped by another.' [3]

It is perhaps profitable now to consider what general *modus vivendi* all these early contacts in Saitic and Persian times established in Eygpt between Greek and Egyptian before the Macedonian conquest established a still closer relationship.

The Persian conquest most probably had not been favourable to Egyptian Hellenism—we have noticed how it affected the trade of Naucratis—nevertheless, the Greeks remained in the country.[4] With Cambyses' conquest a fresh stream of Greeks poured into the country, as Herodotus relates : [5] ' Vast numbers of Greeks flocked thither, some, as was likely enough, to engage in trade, others to take military service, and others again merely to see the country.' (οἱ μὲν, ὡς οἰκὸς, κατ' ἐμπορίην, οἱ δὲ στρατευόμενοι, οἱ δὲ τινες καὶ αὐτῆς τῆς χώρης θεηταί·) Just such a globe-trotter had been Herodotus, as we have seen.

Yet, in spite of the new influx, in spite of the settlement at Naucratis and elsewhere, the two worlds remained strangers to one another. Jardé has an interesting comment to make on this period : [6]

> ' The Greeks may have taken certain technical processes from the Egyptians : the statuaries of Chios learned methods of casting in Egypt, and the export of Egyptian papyrus made the diffusion of literary works possible. But the two civilizations did not interpenetrate or blend. It is remarkable that we at no moment perceive an appreciable influence of the Egyptian language on the Greek. The Greeks were generally ignorant of

---

[1] T. E. Peet, in *C.A.H.* i. 326.
[2] Sather, *Classical Lectures*, Univ. of Calif. Press, 1924, p. 281.
[3] Ibid., p. 273.
[4] At the time of the Macedonian conquest there were Greek centres in the valley of the Nile. Naucratis was still flourishing, and from it the Greeks had sent out swarms into the Delta, and even to Upper Egypt. Stephanus of Byzantium mentions a Hellenic colony at Abydos, and at an early date there was one at Elephantine : Cf. Rubensohn. *Elephantine Papyri*, Berlin, 1907. Greeks were found even in the Oasis (Steph. Byz., *s.v.* ; cf. Herod. iii. 26).
[5] Herod. iii. 139.
[6] A. Jardé, *The Formation of the Greek People*, London, Kegan Paul, Trench Trubner & Co., 1926, p. 209.

the language of the country, lived apart from the natives, and understood neither their institutions nor their manners. Herodotus travelled in Egypt, visited the temples, and saw the sights : but he only saw the outward setting. He accepted popular romances and the yarns of his ciceroni as if they were historical narratives, and was quite unable to criticize them ; he transformed the epithets applied by the story-tellers to the heroes of their tales into illustrious personages. Like a good Greek, for whom Hellas was the centre of the world, he was blind to all the native characteristics of Egyptian civilization, and imagined that he saw everywhere the gods, and even the institutions of Greece.' [1]

While the Saitic Pharaohs had been profoundly influenced by the character of the Greeks, the mass of the native Egyptians were unscathed by it.

' Before the impact of the foreign life [says Breasted] which thus flowed in upon Egypt, the Egyptian showed himself entirely unmoved, and held himself aloof, fortified behind his ceremonial purity and his inviolable reserve. If he could have had his way he would have banished the foreigners one and all from his shores ; under the circumstances, like the modern Chinese, he trafficked with them and was reconciled to their presence by the gain they brought him.' [2]

These two criticisms well-nigh sum up the situation before the Macedonian conquest was to change it beyond recognition.

When the Ptolemies ruled the land of the Pharaohs after Alexander's death we find a closer interpenetration of Greek and Egyptian proceeding—the two peoples were less divided—if we except Alexandria and one or two other πόλεις, a blend of the Greek and Egyptian races gradually took place—a realization of Alexander's ideal, in Egypt, at any rate—which reached its culmination towards the end of the dynasty. This fusion was only retarded—in fact received a setback—when the Romans succeeded the Ptolemies as rulers of Egypt.

[1] E.g. the goddess Neith of Sais, with her bow and her weaving, could only be Athene (Herod. ii. 59), and the best Solon could do, as we have seen, was to borrow one of his laws from Amasis (Herod. ii. 177).
[2] Breasted, *A History of Egypt*, London, Hodder and Stoughton, 1924, p. 570.

CHAPTER IV

ALEXANDER IN EGYPT

IN the autumn of the year 332 B.C. an army of Macedonians and Greeks numbering some 40,000 men invaded Egypt. It was led by Alexander, who had gone forth two years before to assail the Persian Empire. Before he reached Egypt he had defeated an army gathered by the Persian satraps on the River Granicus in Asia Minor and an army commanded by the great king himself at Issus on the Syrian coast. By the autumn of 332 the Persian power had disappeared from the coast lands of the Eastern Mediterranean, except from Egypt. It was necessary for Alexander to obtain possession of Egypt before he plunged into the countries of the East, because his enemies were still strong at sea and he had no fleet with which to counter them: the only plan which would secure his base would be for him to hold all the ports round the Eastern Mediterranean, and leave the hostile fleets in the air with no place in which they could refit or provision.[1]

According to Hogarth,[2] the reason why Alexander after Issus had not marched straight up to Mesopotamia and Persia, but had turned off into Syria and Egypt, was that what was certainly his original plan must have miscarried. For the sea, held by the Greeks, was hostile to him. The treasonable correspondence, which fell into his hands at Issus,[3] sufficiently proves this. Issus had shown that he could be cut off from his base, and that if he were defeated there was no hope of repairing his losses in men and material. He had started prematurely, without being assured that the agreement he had made at Corinth with the Greek states, and whom he represented as ἡγεμών, would be loyally kept. His own Macedonian ships, which had taken to the sea, were over-awed by larger hostile fleets. He was therefore compelled to change the whole course of his campaign and close to the Greeks not only all ports round the Levant, which he had already done, but also all ports right round to Cyrene, the last Greek stronghold in the Mediterranean. Thus it was that Alexander came to Egypt. It seems extraordinary that Alexander's invasion of Egypt met with no opposition. He could march into the eastern desert, to Cyrene, without the slightest fear about his base. Further, after he had left Egypt for good in the spring of the following year, the country remained perfectly quiet under his extortionate governor, Cleomenes, during all the Far Eastern campaigns; and after Alexander's death it accepted his successor as a matter of

---

[1] Arrian, ii. 17; *C.A.H.* vii. 373.
[2] *J.E.A.* (1915), p. 54.   [3] Cf. Arrian, ii. 145, 152.

course. The explanation lies in the events of the past hundred years in the political co-operation of Egyptians and Greeks, arising from their common hostility to Persia, the stage in Graeco-Egyptian relations already mentioned in the previous chapter.

The Egyptians, as we have seen, had long been used to the presence of Greeks, and in their eyes the Greeks were the foremost fighting race in the world, a belief confirmed by the predominance of the Greeks in the composition of successive Persian armies sent against Egypt. In the year 332, therefore, opposition against the Macedonians was unlikely. In fact, they were regarded as coming to deliver Egypt once more from the Persian yoke recently reimposed, for nationalist Egyptian feeling survived the reconquest by Darius Ochus. The famous Alexander-Romance,[1] which was originally composed in or near Alexandria, as its author's local knowledge of the city shows, actually starts with a design to connect the Macedonian regime with the succession of former native kings, and in it Nectanebo II, who had been driven out by the victorious Persians, appears as the real father of Alexander.

This story brings Nectanebo into the select band of national heroes believed popularly to have survived defeat and death to secure the ultimate victory of the lost cause. It also illustrates the effects of stories put about in Alexander's own life-time which threw doubt on Philip's fatherhood and suggested that a god had begotten the conqueror of the world.[2] The chief interest of the story, however, lies in its nationalist tendency. It proves the survival of the old spirit of Egypt and its desire to accept Greek rule.

Alexander's transaction with the Oracle of Ammon in the Oasis of Siwah was an attempt on his own part to establish his son-ship to Zeus-Ammon. It was natural that once he had conquered Egypt he should call himself Son of Ammon, for in this he was simply following traditional usage. It is to be noted that so far as his own followers attributed divinity to him it was expressed as son-ship of Ammon, since there were no other means elsewhere [3] of so satisfactory a kind for deifying a living sovereign. After his death, his successors, whether in Asia Minor, Syria, or Babylon, promoted his apotheosis for their own ends as a divinity in the Egyptian pantheon. For the benefit of Greeks or philhellenic princes, he might appear on coins

---

[1] Narrated in Pseudo-Callisthenes, *Fabulous History of Alexander*, i. 3 ; ii. 26 ; see Budge, *The History of Alexander the Great* (1889), p. 12 ; cf. ' Kallisthenes ' in Pauly-Wissowa, Stuttgart, 1919, xx., espec. pp. 1707 ff ; cf. also M. L. W. Laistner, *A History of the Greek World*, 479–323 B.C., p. 320.

[2] *J.E.A.*, April, 1915, p. 57.

[3] But see Seltman, *Greek Coins*, Methuen, 1933, p. 205 and Pl. XLVIII, 3 ; obverse Heracles ; reverse Zeus Olympios enthroned. ' Though introduced in 336 B.C., these types were destined to appeal equally to Greek and to Oriental subjects of Alexander as yet unconquered ; for the Phoenician was to see in the obverse type his own god Melqart, the Cilician was to regard the seated deity as the great Baal of Tarsus, and the Babylonian, though he might not be able to read the Greek name of Alexander, was to look on pictures that might recall his own Gilgamesh, the lion slayer, and the figure of Bel-Marduk, god of Babylon.'

with attributes of a hero, such as Herakles ; [1] but, if he was to be a full god, the ram-horns of Ammon must protrude from his hair. [2] Alexander's own insistence on the validity of his Egyptian deification throughout his Empire had far-reaching consequences, but at the moment it dealt a serious blow to Hellenic political and social ideals. One soon sees its effects on the most democratic of Greek cities when divine honours are paid in Athens itself successively to Demetrius of Phalerum and to Demetrius the Besieger. Alexander set a precedent that his successors, especially the Ptolemies, were not slow to follow.

In the organization of Egypt, which Alexander arranged before his departure, it is noticeable that he did not concentrate the administration in the person of one satrap. He preferred instead decentralization. Arrian says : [3]

" It is stated he divided the government of Egypt between many officers, both from his surprise at the nature of the country and its strength since it did not appear to him safe to entrust the command of all Egypt to one man.'

He states, moreover, that the Romans, too, learnt a lesson from Alexander and kept Egypt under guard, and never sent anyone from the Senate as proconsul of Egypt, but only those who were enrolled among them as knights.

In another respect, too, Alexander's arrangement presents a special feature. Previously in Caria he had shown by the appointment of Ada, a native princess, that he was ready to pay regard to the national feelings of the subjected people. Similarly in Egypt [4] he placed two natives at the head of the civil administration of Upper and Lower Egypt, while he assigned the western and eastern frontier districts of the Delta, Libya, and Arabia (near Heroonpolis) to the Greek Apollonius and the Naucratite Cleomenes. The two Egyptians were coupled with two Macedonian military governors, and the fortresses of Memphis and Pelusium received their special commandants. In contrast to this decentralization, the whole administration of finance was placed in the hands of Cleomenes of Naucratis ; the heads of districts had to pay the taxes to him after they had raised them in their own districts in the fashion previously adopted. No doubt the population was heartily glad that the collection of taxes was not in foreign but in native hands. When Alexander departed, he was accompanied by the affection of the Egyptians, who felt themselves free of the load which had rested on them since the reconquest by Ochus on the defeat of Nectanebo. Alexander's organization had been one of elaborate checks, but was, however, of short duration. The effective control of the country seems to have been soon gathered into his hands by one man, [5] Cleomenes

---

[1] Seltman, *Greek Coins*, p. 212 and Pl. XLIX. 8.
[2] Idem, ibid., p. 221 and Pl. XLIX. 9.
[3] Arrian, iii. 5. [4] Ibid. 5. [5] *C.A.H.* vii. 378.

of Naucratis, who had become a citizen of the new Alexandria.   He
was apparently clever enough to use his power of financial control to
wrest the real power to himself, and seems soon to have gained a
reputation in the Greek world for dishonesty and extortion.[1]

The Ptolemies devised a system on other lines, and the high
position given in Alexander's arrangement to native Egyptians is a
feature not reproduced under them till the later days of the dynasty.

[1] Arrian, vii. 23.

CHAPTER V

THE PAPYRI AND THEIR VALUE

WITH the establishment of the Ptolemaic dynasty in Egypt Greek became the official language of the country, and maintained that position throughout the period of Roman rule and down to, and indeed some time after, the Arab invasion. At the beginning of the 8th century A.D. Greek was still freely employed by the newly appointed Arab officials, and bilingual receipts written in Greek and Arabic persisted for a century more. Our knowledge of Egypt during this period is derived from literary, epigraphic, papyrological, and archaeological sources, but it is the papyri that constitute our main source of information.

The most significant thing about the papyrus texts found in Egypt is the way they illustrate the history of Hellenic culture in what was a very un-Hellenic environment and the development and gradual transformation of that culture through successive generations.

A scientific pursuit of Greek papyri has been in progress for little longer than a generation. The older collections were based entirely on purchase from dealers, and it was not till the winter of 1895–6 that an expedition was organized for the express purpose of the discovery of papyri.[1] Spectacular finds on the site of the ancient Oxyrhynchus [2] drew general attention to this method of research, and since then excavations have been carried on at a number of sites by explorers from various countries. As a result old collections were enlarged and many new ones formed. Most of the papyri have come from the ruins of ancient towns or villages either from the remains of houses or the rubbish-heaps which surrounded them, as in the case of the Oxyrhynchus papyri. The second main source is tombs, for occasionally, treasured papyri accompanied their owners to the grave.[3]

---

[1] See *J.E.A.* viii. (1922), p. 121, ' Twenty-five years of Papyrology ', for an excellent account of this and further expeditions in search of papyri. These resulted in the publication not only of the Oxyrhynchus, but also of the Hibeh and Tebtunis papyri.

[2] Ibid., p. 129, ' The Library of a Greek of Oxyrhynchus.' The discovery and publication of the Oxyrhynchus Papyri has been an epoch-making work. They are the fruit of a scientific examination of the rubbish-heaps surrounding one of the more important towns of Graeco-Roman Egypt. They range in date from the 1st century B.C. to the 7th century A.D., from the beginnings of Roman rule to the Arab conquest and cover the whole range of life, including, as they do, literary texts, official and administrative documents, legal and commercial papers, pecuniary accounts, and private letters.

[3] Earlier discoveries which preceded that at Oxyrhynchus had been the product, either of an isolated group of mummy cartonnages, like the Petrie Papyri from Gurob, or of a chance discovery of a jar containing documents, like those of the Serapeum at Memphis, or of rolls found in a few tombs, like the Hyperides manuscripts of the middle of the century, or the British Museum acquisitions in 1890.

Though the papyrological evidence is large and important, it has its limitations, for the papyri come only from some parts of the so-called 'country' (χώρα)—from the Fayum, from certain places in Middle Egypt, and from others in southern Egypt. Nevertheless, the material found provides us with such abundant and trustworthy information for the Graeco-Roman period as we have for no other country. ' In the field of ancient history the Babylonian cuneiform tablets and cylinders alone furnish material comparable to this.' [1]

Literary papyri form but a fraction of what has been found. [2] Of the non-literary or documentary kind, [3] those already edited now run into five figures, and there are numbers still awaiting publication.

There is rarely in the papyri any allusion to the events of history, nevertheless they serve to correct the false focus in which we are apt to see the past. [4] Since their great quality is their unconscious and ephemeral character, they differ in a marked respect from inscriptions which were designed for public view. They reveal to us a class neglected by historians, dealing as they do with the common events of daily life, the little vexations or triumphs, the petty schemes of forgotten men.

' Such people neither make nor possess any claim to fame and are seldom to be met with in the pages of the ancient historians, where the limelight is commonly focussed upon outstanding

[1] M. Rostovtzeff, *The Social and Economic History of the Hellenistic World*, Oxford, 1941, i. 259.

[2] See *J.E.A.* viii. (1922), 123–7, and new chapters in the *History of Greek Literature*, edited by J. U. Powell and E. A. Barber. A selection from the new literary Papyri is still in preparation for the Loeb Library (*Select Papyri*, vols. iii. and iv.). Some Literary Papyri have been published in the Oxford series of Classical texts—viz., *Hellenica Oxyrhyncha cum Theopompi et Cratippi Fragmentis; Fragmenta Tragica Papyracea*, by A. S. Hunt.

[3] A convenient selection has already been issued in the Loeb Library (*Select Papyri*, vols. i and ii), but of course they cannot replace Wilcken and Mitteis' standard selection of representative texts or the publications of Papyri by the Graeco-Roman branch of the Egypt Exploration Society, which are periodically distributed among various English museums and libraries.

The following are among the chief editions of non-literary papyri : The volumes of the Graeco-Roman Branch of the Egypt Exploration Society, edited by Grenfell and Hunt, especially :—

The Oxyrhynchus Papyri (17 vols., 1896–1927).
The Tebtunis Papyri (2 vols. 1902–7).
Greek Papyri in the British Museum, by Kenyon and Bell (5 vols., 1893–1917).
The Flinders Petrie Papyri, by Mahaffy and Smyly (3 vols., 1891–1905).
Griechische Urkunden aus den Mussen zu Berlin, by Wilcken, Viereck, Schubart and others (7 vols., 1893–1926).
Papyrus grecs de Lille, by Jouguet and others (2 vols., 1907–23).
Papiri della Società italiana, by Vitelli and others (10 vols., 1912–32).
Catalogue des Antiquites égyptiennes du Musée du Caire, Zenon Papyri, by Edgar (4 vols., 1925–31).
Papyrus grecs d'époque byzantine, by Maspero (3 vols., 1911–16).

There are many other smaller publications as well, some of which are referred to in the following pages.

[4] See H. I. Bell in *J.E.A.* vi. (1920), ' The Historical Value of Greek Papyri,' especially p. 237 for a useful article on the point.

personalities, while the multitudes of humbler folk, the material which the supermen worked with and set their mark upon, are left to lurk in obscurity.' [1]

The study of such documents as the papyri furnishes a wealth and variety of material to which there is no parallel in any other branch of ancient history. The comedies of Aristophanes, the dialogues of Plato, the *Memorabilia* of Xenophon, and the speeches of the Attic orators, in comparison with the papyri of Hellenistic and Roman times, illustrate to but a slight extent society in Classical Athens. As regards Athens of the 3rd century, the New Comedy is too conventional and limited in range to be a satisfactory source of information, and little represents wide circles of Athenian society. When we turn to Roman society, we find the correspondence of Cicero invaluable for the life of the official and upper classes in the last days of the Republic. The Epistles of Pliny give a picture of the life of a busy man of affairs at Rome in the 1st century of our era. Yet neither Cicero's nor Pliny's correspondence throws any great light on the lower grades of the social order comparable to that of the papyri in Egypt. Moreover, their correspondence deals more with the individual, and in the case of Pliny was definitely composed for publication with an eye on posterity and at a time when letter-writing had become a studied art.

It is only in the Greek papyri found in Egypt that we have a fairly representative mass of evidence for the social life of almost all classes, from the well-to-do circles represented in the papers of the strategos Apollonius to the small peasant and artisan. Their letters show us something of their religious and moral ideas and social habits, while the miscellaneous documents reveal the economic processes, the legal transactions, the communal life, the administrative practice of Graeco-Roman Egypt for over a thousand years. Yet what for our purpose is the main thing is the light the papyri throw on race-relations. In this sense they serve in some respects to supplement several of our literary sources for the period, such as Josephus and Philo.

---

[1] *Select Papyri*, Loeb Library, vol. i. Introduction, p. xii.

CHAPTER VI

THE HELLENIZATION OF EGYPT

W E have seen how Egypt in the Saite period and in the intervals of independence between Persian rule had linked herself closely with the Greek world. Persian domination, too, opened the country to many foreigners, both Persian and other subjects of the Persian king. The Pharaohs of the XXVIIIth to the XXXth dynasties had foreshadowed the policy of the Ptolemies and admitted into Egypt both Greek mercenaries and Greek traders, but they failed to solve the problem of how to establish a suitable *modus vivendi* between the immigrants and the native Egyptians, while reserving for the latter political and social superiority.

From the Greek point of view the problem which faced Ptolemy Lagos, one of the foremost of Alexander's lieutenants, first governor, and then, some time after Alexander's death, king of Egypt,[1] and his successors was likewise no easy one. It might have been possible for Alexander to educate Persians in the Macedonian art of war, to overcome the resistance of Macedonians and Greeks, and to bring about a fusion of races and civilizations. But on his early death his successors, the Diadochoi, were forced to rely on the Graeco-Macedonian elements in their kingdoms and to give them an unquestioned position of superiority over the native element. They could not, to take one instance, risk, in their conflicts with one another, the creation of an army based on the native element.[2] Moreover, although the economic potentialities of Egypt were very great, the pace of economic activity was slow, and as no help in the work of readjustment and improvement could be expected from the natives, the first Ptolemy, Soter, was forced to rely upon his Macedonian fellow-countrymen, and upon Greeks and hellenized Semites.

The Successors, the Diadochoi, were so far dominated by Alexander's ideas that each felt it the primary duty of a king to advance the civilization of his kingdom—in other words, to found cities within its boundaries. But it is very doubtful whether they really grasped the ideals underlying Alexander's colonial policy, or, if they grasped them, whether they approved them. Being men of smaller calibre, they were more subject to the prejudice of their race and age. Most of them must have shared the normal contempt of the Macedonians for barbarians.

---

[1] Ptolemy Soter, though practically an independent sovereign, retained the title of satrap till 305 B.C. Cf. *P. Eleph.* i. 2.

[2] *C.A.H.* vi. p. 10.

Alexander had made himself very unpopular with the Macedonians by his policy of putting barbarians on an equal footing with them, but he could afford to be unpopular owing to his vast prestige and the loyalty of the Macedonian people. In the case of the Successors, political necessity compelled them to be more respectful of the prejudices of their followers than Alexander had been. Moreover, they had to win the allegiance of their followers in competition with many other claimants. They had therefore to conform to the ideas of those whom they led. Hence they tended to relegate the barbarians once more to the position of an inferior race. Thus it comes as no surprise to find that for a time the Greeks ruled Egypt as a conquered country, and not as Alexander had meant. But this was a state of affairs that could not last for long, and the policy of the ruling class inevitably changed with the force of circumstances.

It is to the papyri that we are indebted for the story of the interaction of the two races, of the spread of Greek culture and of the influence exerted by that of the natives on their conquerors. The earliest dated Greek papyrus yet discovered was written in the year 311–310 B.C.[1] This document brings us into a purely Greek circle. It is the contract of marriage between Heracleides, whose origin is not stated, and Demetria, daughter of Leptines of Cos. The marriage-law is purely Greek, and unaffected, as were later marriage contracts, by the different Egyptian law; the witnesses, like the principals, are all Greek, one from Gela, three from Temnos, one from Cyrene, one from Cos. The contract was found and probably written at Elephantine, on the southern frontier of Egypt. The future residence of the parties was uncertain : they had at present no settled home : εἶναι δὲ ἡμᾶς κατὰ ταὐτὸ ὅπου ἂν δοκῆι ἄριστον εἶναι βουλευομένοις κοινῆι βουλῆι Λεπτίνηι καὶ Ἡρακλείδηι. (' We shall live together wherever it seems best to Leptines and Heracleides consulting in common.')

The Greeks mentioned are representative of the majority of the settlers at this time in Egypt. The commonest types were mercenary soldiers, merchants, and some of higher class who filled the superior posts in the new bureaucracy. They came largely from the smaller centres of the old Greek civilization rather than from such places as Athens, Miletus, or Syracuse.

They seem to have been living scattered thinly among an alien population, for the contract was not written in a Greek colony, and Greek cities were few in Egypt, and from none of them have we papyrus documents,[2] at least at this period.

In the later papyri from the Fayum, as represented by the archives of Cleon, the Master of the Works,[3] and Zeno, the agent of the

---

[1] *P. Eleph.* i.
[2] Except the Alexandrian laws in the famous Halle Papyrus, *P. Hal.* i. (Dikaiomata, Berlin, 1913).
[3] Edited in the 3 vols. of the *Petrie Papyri.*

Finance Minister, Apollonius,[1] the names mentioned are also for the most part Greek: Zeno, Cleon, Jason, Xenon, Hermolaus, Theodorus, Zoilus, Apollonius, for instance. In these texts of the middle of the 3rd century B.C. we hear frequently of men from the city-states of Greece or Macedonia and from the surrounding non-Hellenic peoples. Many probably were not born in Greece, but had come to Egypt from Greece or Asia Minor to seek their fortunes.

These settlers seem to have maintained their Hellenic traditions. A small group of the letters of Zeno, the owner of a remarkable archive discovered at Gerza in the Fayum, is concerned with the training of a boy who is to compete in a gymnastic contest:[2] gymnasia, in fact, were founded all over the Near East in the Greek cities and villages wherever Greeks had settled.[3] Homer, Euripides, the New Comedy, Plato were read, and the Persae of Timotheus holds the distinction of being the earliest Greek papyrus yet found. Moreover, the earliest non-literary papyri were found in a jar wrapped in another piece of papyrus containing Greek drinking-songs.[4] In an inscription of Ptolemais, reference too is made to tragic, comic, and epic poets and actors, a harpist, a dancer, and other artists.[5]

Clubs and associations, whether for worship, sports, or social purposes, were formed. Greek institutions, like that of the ephebi, were continued, the names and offices of Greek magistrates were transferred to a new setting, and the Laws of Alexandria, as shown by the Halle papyrus, and probably those of Ptolemais, were Greek. Moreover, the Greek language as used in these documents is not the artificial literary Greek, but the developing κοινή or international Greek of the time.

We see thus present all over Egypt a minority of Greek settlers with their Greek tongue and Greek culture in contrast with the mass of the native population, with a language, culture, and highly organized religious system of their own, going back, as Herodotus noted a few centuries earlier, to an antiquity long before Hellas had been heard of. It is the frequent occurrence in the papyri of Egyptian names, the allusions to Egyptian conditions, that remind one of the natives with whom the Greeks were daily in contact and on whom the economic prosperity of the country depended.

It is especially in the sphere of religion and political organization that matters were felt by the Greeks to be different from those in their homeland. The strange environment had begun to tell. We hear of Sarapis, a new deity who was destined to become the national god of Hellenized Egypt and then to spread his cult throughout the civilized world. The most probable view as to the origin of this cult is that Sarapis is a coalition deity—a combination of Osiris and

[1] Published (1) by Societa italiana per la ricerca dei Papiri in vols. iv–vi of its *Papiri greci e latini* (*P.S.I.*); (2) by C. C. Edgar in the *Ann. du Serv.*, xviii and foll. (P. Edgar) (P. Cairo Zen.). Many papyri in the British Museum and elsewhere are still unpublished.
[2] *P.S.I.* 340. [3] Wilcken, *Archiv. f. Pap.* vi. 389, 392.
[4] P. Berol. 13,270 (*B.G.U.*). [5] Dittenberger, *Or. Graec. Sel.* 51 (i. 78–81).

Apis of Memphis designed to form the meeting-point of Greek and Egyptian and adapted to Hellenistic forms of worship and belief.[1] As such, the cult is important for our estimate of the religious policy of the Ptolemies. A letter from Zeno's archive gives us a valuable illustration of the growth of this cult.[2] The earliest Greek papyrus we possess is a curse written by a Greek woman, Artemisia, in which the vengeance of the ' Lord (δεσπότης) Oserapis ' is called down upon a man by whom she had a daughter.[3] This scrap of papyrus may have been laid at the feet of the god in the days of Alexander the Great and proves that even before Ptolemy I established a cult of Sarapis at Alexandria, the Osiris-Apis of the Memphis Serapeum was already a deity of prestige for Greeks in Egypt.

There were other features present in the religious life of the Greek inhabitants of Egypt that showed the influence of their new environment.   Among the Zeno letters is one from the priests of Aphrodite to the finance minister (διοικητής) Apollonius asking for 100 talents of myrrh for a burial.   Aphrodite is here probably the Egyptian Hathor, who was worshipped as a cow, and not as the human figure to whom the Greeks were accustomed to pay obeisance.[4] From this letter we see already that the Greeks had advanced a stage further in their relations with the religion of Egypt than that depicted in Herodotus.

Another new feature was the worship of the living Ptolemy. The official cult was indeed Greek, developed gradually from the worship of a king or queen after death, but it was not till the latter part of the 3rd century B.C. that the reigning Ptolemy and his wife were worshipped.[5] But Greek though it was in its forms, a cult of this kind could hardly have grown up in classical times. It seems to have grown up under the influence of Oriental absolutist ideas; the deification of men recently dead or still living was a feature of the Greek world after Alexander.[6] The Greek, accustomed to live

---

[1] Cf. P. Jouguet, *Macedonian Imperialism and the Hellenization of the East*, London, Kegan Paul, etc., 1928, p. 339.   See E. Bevan, *A History of Egypt under the Ptolemaic Dynasty*, London, Methuen, 1927, pp. 41–8, and especially pp. 44–5, for a detailed discussion on the origin of the Cult.

[2] *P.S.I.* iv. 345 = P. Edgar, 7.

[3] Bevan, op. cit., p. 43 ;   U. Wilcken, *Urkunde der Ptolemaerzeit Berlin*, and Leipzig, 1922, etc., No. 1.

[4] *P.S.I.* iv. 328.

[5] Cf. *P. Lond.* iii. 879, p. 6 (B.C. 123) ' in the reign of Ptolemy the benefactor God, the son of Ptolemy and Cleopatra the Gods manifest and Queen Cleopatra his wife '.

[6] Cf. C. W. McEwan, *The Oriental Origin of Hellenistic Kingship*, Univ. of Chicago Press, 1934, pp. 238 seq.   Divine kingship was normal in the ancient Orient, and this traditional form was the essential pattern of Hellenistic monarchy, yet political theory, in sanctioning deification, gave it an occasional Olympian tinge and inevitably formalized it.   But Bevan (op. cit. pp. 48–9) believes this cult was a Hellenic development, not borrowed from an oriental tradition. Divine honours offered to men was, in 5th-century Athens, a figure of speech (Aesch. *Supp.* pp. 980 ff.), and the forms of religious worship could be used as a mode of flattery, addressed to eminent men of the time.   It began in the Greek world before Alexander.   Nevertheless, the worship of a dead man was much more in accord with the ancestral religion of the Greeks than the new-fangled worship of men still living.

in a small republic, disliked Oriental ideas of absolute monarchy, and had some difficulty in submitting to the will of a mortal god. Yet the Greeks made their illustrious dead into heroes,[1] and as such the object of worship, and Ionian cities had often decreed divine honours to living men.[2] Such customs and beliefs were not unfavourable to the establishment of a worship of kings, and the Hellenic worship of kings existed in most of the Hellenistic monarchies.

Side by side with this Greek cult, moreover, was the Egyptian cult of the Ptolemy as Pharaoh.[3]

Since the earliest days of her history Egypt had worshipped her kings. The kingship had a complex origin, hence the five names which express the divine descent of the Pharaohs.[4] These five names were taken by the Ptolemies, viz. (i) Horus-Ra, (ii) Lord of the Two Crowns, (iii) Golden Horus, (iv) King of Upper and Lower Egypt, (v) Son of Ra, and the name of every Ptolemaic king was Ptolemy, either alone, as with Soter I and Philadelphus, or with an accompanying epithet, as with their successors—for example, Euergetes I was Ptolemy, Living ever Beloved of Ptah. Thus to the Egyptians once the Ptolemies were accepted as Pharaohs they were naturally regarded as gods. Alexander himself, as we have seen, had had no difficulty in being recognized as the son of Ammon in the Oasis of Siwah,[5] nor had his successors in legalizing their dynasty. The Ptolemies only took on this rôle of god-kings gradually, since the first was a Macedonian of the old type with little liking for the mystical despotism of the Orient. They were fond of boasting of their Macedonian blood, and may have accepted rather than sought this profitable assimilation with the gods of Egypt.[6]

Yet they took some time to adopt the characteristics of the true Pharaohs. Greek sentiment had to be considered. The second Ptolemy made a great advance on his predecessor in conforming to Egyptian custom : not only did he take the five names, but married his sister on both sides, a union quite contrary to Greek custom, and a big concession to native ideas. When Philopator likewise married his sister, as did almost all the Ptolemies after him, and openly

---

[1] McEwan, op. cit., p. 24. The Greeks were accustomed to pay post-mortem homage to city-founders and other distinguished founders and benefactors : a few men in the Greek world had even received ante-mortem heroic or divine honours, but deification was not normal in Greece.

[2] Ibid., p. 25. Lysander is cited as the first deified Greek (Duris of Samos in Plut. *Lysander* 18), but possibly the Samians did not really accord him divine honours.

[3] Cf. Wilcken, *Chrest.* 109. ' He that restored the sacred rites and the laws established by the Most Great and Most Great and Most Great Hermes, Lord of the 30 years periods, like Hephaestus the Great, King like Helios, Great King of the Upper and Lower regions, offspring of the Benefactor Gods whom Hephaestus glorified, to whom Helios gave the power, image of Zeus, son of Helios, Ptolemy who liveth for ever, the beloved of Isis.'

[4] Moret : *The Nile and Egyptian Civilization*, Kegan Paul, etc., London, 1927, p. 151.

[5] See *J.E.A.* ii. (1915), 56 seq. ' Alexander in Egypt and some Consequences.'

[6] P. Jouguet : *Macedonian Imperialism and the Hellenization of the East*, Kegan Paul, etc., London, 1928, p. 288.

adopted the royal title of the Pharaohs, the native Egyptian found every characteristic of his national sovereigns in the Macedonian king.

In the sphere of political organization we see, too, a system totally different from that which the Greeks were accustomed to. From the beginning of their rule in Egypt, says Rostovtzeff,[1] the Ptolemies appropriated a politico-religious principle which had always been the basis of the Egyptian state—that the King alone held absolute power and unlimited rights of disposal over the material resources of the country as a whole, and the wealth of individuals in particular. On this system of ' divine right ' the Ptolemies founded their administrative, social, and economic policy. They elaborated it in detail, and forced the feudal element in Egypt, especially the temples and priesthood, to obey it. This system had at its core not Greek but Egyptian ideas and practice, whatever the new elements introduced into it by the Greeks. The whole economic organization of Egypt, in contrast to that of Greece and Italy, was built up on the principle of centralization and control by the Government, as well as the nationalization of all production in agricultural and industrial life.

> ' Nowhere in the whole evolution of mankind can be found so far reaching and so systematic limitations as those which applied to private property in Ptolemaic Egypt.' [2]

Unless, of course, we think of modern parallels in the totalitarian states of to-day !

The main reason for the adoption of such a system was most probably that it was impossible to transform Egypt into a Greek country with free and autonomous cities and at the same time maintain the strength of Egypt as a united state. The Ptolemies wanted to have a rich and strong state, so they sacrificed the interests of the individual to the principle of systematizing and perfecting the old Egyptian administrative and economic system.[3] Yet the chief aim of the Ptolemies was not to enrich themselves or rob the population of the whole amount of what they produced, as some have held : they did not want to be unjust and make their subjects unhappy. The selection of fine names, like Euergetes and Soter, was not always pure hypocrisy. The results achieved were, on the surface, splendid, and the first three Ptolemies were popular among the population but the system had its inherent evils. Egypt became the richest of the Hellenistic states and the Ptolemies the world's bankers. On the other hand, the spirit of the nation was one of indifference—the dull obedience of serfs possessing no initiative or patriotism, whose thoughts were wholly concentrated on the problems of their daily bread and economic interests. To this mood of the masses the

---

[1] Rostovtzeff in *J.E.A.* vi. (1920), 164 seq.   ' The Foundations of Social and Economic life in Egypt in Hellenistic Times.'
[2] Ibid. p. 164.   [3] Ibid. p. 173.

Ptolemies brought little by little the Greek conquerors of the country themselves.[1]

Nevertheless the achievements of the Ptolemies in Egypt greatly influenced the future. The structure they built up furnished valuable data for all those who afterwards sought for suitable methods to create a rich and powerful state in which autocratic government was to be supreme. The Romans continued this system in Egypt, and even adapted it to the organization of their Empire. Even the new European nations which became the descendants of the Roman provinces were influenced by the ideas of the ancient world, and the same questions which the ancient world had proved incapable of deciding cropped up time and again, ' Does the individual exist for the State, or does the State exist to assure for the individual the free development of his creative powers ? ' [2]

Under the system that has been outlined the Ptolemies instituted a dual policy as regards their Greek and native subjects. At the outset they treated the population of the χώρα differently from those of the πόλεις. There was a contrast between the town, Hellenic in character, and the country, the Chora, which remained Oriental. They differed in everything—political system, economic system, language, occupations, habits, and morals.[3] The Ptolemies preserved the traditional division of the country into Upper and Lower Egypt and its further division into nomes. The Egyptian seems to have been attached to his nome by birth, as the Greek citizen was to his city. It was the administrative district. The whole valley of the Nile, except perhaps the domains set apart for the Greek cities —Ptolemais, Naucratis, and Alexandria—was divided into nomes, and Egypt was administered as one vast estate belonging to the Ptolemaic king. The whole country was honeycombed with officials who were his personal servants. At the head of these was the διοικητής, the manager of the economic affairs of the kingdom, who from his office in Alexandria issued to his various subordinates the orders required to make the immense bureaucratic machine function all over Egypt. It is to be noted that nothing in this system resembled the unpaid, temporary magistracies which the citizen undertook as a duty in the Greek city and that all the higher posts were held by Greeks.

The χώρα, as distinguished from the πόλεις, was literally the

[1] Rostovtzeff in *J.E.A.*, etc., p. 170. [2] Ibid. p. 171.
[3] Jouguet, *Macedonian Imperialism and the Hellenization of the East*, p. 396. Yet there were in Egypt Greek agricultural colonies. The villages, especially in the Fayum, were partly inhabited by Greeks. They were not always citizens, but they had a privileged status, and could obtain a Greek education in the gymnasiums scattered about the country. Certain natives could enter this class by naturalization. Greek manners, however, could develop fully only in city life, and gradually the Hellenic population concentrated in the towns. This process was completed by the first Roman emperors when they constituted a Greek municipality in the nome capital round the gymnasium which soon ceased to exist anywhere else.

king's inheritance, and this character is apparent in the system of ownership of the soil. The king's army was raised from the settlers who held plots of land (κλῆροι) assigned to them out of his territory on the condition of rendering him military service. All that was not royal land was the object of concessions in various forms, the king maintaining an eminent right of ownership. The king received a portion of the produce of the land, either as rent from the royal domains leased out to farmers, or as dues from the holders of concessions. The rest was under his control.

Such a system could never be applied to the Greek cities. The law of every Greek city included the right to own the soil. The citizens of Alexandria and Ptolemais were complete owners of their fields. Such land had originally been detached from the king's domain, and once it was divided among the citizens, they must have managed their allotments as they pleased.

The native Egyptians of the χώρα possessed no economic liberty. From the Revenue Laws of Ptolemy Philadelphus [1] we learn that the tenants of the royal lands and workers in the oil monopoly were limited in their personal liberty. They were bound to the soil, forbidden as they were to remove to another nome. They were at once free and unfree; tenants paying rent or artisans receiving wages, yet at every point subject to restrictions and tied to their homes, semi-serfs. They were merely part of the machinery of a system of centralization and absolutism at whose summit was the expression of the king's will. One of the signs of this servitude of the native Egyptian was the poll-tax, syntaxis. His person was catalogued on the registers of that tax, which were called laographiae.

The Greek city, with its small territory, stood in direct contrast to the great region of the χώρα in which the king exercised direct authority as absolute master. Although the Macedonian king had now become an oriental monarch with absolute power, yet his history and origin made it impossible for him to treat his Greek subjects on the same level as the native Egyptians. Of necessity there had to be a dual system, the component parts of which—the principles of Oriental civilization, with its absolutism, and those of Hellenism, with its emphasis on the free play of individual initiative— in the civilization of the πόλις on which Western civilization is based, were irreconcilable. Whether the Ptolemies wanted it or not, there had to be Greek cities in Egypt as a compromise with the past and as an outlet for those who were as yet incapable of adapting themselves to the idea of the king as a god, the master, and even the owner of the country.

The Ptolemies had incorporated several Greek cities in their Empire, but in Egypt itself there were only three, or perhaps four, the old Ionian city of Naucratis, and the new foundations of Alexandria, the capital, Ptolemais in the Thebaid, and perhaps Paraetonion (Mersa Matruh), supposed to have been founded by Alexander.

---

[1] *J.E.A.* viii. (1922), p. 145. *P. Rev. Laws* (259 B.C.), Col. 44.

To these few cities at least the kings allowed the institutions of genuine independent poleis. Naucratis perhaps kept its old constitution, with its aristocratic Council of Timouchoi,[1] and struck coins. In the time of Philadelphus and Euergetes, Ptolemais,[2] and probably Alexandria as well [3] had an Assembly of the people, a Council, and a board of six executive magistrates called Prytanes, although these were not the only magistrates.

Citizens, or, at least, those with full rights, were divided into tribes and demes, and the latter appear to have been territorial divisions. But it seems there were also citizens outside the demes, who, like the women, had only the private rights, and not the political rights, enjoyed by full citizens. The local government of Alexandria has been described as a tempered aristocracy, and the definition applies perhaps to Ptolemais as well.

The Ptolemies, however, did not forget their position of Absolutism. It pleased them to see their Greeks form their associations, indulge in their ancestral pursuits, and play at self-government, with their senates and assemblies, their Greek laws and their popular decrees ; but it was in the last resort only play, and self-government inevitably gave way to the will of the Ptolemies. The cities betray their position of dependence by dating documents by the King's years, celebrating his anniversaries, and stamping his image on their coins. The orders or desires of the central power would meet with no difficulty in being transformed into laws or decrees of the city by the vote of the Council and popular Assembly. Moreover, the officials of the king took direct part in the administration of the city. Ptolemais honoured Euergetes ' with maintenance in the Prytaneion for his whole life, a front seat at the Games, and the citizenship ', according to the time-honoured practice of Greek cities, in the case of a benefactor.[4]

This system of government, on the whole, was fairly liberal, but was not maintained to the end of the dynasty. The cities kept ' their liberties ' to a varying extent, and remained the essentially Greek territory of Egypt and the centres from which Hellenism spread over the country.

Although both Egyptians and Greeks were subject to a despotic master, who might send out from Alexandria laws (νόμοι)—that is, general ordinances intended to be permanent till repealed—or rescripts (διαγράμματα), edicts (προστάγματα), declarations of the royal will in regard to some particular point, it was the policy of the Ptolemies to allow the Egyptians to go on living under their traditional laws and customs, οἱ τῆς χώρας νόμοι in contrast with the πολιτικοὶ νόμοι, the Civic Laws ordained by the king for those who had the

---

[1] P. Jouguet : *La Vie muncipale dans l'Égypte romaine*, Paris, 1911.
[2] *O.G.I.* 47–9.
[3] P. Jouguet in *Journal des Savantes*, 1925, p. 12.
[4] *O.G.I.* No. 49. Cf. *Apology* of Plato, 36 E, ἐν πρυτανείῳ σιτήσεως. For a good account of Ptolemais see Bevan, *A History of Egypt under the Ptolemaic Dynasty*, pp. 104–8.

E

status of ' citizens ' of Greek cities.   But there were Greeks all over
the country, and this made a somewhat complicated system necessary.
Thus there were two systems of law in operation, but each to some
extent modified the other, especially as mixture of blood between
the two peoples took place, and in many disputes one party was
Greek and the other Egyptian.   Such mutual modification can be
traced in marriage law, where in the Egyptian, as contrasted with
the Greek : [1]—

   (i) brother-and-sister marriage was allowed ; [2]
  (ii) the woman had greater independence, and might choose
      her husband freely as a person *sui iuris*, and separate from
      him whenever she liked,[3] or, if he divorced her, reclaim her
      dowry; [4]
 (iii) various grades of marriage—e.g., a trial union [5]—were
      recognized.

A double system of administering justice necessarily followed from
the double system of law.   The Egyptians could bring their civil
disputes before native judges (λαοκριταί), who decided them according to the Pharaonic tradition.   But for criminal justice, and for
suits between Greeks, the king's deputies or the king himself constituted the judicial authority.

It is remarkable that there is no part of the Ptolemaic system in
Egypt that presents such an appearance of elaborate confusion as the
judicial arrangements.   In theory every subject of the king could
make appeal for judgment to the king direct, but since it was physically
impossible for the seven or eight million inhabitants of Egypt to do
so, we find the institution of a Greek judicial body for particular
nomes or groups of nomes, called χρηματισταί, who went on circuit
and delivered judgment in the king's name.   Actually anyone who
desired justice might appeal to the civil governor of his nome
(strategos) or the chief of police (epistates).   The chrematistae seem
to have had concurrent jurisdiction.

---

[1] *P. Eleph.* i. (311 B.C.), already quoted, is a good example of a very early Greek
marriage contract in Egypt as yet uninfluenced by the very different Egyptian
marriage law.
[2] It is hard to get data from the papyri in brother-and-sister marriage among the
Greeks in Egypt because (1) Greek names cease from the 2nd century B.C. to be a
sure indicatioa of Greek race and (2) the term ' sister ' may be a conventional form
of speech for a wife who was not really a sister (cf. *Song of Songs*, iv. 9).
[3] Cf. *P. Tebt.* 104, i. 30–32 (92 B.C.): ἐὰν δὲ Ἀπολλωνία ἐκοῦσα βούληται ἀπαλλάσ-
σεσθαι ἀπὸ Φιλίσκου, ἀποδότω αὐτῆι Φιλίσκος τὴν φερνὴν ἁπλῆν ἐν ἡμέραις δέκα ἀφ' ἧς ἐὰν
ἀπαιτηθῆι.
[4] Cf. *P. Ryl.* 154, i. 24–7 (A.D. 66): ἐὰν δὲ διαφορᾶς αὐτοῖς γεναμένης χωρίζονται ἀπ'
ἀλλήλων, ἤτοι τοῦ Χαιρήμονος ἀποπέμποντος τὴν Θαϊσάριον ἢ καὶ αὐτῆς ἑκουσίως ἀπαλλα-
σομένης ἀπ' αὐτοῦ, ἔστωι τοῦ τῆς Θαϊσαρίου πατρὸς Σισόιτος, ἐὰν δὲ οὗτος μὴ περιῆι αὐτῆς
Θαϊσαρίου ὁ σημαινόμενος κλῆρος τῶν ἀρουρῶν δέκα ἡμίσους τετάρτου καθὼς πρόκειται.
[5] In one document—Louvre, No. 13—we find a Greek contract for a trial
marriage for a year, which may show an influence of Egyptian customs upon the
Greeks (Wilcken, *U.d.* Pt. i. p. 322).

'We see the chrematistae intervene concurrently with the officials, sometimes before the officials, sometimes after them, sometimes sitting together with them : we see them issue summonses which are not obeyed, and pronounce decisions which leave the matter submitted to them as unsettled as ever.' [1]

It is possible that ' baksheesh ' ($\sigma\tau\acute{\epsilon}\phi\alpha\nu\sigma\iota$) and personal interest,[2] only occasionally to be traced in the written documents, played a part in these transactions.

An important document relating to the delimitation of the province of the native $\lambda\alpha\sigma\kappa\rho\iota\tau\alpha\acute{\iota}$, as against that of the Greek authorities, is the law of Ptolemy VI (118 B.C.), rehearsed in one papyrus.[3] In cases where one party is Greek and the other Egyptian, the question of the proper court is to be decided by the language of the documents with which the dispute is concerned. If they are in demotic, the case is to go before the laokritai, to be decided according to Egyptian law ; if they are in Greek, the case is to go before the chrematistai. Where both parties are Egyptian, the case is to go before the laokritai. Such cases the chrematistai are not to draw into their sphere— an indication that there had actually been a tendency for the Greek judge to encroach upon the sphere of the native judges.

An exceptional phenomenon in the Fayum under Ptolemy III is a board of $\delta\iota\kappa\alpha\sigma\tau\alpha\acute{\iota}$, who try cases mainly between soldiers. One is the case of a Jew belonging to the Epigone against a Jewess who has as her Kurios an Athenian. It suggests that the Ptolemaic system of justice may have had all kinds of temporary and local varieties of which we know nothing. Commonly, those desiring justice appeal to someone in an official position, whose functions were not primarily or principally judicial, and if the verdict is adverse they can try to get it upset by appealing to a yet higher authority.[4]

It seems that the kings were concerned to ensure speedy and fair justice to their subjects, but the task was rendered difficult by the diversity of the population living side by side in the valley of the Nile, who were accustomed to very different laws. The great weaknesses of the system were the arbitrariness inherent in despotism and authority of a personal character, and a certain confusion in the competence of various courts.

In spite of the dual policy of the Ptolemies towards the two chief races settled in the country, Greek and Egyptian began to influence one another. We have seen this tendency at work in the spheres of religion, in legal administration, and in the adoption by the Ptolemies

---

[1] Bouché-Leclercq, *Histoire des Lagides*, Paris, 1903–6, iv. 214.
[2] Cf. *P. Tebt.* i. 34. An official gives it to be understood that Horus, being under the protection of a great personage, must be set free. Cf. *P. Petrie* iii. 28. A burglar, caught red-handed, gets off by paying 200 drachmas to the police-agent.
[3] *P. Tebt.* i. 5, C. 207 seq.
[4] Cf. *P. Grenfell* i. 11 ; *P. Tebt.* i. 54 ; *P. Tebt.* i. 50 ; *P. Petrie* ii. 18. 1.

of the principle of absolutism in their political organization—a principle which though it weighed heavily on the native Egyptians, to some extent affected the Greeks as well, those of the cities less, those settled in the χώρα more directly. It remains to consider to what extent assimilation between the two peoples took place and what was to be the fate of Hellenism in this environment.

' No modern country ' [says Bevan] [1] ' in which a European race bears rule over a more numerous native race is quite like Ptolemaic Egypt. South Africa so far resembles it, that the European there too has settled in the country as his permanent home, a minority amongst a native population, but the situation is different in so far as the natives of South Africa are primitive people, not, like the Egyptians, representatives of an ancient civilization of which the European immigrants stood in a certain awe.'

Bevan holds that India would seem more analogous than South Africa to Ptolemaic Egypt but for the fact that the Europeans there form only a transient community of officials, soldiers, and merchants who have not settled in the country as their permanent home. Yet there are far more analogous instances in the modern world that seem to have escaped notice. The Spanish, who under Cortes and Pizarro conquered Mexico and Peru, did not by any means discover in these countries primitive peoples, but races which had long been possessed of a high civilization,[2] in some respects superior, in spite of the lack of knowledge of coined money, to the harsh imperialism of white civilization as exemplified by the chief European race of the day. The European newcomers settled permanently as a minority, as did the Greeks in Egypt amid the vast mass of the native population, and what happened ultimately in Egypt happened likewise in Central and South America. The natives, though dominated for centuries by Europeans, at last reasserted themselves. In Egypt the process was very gradual, but culminated with the Arab conquest, and today, as most writers agree, the modern population bears no trace whatever of Greek admixture : the fellahin who till the fields in modern Egypt seem no different in appearance from those depicted

---

[1] Bevan, *A History of Egypt under the Ptolemaic Dynasty*, p. 86.
[2] Cf. W. H. Prescott, *History of the Conquest of Mexico*, Routledge, 1899, p. 13. ' The history of the Aztecs suggests some strong points of resemblance to that of the ancient Romans not only in their military successes, but in the policy which led to them ' (p. 25). ' In respect to the nature of it (their civilization) they may be better compared with the Egyptians : and the examination of their social relations and culture may suggest still stronger points of resemblance to that ancient people ' (p. 69). ' The traffic was carried on partly by barter, and partly by a regulated currency, of different values. This consisted of transparent quills of gold dust : of bits of tin, cut in the form of a T : and of bags of cacao, containing a specified number of grains ' (p. 592). The architectural remains ' are of sufficient magnitude and wrought with sufficient skill, to attest mechanical powers in the Aztecs not unworthy to be compared with those of the ancient Egyptians '. Cf. also L. Spence, *The Civilization of Ancient Mexico*, Cambridge University Press, 1912.

on the Pharaonic monuments of Old Egypt before the Greeks came.[1]

In Central and South America the Indians in many of the republics have superseded those who proudly claim pure Spanish blood as the political rulers of their country. In both Egypt, Central and South America a great deal of admixture between Europeans and natives went on. The modern population of the Central and South American states varies in the percentage of Spanish blood each contains. Perhaps centuries hence Spanish blood will disappear altogether, but not Spanish civilization, and this is where the similarity with Egypt breaks down. The Greeks, too, imposed their civilization and culture on the natives, and if it had not been for the Arab conquest of the 7th century, whether the conquered absorbed their conquerors or not, the civilization and culture of Egypt would have remained in their main essentials Hellenic, just as those of the Central and South American states remain to-day essentially Spanish.

A contrast is usually made between the position of European and native in Ptolemaic Egypt and the position to-day of European and native, mainly in countries governed by Anglo-Saxon or English-speaking rulers. In these countries the chief barriers against assimilation of rulers and ruled are the horror of intermarriage and the difference in religion. Yet the Dutch in Java have no horror of intermarriage, nor have the French in their Empire any objection to their coloured subjects commensurate with the race-prejudice felt in English-speaking countries. Religion, of course, to-day counts for little, as any man, whatever his race or colour, can belong to a denomination of the Christian faith, so successful has been missionary propaganda, except where it has come into contact with Mohammedanism. As regards race-prejudice, the attitude of the Greeks in Egypt can be compared most aptly with the attitude prevailing in non-English-speaking countries. Although the Greeks and Macedonians held themselves the superior type of humanity,[2] the ordinary Greek or Macedonian settler (except most probably the great families, as was the case in the American countries conquered by Spain) had

---

[1] Cf. H. V. Morton, *Middle East*, Methuen, 1941, and T. G. Garry, *African Doctor*, published for the Book Club, 121 Charing Cross Road, by the London Trinity Press, Worcester and London, 1939, pp. 115 seq. The latter contains some very interesting observations on the modern Egyptian by one who had spent several years before and during the Great War as a doctor at Cairo. '. . . during the seven thousand years of Egyptian history there has been little change in the essential characteristics and pursuits of the inhabitants. The manners and customs and even the physiognomy of the people in Upper Egypt bear a striking resemblance to the Egyptians of the Pharaohs as revealed by ancient monuments and literature. Nor has there been much change in their moral, material and intellectual conditions' (p. 123). 'It is a remarkable fact that the race, subdued again and again by the advancing hordes of Semites, Phoenicians, Persians, Greeks, Romans and Arabs, has been able not only to assimilate but also to fuse them into the common mould. It seems as if the soil of Egypt demanded one uniform stock and that the climatic conditions would tolerate no other. Although temporary racial variations may have sometimes appeared, there has always been a reversion to the original type which has remained obstinately Egyptian' (p. 124).

[2] Cf. Herod. i. 60.

no horror of intermarriage with Egyptian women. Generally speaking, in ancient times there was no colour-bar. Since the Greeks and Macedonians largely came into the country as soldiers, the men amongst them must have been far more numerous than the women. Though many, according to the papyri, had European wives, the supply of European wives could hardly have gone round.

The feeling of contempt for the enslaved barbarian felt by some of the earliest immigrants in their pride as free citizens must have grown weaker with time. In any case, it became almost extinct in the Greek born in the χώρα, who had never known city life and had probably taken a wife of the country. From this continual mixture of blood the racial differences in Ptolemaic Egypt grew less and less with succeeding generations. Later on large numbers of people who called themselves Greeks were mainly Egyptian in blood.

It was the three Greek cities in Egypt—Naucratis, Alexandria, Ptolemais—that most probably formed an exception to the general trend. Here a conservative policy was followed—the aim being to keep the source of Hellenism pure. The members of the citizen body were forbidden to contract marriages with natives. Citizenship was not made too easy for foreigners to acquire, although there were some cases of naturalization. The statutes of the cities placed obstacles in the way of mixed marriages, and the charter of Naucratis refused to recognize marriages between citizen and native as lawful.[1] Great importance was attached to purity of race, since the citizenship was refused to the illegitimate son of a citizen,[2] and in the Roman period Alexandria definitely did not have connubium with the Egyptians.[3] The same must have been the case in Ptolemais, for the names borne by the Ptolemaites, in contrast to what we notice in the Greeks of the χώρα, always preserve their Hellenic character.[4]

It was otherwise, however, with the multitude of Greeks resident in Egypt, who did not belong to the citizen-body of one of the three cities, whether they were domiciled in the cities or had their homes in some Egyptian town or village. To prohibit such unions in their case was virtually impossible, and would have been a mistake if the aim of the Ptolemies was to Hellenize the natives. The legal status of these mixed marriages and the condition of the children born of them are unknown—probably they did not all get Hellenic status by their birth, though Hellenism in Egypt does not seem to have been exclusive and closed.[5] Possibly a man might become the equal of a Greek if he had received a Greek education, such as was given in the schools and gymnasiums. Thus the idea of Iso-

---

[1] Wilcken and Mitteis, *Grundzüge und Chrestomathie des Papyruskunde*, Leipzig und Berlin, 1921, ii. 27. The text is of the 2nd century A.D., but the regulation was probably more ancient.
[2] Ibid. ii. 372, col. 4.
[3] T. Reinach, *Un Code fiscal de l'Égypte romaine*, pp. 82–3.
[4] Wilcken, *Archiv für Papyrusforschung und verwandte gebiete*, iv. 537.
[5] Jouguet, *Macedonian Imperialism and the Hellenization of the East*, Kegan Paul, etc., London, 1928, p. 340.

crates, that not blood but education (παίδευσις) made the Hellene, could be applied.[1] When a man became a Greek, he took a Greek name. He bore both together, one often being a translation of the other, as in the case of Dionysios Petoserapis.

From about 150 B.C. it becomes common in the papyri to find people who bear both a Greek and an Egyptian name.[2] Probably few Greeks of pure blood took Egyptian names, but many pure Egyptians must have assumed Greek names. This shows to what an extent Hellenization of the Egyptians had succeeded, just as to-day in many English-speaking countries the English language and culture have been adopted by varied races. Yet, in spite of this surface veneer, the language and customs of the natives by no means died out, though after the middle of the 2nd century it becomes impossible to tell by name alone whether a man or woman is Greek or Egyptian, as is often the case, for instance, in South Africa, Canada, or the United States, where a change of name has brought advantages to many an immigrant. The parallel with Egypt is, indeed, not quite a true one, since in modern times it is the immigrants, and not the settled population, who have adopted the culture and official language or languages of the other. But the reasons for this tendency to assimilation were the same both in ancient and modern times. Similarly, we find that the Jews in Alexandria were Hellenized to a great extent, as is evidenced by the translation of the Old Testament into Greek (the Septuagint) and the philosophical works of Philo, which imply an intensive study of Greek literature, and of Platonism in particular.

The distinction between the higher stratum of Greeks and lower stratum of natives did not cease, but it became more a matter of culture and tradition than of physical race. A family which had Greek names (even if it had Egyptian ones, too), which talked and wrote Greek [3] and had learnt something of Greek literature, which followed the Greek tradition in manners, would count as belonging to the privileged race : those who talked Egyptian and lived in the native way would count as belonging to the subject race. If Ptolemaic rule had gone on the difference between Greek and Egyptian might have gradually faded away. The native element asserted itself more under the later than under the first Ptolemies, as we shall see, but with Roman rule the native Egyptian-speaking mass was again thrust definitely into a subject position beneath Greeks and Romans. A proof of how comparatively well-treated the natives

---

[1] Isocrates, *Panegyricus*, 50.
[2] Cf. W. Otto, *Priester und Tempel in hellenistichen Ägypten* (Leipzig und Berlin, vol. i. 1905, vol. ii. 1908).
[3] The Greeks, on their side, did not, in some cases at least, disdain to learn Egyptian. In a letter of the 2nd century B.C. [P. London i. 43 (p. 48) = Witkowski, *Ep. Priv. Graec.* 50, Wilcken, *Chrest.*, p. 136] a mother writes to her son : ' I congratulate you and myself on the news that you are learning Egyptian, for now when you get to the city you will teach the children at the house of Phalou ... es the physician, and will have a provision for your old age.' A knowledge of the native language apparently improved the prospects of a Greek schoolmaster in a nome capital.

were from the point of view of their language and culture—which, after all, are the main things, since they are more important than economic factors—is the fact that these still flourished under the Greeks and Romans. It was left to the Arabic conquest of the country, however, to bring a definite period not only to Hellenic culture and civilization, but also to the old culture, civilization, and above all religion of the Pharaohs.

These tendencies to assimilation were more and more encouraged by the kings as they came to identify themselves more and more with the Pharaohs. Their policy aimed at creating between the fellahin in the country and the aristocracy of the cities and Court, a mixed Graeco-Egyptian population, which might be penetrated with Oriental ideas, but in the higher classes was dominated by Hellenic culture. This framework enabled the dynasty to resist when rebellion broke out, since the Graeco-Egyptian classes as a whole, Hellenized as they were, had no reason for regarding a Greek dynasty as an anti-national dynasty. But there was another side to the picture. If there was Hellenization of the Egyptians, there was corresponding de-Hellenization of the Greeks.

'The externals of Hellenism, the Greek tongue, Greek law modified of course by Egyptian custom and local conditions, Greek institutions so far as they could be adapted, some elements of Greek religion, Greek social life, even Greek education and the study of Greek art and literature—all these could be and were transplanted to the new environment; but the spirit of Hellenism, that mental freedom, that fulness of humanity, that exquisite balance, that fearless, cloudless facing of concrete reality, which are the glory of Hellas, could not but wither in such an atmosphere.'[1]

Three or four Greek cities were not enough to Hellenize the country, especially as they were closed to the Egyptians and withdrawn in themselves. Moreover, there was a great difference between the half-Greeks of the χώρα and the genuine Hellene. These Greeks, distributed among the villages or nome-capitals of Egypt, knew nothing of the city-life which was the only true Greek life, and were imbued with Oriental superstitions. They read and wrote Greek, but they wrote it more and more incorrectly. In the 2nd and 1st centuries the letters, ordinances, and circulars, issued by high officials are drafted in a pretentious, incorrect, and hopelessly involved style.

Egyptian customs, too, gained ground. The marriage of brother and sister common in Egypt, but probably at first unpopular with the Greeks, is found in the Roman period even among the well-to-do.[2] In religion the borrowing from Egyptian usage went on apace.

---

[1] H. I. Bell in *J.E.A.* viii. (1922), 145–6.
[2] Wilcken, *Archiv. f. Pap.*, vi 426; cf. the case of the strategus Apollonius in the 2nd century.

In the years 98 and 95 B.C. ex-ephebi are found, in the Fayum, a nome where the Hellenic element was specially strong, dedicating shrines to ' Suchus the great, great god ', the crocodile god of the Fayum. There was nothing in the Greek religion to make the Greek regard the Egyptian religion as heathenish or as idolatrous or as a religion essentially inferior to his own. Here, too, his attitude differs from that of many European races to the native. His religion made no exclusive claims, as do the modern religions, and the mixed Graeco-Egyptian race which sprang up through inter-marriage absorbed a good deal of popular Egyptian religion through the Egyptian mothers. We have seen in the pages of Herodotus how the Greeks tended to identify the Egyptian gods with their own. This process went on apace in Ptolemaic Egypt. Setet and Anuquet, the goddesses of the Cataract, became Hera and Hestia, the falcon Horus of Edfu Apollo, Amon-Ra-Sonther of Thebes Zeus. At Tentyris, Hathor was Aphrodite ; at Hermopolis, Thoth was Hermes ; at Heracleopolis, Herishef was Heracles ; Neith of Sais had long been Athene ; Ptah was Hephaestus. Very often, too, when they used the Greek name they meant an Egyptian god, and sometimes both Egyptian names (in a Grecized form) and Greek names are given side by side.[1]

The Greeks had no objection to worshipping the oddest of them, under names scarcely Hellenized—Thueris, the She-hippopotamus of Oxyrhynchus, Suchus, Socnebtynis, Pnepherus, and Mestasutmis, the crocodiles of the Fayum. A papyrus from the Fayum of the mid 3rd century B.C. shows us the daughters of a Greek father from Cyrene, Demetrius, and an Egyptian mother, Thasis, dedicating a shrine to Thueris. The daughters have both Greek and Egyptian names.[2] It is significant, however, that the more human less remote gods of the Greeks, do not seem to have attracted the Egyptians.[3]

Apart from the absence of race-prejudice which resulted in inter-marriage and the assimilation in religion, certain important economic and political changes which took place at the end of the 3rd century B.C. hastened on the process of de-Hellenization.

The alteration in the position of the cleruchs or military settlers was significant. At first the Kleroi or allotments were held on a contingent and precarious tenure, not heritable, not to be sold or mortgaged, resumed by the king on the holder's death ; but by the

---

[1] O.G.I. No. iii. The Greek, however, did not cease to worship his own gods, even outside Alexandria, Ptolemais, and Naucratis. Zeus, Apollo, Demeter, Aphrodite, or any other deity could be worshipped with Greek rites at little temples, set up wherever any number of Greeks were living together in Egypt.

[2] Wilcken, Chrest. i. No. 51.

[3] Nevertheless there was one mark of Hellenic influence upon the native population that deserves notice. There was one thing new to Egypt which came in with the Greek population—the voluntary associations with the cult of some deity as the ostensible object, serving really the purposes of a convivial club or trade guild, which sprang up everywhere, in the times after Alexander, over the Greek world and called Thiasoi or Synodoi. Such associations, too, began to be formed among the native population, centring in the cult of Egyptian gods—Osiris, Isis, Anubis, Chnubis-Ammon, or some local deity. Cf. Otto, op. cit., i. 125 ff.

end of the 3rd century it was taken as a matter of course that the cleruch would be succeeded by his son, and gradually the right, first to sell and afterwards to bequeath the kleros was established. The Romans further recognized the *catoecic* land, as it was called, as being in effect the property of its holders.[1] This development had its influence on the de-Hellenization of the settlers : for while they were primarily soldiers, holding their land on a precarious tenure, they were less exposed to the influence of the Egyptian environment than when they had become regular landowners with a permanent stake in the country. In a deed of 215–214 B.C. we find a Greek of Cyrene and an Egyptian as joint tenants of land leased by an Athenian settler.[2] The new change thus meant co-operation to a great extent with the native race.

The process of de-Hellenization was further hastened by the policy of the feeble rulers who followed the first three kings of the dynasty, a policy which took its rise from an event of great importance in Egyptian history—the Battle of Raphia in 217 B.C.

In Alexander's system the civil government had been entrusted to Egyptians : the nomes remained under native nomarchs, and he appointed native governors instead of a Macedonian satrap. Europeans managed only finance and the army of occupation. Even Ptolemy I, while satrap, did not entirely discard Alexander's idea, and gave more place to natives than they subsequently possessed. The change came when he initiated a policy of oversea conquest.[3] His immediate successors aimed at the Empire of the Aegean, and treated Egypt as a conquered country and money-making machine, but by the end of the 3rd century there was a significant alteration in this policy of exclusiveness. The political and economic situation left much to be desired. No other foreign domination, not even the Assyrians nor Persians, had taken possession of all the resources of Egypt to such an extent. The natives must have felt themselves despoiled. The people was subject not only to a foreign reigning house, but a whole new race which spread and insinuated itself all over the country. Discontent must have smouldered for a long time, and we hear of disorders as early as the beginning of the reign of Euergetes.[4]

Early in the reign of the weak debauchee Ptolemy IV Philopator, Antiochus III of Syria resolved to reconquer Palestine. The Egyptian army had been grossly neglected, so that Ptolemy was forced to enrol a large number of Egyptians, arming and training them in the Macedonian manner. He met Antiochus at Raphia, and it was the army of Egypt that won the day, but it was a Pyrrhic victory for Egyptian Hellenism and the Ptolemaic dynasty.[5] Rendered

[1] Bell in *J.E.A.* (1922), p. 146.   [2] *P. Frankf.* 2.
[3] Tarn, *Hellenistic Civilization*, Arnold & Co., London, 1927, p. 143.
[4] Just. xxviii. i. 9 ; Jerome, *In Dan.*, ii.
[5] Jouguet, *Macedonian Imperialism and the Hellenization of the East*, London, Kegan Paul, etc., 1928, pp. 214–61. ' By an innovation which was to have important consequences, a Macedonian phalanx had been made up of Libyan and, above all,

confident by their share in the triumph, and utilizing their new military knowledge, the Egyptians began to offer a bolder front to their Macedonian and Greek masters, and revolts soon became frequent. The uprising was long and terrible, beginning in Central Egypt and the Delta, and even spreading to the South. The troubles continued everywhere till the reign of Epiphanes, who at last repressed it with severe measures.

During the reign of Philometor a civil war was fomented by Dionysios Petoserapis,[1] a native who was esteemed for his military talents and had the rank of ' Friend ' at the Court. This movement had repercussions in Memphis, the Fayum, and even in the Thebaid. The disturbances continued into the reigns of the succeeding kings. Finally, Soter II decided to destroy the old native capital. Thebes was taken, looted and partly destroyed, so that it was no more than an agglomeration of villages as Strabo saw it later.

Though the Egyptians emerged defeated from a struggle of more than a hundred years, the kings found themselves obliged to make concessions, probably to the warriors and the priests who had been the soul of the revolt.

Philopator and his successors, despite some attempts at reaction, made more and more concessions to their Egyptian subjects, more and more tended to convert their rule into a national Egyptian monarchy. Egyptians who served in the army or police received, like the Greeks, their kleroi, and the size of their holding increased, while those of the Greeks grew smaller. The Greek settlers had to the end larger kleroi than the Egyptians, but the difference between the two races was far less in the first than in the 3rd century B.C. Egyptians, moreover, began to rise to high office in the state. Already in the 2nd century we hear of an Egyptian Paôs with the titles ' Kinsman and general of the Thebaid ',[2] and a son, writing in the year 131–130 B.C. to his father in the Thebaid, where a revolt had broken out, bids him keep his spirits up, ' for the news has come that Paôs is sailing up in Tybi with adequate forces to put down the insurgents at Hermanthis and treat them as rebels '.[3] Things had indeed altered when a Ptolemy had to rely on an Egyptian general to suppress insurgents !

The power of the priesthood, kept severely in check by the early Ptolemies, grew steadily ; the right of asylum was extended to

---

Egyptian subjects, largely recruited from the mass of the natives outside the warrior class. This Egyptian phalanx numbered 20,000 men.' Cf. Polybius v. 107, 2–4, who regards this step as marking the beginning of Egypt's decline : ὁ γὰρ βασιλεὺς καθοπλίσας τοὺς Αἰγυπτίους ἐπὶ τὸν πρὸς Ἀντίοχον πόλεμον πρὸς μὲν τὸ παρὸν ἐνδεχομένως ἐβουλεύσατο, τοῦ δὲ μέλλοντος ἠστόχησε· φρονηματισθέντες γὰρ ἐκ τοῦ περὶ Ῥαφίαν προτερήματος οὐκέτι τὸ προστατ τόμενον οἷοί τ' ἦσαν ὑπομένειν, ἀλλ' ἐζήτουν ἡγεμόνα καὶ πρόσωπον ὡς ἱκανοὶ βοηθεῖν ὄντες αὐτοῖς. ὃ καὶ τέλος ἐποίησαν, οὐ μετὰ πολὺν χρόνον.

[1] Diod. xxxi. 15a.
[2] Strack, Dyn. der Ptol. p. 257, No. 109.
[3] P. Louvre 10595 = Wilcken, Chrest. 101.

temple after temple, and the priests became once more a formidable power in the state.[1]

These tendencies were accentuated by the concessions of Euergetes II, in the 2nd century [2] to his Egyptian subjects—concessions, which were just and reasonable enough in themselves, though probably made, partly at least, to gain support in the civil wars which occupied so much of his reign : but they certainly helped to assimilate Greek and Egyptian and so to weaken still further the influence of Hellenism. Another factor that contributed to the victory of the kings in the revolt was that Hellenism had penetrated the whole country. Nevertheless, Greek immigration having ceased, the Egyptian element gained ground at the expense of the Greek, and would ultimately have absorbed it but for the intervention of Rome.

It can thus be seen that while race mixture and assimilation brought about a certain amount of Hellenization among the natives, it inevitably caused a de-Hellenization of the Greeks living in the χώρα.

It is surprising that this de-Hellenization did not take place more quickly—an immigrant race, even of conquerors, when it mingles with that of the country where it has settled, is usually absorbed by the conquered and begins to lose its identity. The Greeks of the χώρα were hardly Greeks any longer. Yet for several centuries they had no other civilization than Hellenic, and once this was removed by the Arab conquest the whole façade of Hellenism collapsed. Till then, de-Hellenization did not do its work more quickly, because it was the Greek cities, Alexandria in particular, that kept Hellenism alive and radiated it out to the χώρα.[3]

The Roman conquest caused no immediate change of importance in the internal organization of the country, it being the general policy of Roman statesmen to interfere as little as possible with existing institutions of any country which had a fully developed system of local government when it was added to their empire. In fact, the Roman conquest amounted to little more than a change of dynasty, the highest official, the Prefect, representing the emperor and taking the place of the Ptolemy, while a firmer rule was instituted than had been the case previously. As Egypt was important to Rome from the point of view of its corn supply and its general economic value, it was, by reason of its isolated situation, a more natural and convenient unit for separate administration than any other area in the Near East. Just as the Ptolemies had taken over and modified the politico-economic system instituted by the Pharaohs based on the principle of absolutism, so did the Romans, with but little change. Egypt was therefore treated as the personal domain of the Roman

[1] *Ann. du Service*, xix. 37 ff.
[2] P. Teb. 1. 5 = Wilcken, *Chrest.*, 65 and 260; cf. Preisigke, *Archiv. f. Pap.*, v. 301–16.
[3] Jouguet : *Macedonian Imperialism and the Hellenization of the East*, London, Kegan Paul, etc., 1928, pp. 343–4.

emperor: and from him, directly or indirectly, all Egyptian officials held their posts. But it was only a few high functionaries in the central administration at Alexandria who were sent from Rome: the great mass of the work was done by residents or natives selected locally. These high posts were filled normally by Romans of equestrian rank: to guard against the possibility of senatorial interference, no member of the Senate was allowed to take office, or even to set foot, without the special leave of the emperor,[1] in Egypt. During the latter part of the reign of Augustus and most of that of Tiberius Egypt remained in a state of comparative tranquillity. The strict watch Tiberius kept on his ministers in the interests of the provincials tended to preserve this tranquillity, by checking any exaction or oppression on the part of officials which might have given occasion for disturbances among the people. It was only under the later emperors that this tranquillity was disturbed.

Greek continued to be, for most purposes, the official language, used even by the prefects in their decrees and correspondence with the local officials, and the Greeks were left in their privileged position of exemption from that mark of subjection, the poll-tax. But it seems clear that Augustus had no intention of founding his rule in Egypt on the good-will merely of the Hellenic element in the population, for, instead of being a governing class, they were now in a subservient position.[2] Alexandria had been under the later Ptolemies the most dangerous focus of disturbance in the lower part of the country, so that besides keeping a substantial force nearby to overawe the populace, the Roman Government, most probably at this time, deprived the city of its senate and confirmed the Jews, their constant rivals, of all the rights and privileges they had enjoyed under the Ptolemies.

The effect of the Roman conquest was at first, in a sense, to strengthen the position of Hellenism against Egyptian influences, since it deepened and made more definite the gulf between Greek and Egyptian. It was the Roman citizen who was now what the Macedonian or Greek had been under the early Ptolemies, who took precedence. Only Roman citizens could serve in the legions, but in practice Greeks—at first those only of the Greek cities, later even residents in the nome-capitals—were given the citizenship as a preliminary to enlistment, while from the first they were admitted freely to service in the auxiliary forces and fleet, receiving the citizenship

---

[1] Cf. J. G. Milne, *A History of Egypt under Roman Rule*, Methuen, London, 1924, p. 13. Germanicus Caesar, when sent out as governor of the East, took the opportunity of visiting Egypt without obtaining the emperor's permission, thus breaking Augustus' law which forbade any Roman citizen of Senatorial rank, without such permission, to enter Alexandria. 'This visit was capable of a treasonable interpretation especially as Egypt was the province which gave to its possessor the command of Rome, and which was always ready to embark on a new course of sedition, with any leader who might call to it: and it was visited with severe reproof by Tiberius.'

[2] J. G. Milne, *A History of Egypt under Roman Rule*, Methuen, London, 1924, p. 4.

on discharge.[1] The ability to enlist in the army was a short cut to full citizenship and a substantial privilege.

The native Egyptians, however, throughout the Roman period were denied access to the legions, and till the 3rd century to the auxiliary corps.[2] Moreover, they still paid the full poll-tax. The power of the priesthood—the focus of national feeling—was severely curbed, and the whole hierarchy placed under strict control. The temple lands were even annexed to the imperial domain by Petronius (prefect, 25–21 B.C.), though the priests might be allowed to cultivate some of the former property of their gods in lieu of receiving a stipend.[3]

The Hellenized inhabitants of the nome-capitals, usually of mixed race, were not quite exempt from the poll-tax, but were assessed at a lower rate, which varied from nome to nome.

It seems that what now helped the cause of Hellenism was the growth in municipal pride and self-consciousness brought about by the Roman conquest. The nome-capitals did not become Greek πόλεις or Roman *municipia*, but in practice the tendency was to assimilate them more and more to the self-governing cities. Their magistrates were arranged in a regular hierarchy, and it became usual for a magistrate to give the list of offices he had held in the past, his *cursus honorum*, just as in the *municipia* ; [4] while the whole body of magistrates formed a κοινόν or corporation, which carried on correspondence with the state officials and undertook other duties as a corporate body, fulfilling many of the functions of a Senate. The tendency in the nome-capitals was to look down on the Egyptians of the villages as barbarians,[5] just as the Alexandrians had always done. Thus we see how the Roman conquest widened the gulf between Egyptian and Greek in the Chora, a tendency that hardly existed in Ptolemaic times—in the cities, of course, it had always existed. The Greeks, too, who were scattered about the nomes seem at some time to have been formed into associations, probably modelled on those of the free cities, and apparently possessing some political significance.[6] The revival of Hellenism received an added impulse from the foundation in A.D. 130 of Antinoopolis by the Philhellenic Emperor Hadrian. At Alexandria the pride in Hellenic traditions led, on the one hand, to violent outbursts of anti-Semitism, and, on the other, to constant friction with the Roman Government,

---

[1] Lesquier, *L'Armée romaine d'Égypte*, pp. 203–26.
[2] Lesquier, op. cit., p. 225.   [3] Milne, op. cit., p. 11.
[4] *P. Oxy.*, xii. 28–30 gives a discussion of the ' *cursus honorum* ' in Egypt.
[5] Cf. *P. Oxy.*, xvi. 1681. The writer of this 3rd century A.D letter found at Oxyrhynchus declares : ἴσως με νομίζετε, ἀδελφοὶ βάρβαρόν τινα ἢ Αἰγυπτίον ἄνθρωπον εἶναι. ἀλλὰ ἀξιῶ μὴ οὕτως ἔχειν. (' Perhaps, my brothers, you are thinking me a barbarian or an inhuman Egyptian : but I claim this is not so.') It is, of course, possible that he was an Alexandrian living in the χώρα and writing to Alexandria.
[6] We hear in the Fayum of the ' 6475 Greek men of the Arsinoite nome ' (Plaumann in *Archiv. f. Pap.*, vi. 176–83 : Plaumann, however, thinks this body was formed under the early Ptolemies, but there is no evidence for this). Further, the Greeks of the Delta and the Thebais are found uniting with other bodies to erect an inscription in honour of a rhetorician (Dittenberger, *Or. Graec. Sel.* 709 (ii. 446–8)).

which tended to favour the Jews, at least till the revolt of Judaea, and even after that event it had at times to protect them from their Greek neighbours. As in the Greek cities, so in the nome-capitals, the centre of Hellenic life was the gymnasium and οἱ ἀπὸ γυμνασίου, as they were called, formed a special class socially and politically. Athletics, music, and rhetoric were essential parts of this education. Classical Greek literature, with, needless to say, Homer in the place of honour, was studied and read.[1]

Although the Roman Government might on paper make clear-cut distinctions between Greek and Egyptian, and so widen the gulf between them, such distinctions could only be theoretical, not based on purity of blood, but on external criteria. Hellenic culture, the possession of catoecic land, citizenship of a Greek city were the lines of division, and even they were shifting and uncertain. Purity of race was hard to find, and there were few pure-blooded Greeks in Egypt except at Alexandria, and possibly Naucratis and Ptolemais— the process of intermingling and assimilation had gone on for too long, and there were probably even few pure-blooded Egyptians in most districts.

The fate of Hellenism, as can be gauged from the preceding pages, was bound up with the cities and with the Greek municipalities in the nome-capitals constituted round the gymnasium. But these— the chief barrier to de-Hellenization—broke down. The system of *munera* developed by the Roman Empire, by which the costs of the municipality were laid upon the citizens, until at last all their activity and wealth were absorbed in very onerous offices, contributed greatly to the ruin of the municipalities. Already at the beginning of the 2nd century A.D. the enormous changes these *munera* involved and the increasing economic difficulties made it hard to obtain candidates, and compulsion had to be resorted to.[2] The municipal magistracies had, in fact, a fatal influence on the economic history of Egypt, and led at last to the ruin of the urban middle class.[3]

---

[1] *P. Oxy.* vi. 930 = Wilcken, *Chrest.* 138 A mother writing to her son remarks : ἐμέλησε δέ μοι πέμψαι καὶ πυθέσθαι περὶ τῆς ὑγίας σου καὶ ἐπιγνῶναι τί ἀναγεινώσκεις καὶ ἔλεγεν τὸ ζῆτα. ' I took care to send and enquire about your health and learn what you were reading. He said it was the 6th book.' (cf. the *Iliad*).

[2] Cf. *P. Ryl.* ii. 77, A.D. 192, which well illustrates the shifts and subterfuges to which a man might be driven to escape service (line 38 : Ἀχιλλεὺς εἶπεν ἐγὼ ἀνεδειξάμην ἐξηγητείαν ἐπὶ τῷ κατ' ἔτος δύο τάλαντα εἰσφέρειν, οὐ γὰρ δύναμαι κοσμητείαν). Achilles had been nominated for the office of cosmetes, and the matter was referred to the strategus sitting in public audience. As a means of escaping this burdensome duty, Achilles offers to undertake, on certain conditions, the office of exegetes, which was superior in rank, but, according to him, less expensive. His opponents imply that Achilles' proposal is a mere pretence, and that in any case a law of the Emperor Antoninus refuses to absolve him from the office of Cosmetes. He is accordingly appointed, unwilling though he is, but Aspidos, father of the ex-cosmetes, guarantees the expenses of the office. It is noteworthy that by the so-called ' cessio bonorum ', the surrender of two-thirds of his property, a man nominated to office might escape the duty.

[3] *J.E.A.* iv. (1917) pp. 86–106, ' The Byzantine Servile State, in Egypt ', gives a summary-sketch of the effects of liturgies and magistracies on the economic and eventually the political history of Egypt.

The status of the Hellenized inhabitants was, however, enhanced by two measures on the part of the Roman Emperors. Septimius Severus in 202 gave the nome-capitals a senate or βουλή.[1] This was a considerable step in the direction of assimilation to the free cities. Caracalla in 212, by the famous ' Constitutio Antoniniana ',[2] extended the Roman citizenship throughout the Empire. The native Egyptians, who ranked as dediticii, were probably excluded from the benefits of the edict ; but a very large addition to the roll of citizens was nevertheless made in the population of the nome-capitals. These measures widened the gulf between the rural peasantry and the people of the nome-capitals who adopted high-sounding titles in their civic pride and advertised their Hellenic culture. But these things could not check their steady drift to ruin, which accompanied and was doubtless accentuated by the economic crisis throughout the Empire and the slump in the value of money without parallel in history except in modern times. The end of the process was the ruin of the urban middle class ; and its ruin meant, ultimately, the ruin of Hellenism as an effective force in Egypt.

By this time there had appeared another force which was to prove

[1] Milne, op. cit., pp. 61–2, ' It was probably part of a considered policy which aimed on the one hand at a strengthening of Roman influence under Greek forms in the towns, and on the other at an improvement in the machinery for tax-collection.'

[2] P. Giessen, 40, col. 1, is a fragmentary Greek translation of the edict. The actual words of the important clause (as translated by F. M. Heichelheim in *J.E.A.*, xxvi. (1940) 10) are : ' I grant, therefore, to all (free persons throughout the Roman world) the citizenship of the Romans (no other legal status remaining) except that of the dediticians.' The dediticii were the unprivileged classes, paying the full poll-tax ; in Egypt, therefore, the native Egyptians, not sharing in Hellenic culture. Several other sources refer to this franchise which granted Roman citizenship to most of the inhabitants of the Roman Empire. Dio Cassius LXXVIII, 9, 5, says (Prof. Cary's translation in Loeb Library) ' This was the reason why (the Emperor Caracalla) made all the people in his Empire Roman citizens. Nominally he was honouring them, but his real purpose was to increase his revenues by this means, inasmuch as aliens did not have to pay most of the taxes, which he had introduced or reorganized.' Οὗ ἕνεκα καὶ Ῥωμαίους πάντας τοὺς ἐν τῇ ἀρχῇ αὐτοῦ, λόγῳ μὲν τιμῶν, ἔργῳ δὲ ὅπως πλείω αὐτῷ καὶ ἐκ τοῦ τοιούτου προσίῃ διὰ τὸ τοὺς ξένους τὰ πολλὰ αὐτῶν μὴ συντελεῖν ἀποδείξειν.

Ulpianus states in Dig. i. 5, 17 : ' In orbe Romano qui sunt, ex constitutione imperatoris Antonini cives Romani effecti sunt,' St. Augustine in his *De Civ. Dei*, v. 17 : ' fieret . . . ut omnes ad Romanum imperium pertinentes societatem acciperent civitatis et Romani cives essent ac sic esset omnium quod erat ante paucorum ' ; and a short statement in *Script. Hist. Aug.* x. 1, 2 : ' civitatem omnibus datam '. As to the term dediticii, Heichelheim in *J.E.A.*, xxvi. (1940) 16, 17, observes that it can be considered as certain that several small groups of inhabitants of the Roman Empire—e.g., freedmen of minor status, prisoners of war, as well as barbarian settlers and soldiers of minor status—were excluded from Caracalla's franchise. The term referred originally to all provincials who had been conquered by Rome by force, but later often included the small groups which preserved a minor status after Caracalla. Yet Ulpian and Dio Cassius, who were both living under Caracalla, assert that all people received Roman citizenship under this Emperor. Heichelheim is of the opinion that this was due to the fact that the exclusion of certain groups from the franchise was not directly mentioned in the main sentence of the law, but only stated indirectly in the ' Constitutio Antoniniana ' See Part III, Ch. 2 of the present work, for a fuller discussion of the problem of the ' Constitutio '.

hostile to Greek culture, Christianity. Directly through fixing attention on the future life and the salvation of the soul instead of the cult of bodily fitness so characteristic of Hellenism, on theology rather than on classical literature, and indirectly by acting as a solvent on the unity of the Graeco-Roman world in the East in contrast with the Papacy and the Church in the West, Christianity helped in Egypt, as elsewhere, to reawaken the slumbering national consciousness, to revive the national tongue, and so to weaken Hellenism, though Hellenism did not die without a struggle, as witness Hypatia and the pagan schools of philosophy at Alexandria. But this pagan circle was by no means merely Hellenic ; on the contrary, it represented a strongly national tendency, attempting a revival of the ancient Egyptian religion.

It is clear, in fact, that Greek was now in Egypt a doomed language, kept alive only by its use as the official tongue of the Byzantine Government ; when that Government ceased with the Arab conquest, Greek soon died out. For nearly a century, it is true, it lingered on for official use, and there were Greek notaries in the chancery of the Arab governor.[1]

Bell says :—

> ' With good reason did Mommsen call Islam " the executioner of Hellenism ". In this new world of dogmatism and religious bigotry, Christian or Mahommedan, there was no room left for the clear-eyed sanity of Hellas. Egypt had become once more a part of that Oriental world from which the fiery genius of Alexander had separated her for a thousand years.' [2]

[1] P. Lond. iv. 1380 = Wilcken, *Chrest.* 285.   [2] *J.E.A.* viii. (1922), 155.

CHAPTER VII

ALEXANDRIA

THE thing of most enduring importance, says Bevan, which Alexander did was the founding of Alexandria.

On the surrender of Egypt by the Persian satrap in the autumn of the year 332 B.C., Alexander, after reaching Canopus and sailing round Lake Mareotis, came ashore just where now is the city of Alexandria. It struck him that the position was admirable for founding a city there in his name, and that such a city was bound to be prosperous.[1]

In the summer of the same year he had destroyed the great commercial port of the eastern Mediterranean, Tyre, which had given him more trouble than any other city to reduce. Hogarth believes that he was convinced that some measure had to be devised to prevent its revival,[2] and that this measure had to be taken by his founding of Alexandria—his creating of a new port in Egypt, a ' Macedonian Tyre ' which would take the place in world commerce which Tyre had taken. He chose a site some forty miles away from the old Greek city of Naucratis, communicating with the interior by the Canopic branch of the Nile. The Canopic mouth of the Nile had long served for the comparatively little sea-borne commerce with the alien Levant, which Egypt had hitherto had, while, of the other mouths, the Pelusiac alone remained open. At Rhacotis, a few miles west of Canopus, which Strabo[3] gives us to understand was occupied only by a fishing village when Alexander found it, was a dry limestone site, raised above the Delta level, within easy reach of drinkable and navigable inland water by a canal to be taken off the Nile. The set of the current in the Mediterranean eastwards involves for the other coastal harbours a constant tendency to silt up from which Alexandria is free, a fact probably made known to Alexander by the Greeks of Naucratis. The site was covered by an island, Pharos, which, when joined to the mainland by a mole, the Heptastadion, gave alternate harbours, the Great Harbour and Eunostus, against the sea-winds from whatever direction they blew. Thus the site was the only possible one in Egypt for a healthy open port to be used by Macedonian sea-going fleets, especially as by that time warships tended to increase their tonnage and draught.[4]

Bell holds there may also have been a reason of a political kind in the choice of the site. Rhacotis had no special associations or prestige,

---

[1] Arrian, iii. 1.
[2] *J.E.A.* (1915), p. 55. ' Alexander in Egypt and some Consequences ', *C.A.H.* vii. 377.
[3] Strabo, xvii. 792.   [4] *J.E.A.* (1915), p. 55.

and a Hellenistic foundation there could develop its Hellenic culture
unthreatened by the weight of native tradition. Alexander laid out
his city on the straight rectangular plan which had been brought into
fashion for new cities by Hippodamus of Miletus a century before.
This grid-iron scheme on which the streets were projected was
destined to determine the lay-out of typical Hellenistic foundations
all over the Near East, such as Priene and Pergamum, the plans of
which have been recovered by excavation. The city as Alexander
planned it formed an extended oblong along the neck of land between
Lake Mareotis and the sea, and it was about 20 January in the year
331 B.C. that the actual ceremony of foundation took place.

Of the earliest history of Alexandria we know little. Alexander [1]
had apparently no idea of making his foundation the capital of the
country, and it was probably from Memphis that his representative
governed. Even Ptolemy son of Lagus, who obtained Egypt as his
province, took up his residence at Memphis, where Alexander's body,
which he had secured on the latter's death, was at first buried. It
was not till several years later, owing probably to a change of policy,
that he transferred the capital to Alexandria. [2] He abandoned
Alexander's lead in favouring the amalgamation of Greek and
Egyptian, and adopted towards the natives the attitude of conqueror
to conquered which, as we have already noticed, was maintained by his
successor until the growing weakness of the dynasty forced them to
make concessions to their Egyptian subjects. The outward signs of
this new course were the removal of the seat of government to Alexandria, the establishment there of the cult of the new god Sarapis, evolved
at Memphis, whom Ptolemy had made the meeting-point of Greek
and Egyptian and in some sort the national god of his dominions, and,
further, the removal thither as well by Ptolemy II of the body of
Alexander, which became the object of an elaborate cult, with its
eponymous priest.

From the first Alexandria seemed destined for its rôle of melting-
pot in which East and West, Greece and Egypt and Asia, and countries as yet hardly known, could meet and contribute their several
quotas.

There were Macedonians who, according to Bell, [3] at a later time
certainly, and possibly from the first, were not a part of the regular
citizen body, but formed a special class of the population, with their
own privileges. Bevan [4] holds that the original citizen-body must
have consisted of Macedonians and Greeks, but how Alexander got
together the families which constituted the first nucleus is unknown.
The mass of the ordinary citizens were Greeks, but may have included Hellenized representatives of non-Greek races. The Greeks

---

[1] *J.E.A.* (1927), Alexandria, p. 172.
[2] Ibid. 172, Bell quotes Kornemann, ' Die Satrapenpolitik des erstenlagiden ',
in *Raccolta Lumbroso*, pp. 235–45, for this point of view.
[3] Ibid. xiii. (1927), 173.
[4] Bevan, *A History of Egypt under the Ptolemaic Dynasty*, Methuen, London,
1927, pp. 8, 98.

68 RACE-RELATIONS IN ANCIENT EGYPT

came from many parts of the Greek world, and many different dialects were to be heard in the streets until they gave place to the so-called koine of the Hellenistic Age. In this respect one is reminded of the altercation in the 15th Idyll of Theocritus,[1] where the stranger, exasperated by the chattering of Praxinoa and her friend, exclaims : ' My good women, do stop that everlasting prattling, like a couple of doves! they wear me out with their broad Doric,' and Praxinoa replies : ' Good gracious, where does the fellow come from ? What is it to you if we do prattle ? You buy your slaves before you order them about. It's Syracusans you're giving orders to. I'd have you know we're Corinthians by extraction—like Bellerophon you know ; we talk Peloponnesian. I suppose Dorians are allowed to talk Doric ? '

In a papyrus which contains a contract for a commercial expedition to the land of Punt to buy spices [2] we find among the parties and their sureties men from Sparta, Elea in Italy, Carthage, and Marseilles, and one who from his name may be a Roman ; and in a contract of loan dated in 252 B.C.[3] occur a Persian of the royal guard, a Roman, and three men of Barca.

Besides the full citizens there were, not perhaps at first, but certainly later, other Greeks not enjoying the Alexandrian citizenship. There were also in the city Jews whose numbers in later times grew very greatly. Bevan [4] doubts the truth of the statement of Josephus about Alexander encouraging the Jews especially to settle in Alexandria and giving them citizen rights, on the ground that the Jews were not in those days what they afterwards became—a people connected to a pre-eminent degree with finance.[5] The Greeks, of course, were the commercial people *par excellence* of these days. Nevertheless, whether the Jews were there from the very foundation, as Bell believes, or were attracted by this city from their isolated Judean hills, as Hogarth holds, already prepared as they were by the great experience of the Babylonian captivity to expand, associate with foreigners, live abroad, and take avidly to trade, it was Alexandria which was the chief agent in their Hellenization, which possessed eventually the largest urban Hebrew population in the world and which gave them most of their primary education as bankers and middlemen of the civilized world.[6]

Alexandria with its territory was not considered as being in Egypt. It was regarded as adjacent to Egypt—' Alexandria ad Aegyptum ' (πρὸς Αἰγύπτωι or κατ' Αἴγυπτον).

In the papyri people sometimes speak of making the journey from Alexandria to Egypt. This is significant. The total population of Alexandria in the latter years of the Ptolemaic Dynasty may have

---

[1] Theocritus, *Idyll*, p. 15.   [2] Wilcken, *Zeitschr. f. äg. Spr.*, lx. 86–102.
[3] *Archiv. Pap.* vii. 19 f.
[4] Bevan, *A History of Egypt under the Ptolemaic Dynasty*, Methuen, London, 1927, p. 8.
[5] Cf. Josephus, *c. Apion.*, I, par. 60 ; *Antiquities*, xii. 1, 8.
[6] *J.E.A.* ii. (1915), 59–60.

been little short of a million, but the population of Alexandria, not counting strangers of passage, included a great multitude who did not belong to the body of those who proudly called themselves 'Alexandrines'. Diodorus [1] gives the numbers of the citizen-body at the end of the dynasty as 300,000. Of course all the native Egyptian element in Alexandria, which was considerable in later times, was excluded from the citizen-body—perhaps also the Jews domiciled in the city, though the question whether the Jews were or were not included is still debatable (this question will be dealt with in another chapter). The citizen-body claimed to be a community of genuine Greeks, with the interests and social organization which belonged to the free citizens of a Greek city as such. The Alexandrines considered themselves Greeks and Macedonians. As a matter of fact, it does not seem likely that there was any considerable infusion of native Egyptian blood in the Alexandrines, since at Naucratis, as we have seen, marriage between a citizen and an Egyptian woman was illegal; [2] probably this was also so at Alexandria and at Ptolemais. [3]

In a well-known fragment of Polybius [4] the population of Alexandria in the later days of the dynasty is said to consist of three elements:—

    (i) the native Egyptian element, 'sharp-witted and amenable to civil life';
    (ii) the mercenary troops insubordinate and apt to impose their will upon the government;
    (iii) the 'Alexandrines' who showed some tendency themselves to break through the restraints of civil order though less turbulent than the soldiery.

'for even if they were mixed (μιγάδες) in stock, they were Greek by origin and had not forgotten the general Greek mode of life'. This classification is obviously inexact. Polybius says nothing of the regular army, and under the term 'Alexandrines' he apparently includes the whole free Greek civil population, whether they belonged to the citizen-body or not. He does not mention the Jews; possibly, Hellenized as they were in speech and dress, they were not easily distinguishable in appearance from the Greeks.

Both Polybius and Philo speak of the Alexandrines as 'people of mixed blood' (μιγάδες), but it seems likely that what is meant is

---

[1] Bevan, op cit., p. 352. Diod. Sic., xvii. 52. 6.
[2] Wilcken and Mitteis, *Grundzüge und Chrestomathie der Papyrus-kunde*, Leipzig and Berlin, 1912, ii. 27.
[3] T. Reinach, *Un Code Fiscal de l'Égypte romaine*, pp. 82–3.
[4] Polybius, xxxiv. 14, 2–5: ὁ γοῦν Πολύβιος . . . φησι τρία γένη τὴν πόλιν οἰκεῖν, τό τε Αἰγύπτιον καὶ ἐπιχώριον φῦλον, ὀξὺ καὶ πολιτικόν, καὶ τὸ μισθοφορικόν, βαρὺ καὶ πολὺ καὶ ἀνάγωγον· ἐξ ἔθους γὰρ παλαιοῦ ξένους ἔτρεφον τοὺς τὰ ὅπλα ἔχοντας, ἄρχειν μᾶλλον ἢ ἄρχεσθαι δεδιδαγμένους διὰ τὴν τῶν βασιλέων οὐδένειαν. τρίτον δ᾽ ἦν γένος τὸ τῶν Ἀλεξανδρέων, οὐδ᾽ αὐτὸ εὐκρινῶς πολιτικὸν διὰ τὰς αὐτὰς αἰτίας, κρεῖττον δ᾽ ἐκείνων ὅμως· καὶ γὰρ εἰ μιγάδες, Ἕλληνες ὅμως ἀνέκαθεν ἦσαν καὶ ἐμέμνηντο τοῦ κοινοῦ τῶν Ἑλλήνων ἔθους.

that the citizen-body was a medley of Greeks of all kinds—Ionians, Dorians, Aeolians, Greeks from Hellas, and Greeks from all the outlying cities, east and west—not that it had an admixture of Egyptian blood.[1]

But not even all the Greek population of Alexandria was included in the citizen-body of ' Alexandrines '. Schubart thinks, indeed, that the citizen-body included only a minority of the Greeks resident in Alexandria. The multitude of men who called themselves Hellenes, talked Greek, and lived like Greeks, but had not the privileges of citizenship—like the Greek ' metoikoi ' living in Athens or any other Greek town—were perhaps largely not Greek in blood : the offspring, for instance, of marriages between Greek and Egyptian women in the country outside Alexandria who had come to settle in the city. Certain privileges probably belonged to all Greeks, as such, in distinction from natives. Egyptians, for instance, might be punished by bastinado, but the ' Alexandrines ', Philo [2] tells us, might be beaten only with flat sticks (*spathai*).

The Jews in this matter were classed with the ' Alexandrines ', and it is probable that by the ' Alexandrines ' we are here to understand all resident Greeks, not members of the citizen-body only.

In every city of Greek type the citizen-body was organized in smaller social groups. At Athens the citizens were divided into ten tribes φυλαί and between 100 and 190 demes, δῆμοι. A similar organization into tribes and demes existed for the Alexandrine citizen-body,[3] though it does not seem to have been extended to the whole citizen-body.

There were numbers of people who were ' Alexandrines ' but not members of a deme. The members of the demes formed the social aristocracy of Alexandria, perhaps largely the descendants of the original citizen-body, at the beginning of the 3rd century. Marriages, however, between members of demes and Greeks, or even Persians outside the demes, were apparently quite in order.

About the constitution of Alexandria we know little. Whether it possessed a Senate is a matter of dispute. It is a matter of controversy whether Augustus found there a senate, which he abolished,[4] but it is certain that it had none under the Romans until the time of Septimius Severus. The most probable hypothesis is that Alexander

---

[1] Lumbroso, *Archiv.* v. 400.   [2] *In Flacc.*, par. 78.

[3] A papyrus from Hibeh of the earlier part of the 3rd century indicates that in a city which must be either Alexandria or Ptolemais there were five tribes, with twelve demes to each tribe and twelve phratries to each deme (Chrest. No. 25). The member of a deme is described in legal documents by his deme-name (e.g. Antaeus a Temenean—i.e., belonging to the deme called after Temenus), just as another man might be described as ' Athenian ' or as ' Thracian '. It was not necessary to put ' Alexandrine ', this being implied in the deme-name, and it was not the practice for the tribe to be mentioned as well as the deme.

[4] Cf. Dio Cassius, li. 17 : τοῖς δ' ᾿Αλεξανδρεῦσιν ἄνευ βουλευτῶν πολιτεύεσθαι ἐκέλευσε· τοσαύτην που νεωτεροποιίαν αὐτῶν κατέγνω.

Cf. Bell, *Jews and Christians in Egypt*, pp. 8–10.   J. G. Milne, *A History of Egypt under Roman Rule*, 3rd edition, pp. 282–6.

gave the city a senate, which some Ptolemaic king took away, perhaps after one of the civil wars in which Alexandria espoused the losing side. There was probably an *ecclesia* or popular assembly with little real power, and there were the usual magistrates, the *gymnasiarch* or head of the gymnasium, the *exegetes*, a high official with various functions, including that of keeping the register of citizens, the *eutheniarch* in charge of the food supply, and the *cosmetes*, the leader of the *ephebi* or young citizens.

As the Gymnasium was the centre of the social life of a Greek city, the Gymnasiarch was, in a way, the social head of the citizen-body. When, in Roman times, there are repeated outbreaks of violence between Greeks and Jews in Alexandria, it is the Gymnasiarch who represents the Greek citizens, who heads the cause of the Greeks at Rome before the Emperor and stands for Greek republican freedom.[1] The gymnasiarch of Alexandria must have been a very important person under the Ptolemies. Citizenship was secured through enrolment among the ephebi. An attested record of such enrolment of the imperial period [2] is extant.

> ' Date of entry among the ephebi 13th year of Imperator Caesar Titus Aelius Hadrianus Antoninus Pius, 12th Sebastos (Thoth). Theon son of Theon of the Propapposebastian tribe and Althaean deme, thirty years old, and his wife Sarapias daughter of Dion, citizeness, thirty years old, with her legal guardian assigned her by minute of the prytaneis dated in the prytaneum of the current year and month, namely Theon son of Tryphon of the Musopaterian tribe and Althaean deme, fifty-eight years old, of Arsinoe Nike Street, stating that they are united in a marriage without contract, (enter) their son Theon, one year old in the 29th year of Imperator Caesar Trajanus Hadrianus Augustus Pharmouthi 22 . . . of the detachment of Ptolemy son of Antipater.'

It is noteworthy in this respect that the penalty for fraudulent enrolment of youths not entitled by birth to the honour was con-fiscation of a sixth of the income.

Alexandria, moreover, had its own law courts and its own code of laws, known as ὁ πολιτικὸς νόμος or ' the civic law ', which were recognized even in the royal courts. These laws were founded largely on Attic law, with modifications derived from other systems and the special circumstances of Alexandria. They were supple-mented from time to time by decrees of the citizens.

The city was in a somewhat hybrid position as a royal residence and the capital of the Empire, for, besides strictly civic officials, there were also royal officials, besides civic decrees, the inhabitants were subject in addition to royal ones. In a Greek city which was

---

[1] Wilcken, ' Zum Alexandrinischen Antisemitismus ', *Abh. der sächs Ges d. Wiss. phil. hist.* Kl. XXVII (1909).
[2] Wilcken, *Chrestomathie*, 146.

also the residence of a despotic court, even where the forms of autonomous government existed, they could not but be really under the
control of the court, as we know was the case at Pergamum.

Reforms must have taken place in the constitution of Alexandria
probably in the time of the earliest kings. However, though the
Greek city was mutilated by the royal power, the citizen-body was
one of the mainstays of Hellenic civilization, and the kings were the
patrons of Greek culture. Its centres were the Library and the
Museum, royal institutions attached to the Palace buildings.

Here we have one of the essential features of Alexandrian Hellenism and the Hellenism of all Egypt. It was based on the power of
the kings, which was a contrast to the past, and even the present of
Greece. The effect on the literature and thought of Alexandria was
bound to be serious. Philosophy usually lost interest in the destiny
of the state, and cultivated the ideal of the wise man, the Citizen of
the World. Literature was a Court literature. Alexandrian
literature will not bear comparison with that of the classical period,
but it has a real importance. The Alexandrines were too much
dominated by the classics of the great age as regards the forms of
their poetry, while to balance this they aimed at novelty in the matter
of theme and treatment : they were continually pouring new wine
into old bottles, sometimes with distressing results, yet the hymns
of Callimachus and the Epic of Apollonius Rhodius have very real
merits, and the Idylls of Theocritus give us a new genre the handling
of which has not been equalled since. The great poetical geniuses
of the time—Theocritus, Callimachus, Apollonius of Rhodes—were
Court poets. The nature of their inspiration is purely Greek, and
of Egypt they know and say hardly anything, for they wrote for an
essentially Greek circle—the Court folk, among whom the natives
did not appear till later, and the citizens of the cities, who stood aloof
from the people of the country and did not intermarry with them.[1]
Yet by the side of this truly Alexandrian literature a whole body of
semi-literary writings sprang up for the mixed Greek population of
the nomes—tales and novels full of magic and mysticism, sometimes
of a coarse kind.

The Greeks of Alexandria must have been affected by the cosmopolitanism of the city which was a meeting-place of the world.
The Alexandrians had not connubium with the natives, but they
might have had it with the Greeks of the Chora, and these were

[1] Cf. J. W. Mackail, *Lectures on Greek Pottery*, Longmans, Green & Co., 1926,
pp. 177 seq., for a sympathetic view of the Alexandrians. Though their poetic
production was mingled with pedantry, they were trying their best to find the centre
of poetry which had been lost, and the Latin genius entered the field they had
prepared. ' But for them Greek poetry might have perished out of the world.
But for them Latin poetry might never have come to the birth ' (ibid., p. 184).
Cf. also *C.A.H.*, vii. Ch. VIII, for an excellent account of Alexandrian literature.
As regards prose, it was the technical sciences (geography, mathematics, physics,
medicine, natural history, philology) which chiefly engaged the Alexandrian prose-
writers. Just as in the Silver Age of Latin literature there was no room for the
political oration, so, too, in the Hellenistic monarchies there was no place for it.

Egyptianized. The truly original creations of Alexandrian thought had a Graeco-Oriental character. The Ptolemaic monarchy was not a national state. The Lagids neither wished to revive the Egyptian nation nor to create a new national state, Macedonian or Greek. From Egypt they took the principle of the divine right of kings and the bureaucratic organization of the State. But the world had been drawn into the current of Greek civilization, and they themselves had adopted that culture. Their work could be accomplished only with the help of Greeks. They therefore gave an important, but limited, place in their kingdom to the city. They propagated Hellenism by agricultural colonization, taking care not to group their colonists in autonomous centres like Greek cities.

To Hellenize their realm they selected those institutions of the city which were educational rather than political in character.

PART II

CHAPTER I

THE EARLIEST HEBREW CONTACT WITH EGYPT

THE Hebrews, Greeks, and Romans, though sharing in a common Mediterranean habitation, were sundered by a difference of racial origin which goes far to account for the distinctive character of their civilizations.

The Hebrews were a branch of the Semitic stock, whose home was Arabia. The Greeks and the Romans belonged in the main to the Indo-European family, whose home was probably the steppe lands north of the Caucasus, though some have placed it in the plain of Hungary.[1]

The home of the Hebrews themselves was on the west end of what Breasted describes as the Fertile Crescent of Arabia, a great semicircle with the open side towards the south, the west and at the southeast corner of the Mediterranean, the centre directly north of Arabia, and the east end at the north end of the Persian Gulf.[2]

By a not too bold generalization the history of South-west Asia has been styled an age-long struggle between the mountain peoples to the north and the desert-wanderers of the scanty grasslands to the south for its possession. As early as 3000 B.C. the desert-wanderers were drifting in from the desert and settling in Palestine on the western end of the Fertile Crescent, where they are found in possession of walled towns by 2500 B.C.[3] The actual predecessors of the Hebrews in Palestine were a tribe called Canaanites ; farther north settled a powerful tribe known as Amorites,[4] while along the shores of North

---

[1] Cf. *Ency. Brit.*, 14th edition (1937), xii. 263. Article ' Indo-Europeans ', by Dr. P. Giles.

[2] J. H. Breasted, *Ancient Times : A History of the Early World*, Ginn & Co., p. 101.

[3] Ibid., p. 104.

[4] The Babylonians, who were in relations with Syria in the 3rd millennium B.C., called Syria-Palestine Amurru or the country of the Amorreans or Amorites. The Canaanites, properly so called, had their share in the supremacy of Syria about the middle of the 2nd millennium, for it is roughly this region which bears this name in the Egyptian texts from about 1600 onwards. From the linguistic point of view both Canaanites and Amorites were Semitic, and moreover the excavations in Palestine have definitely not established that a new civilization displaced an older one about 1500 B.C. From an ethical or cultural viewpoint there were probably hardly any essential points of difference between Amorites and Canaanites. Eyre, *European Civilization, Its Origin and Development*, Oxford Univ. Press, 1935, i. 298.

Syria a Semitic [1] people had taken to the sea, and had become the Phoenicians.

By 2000 B.C. all these settled communities of the Western Semites had developed no mean degree of civilization, drawn for the most part from Egypt and Babylonia. Their home along the east end of the Mediterranean was on the highway between the two countries, and they were in constant contact with both. Similar movements of Semitic tribes had long before taken place at the eastern end of the Fertile Crescent along the lower courses of the Tigris and Euphrates. Here, however, there were two parts of the plain of Lower Mesopotamia standing in sharp opposition to one another, distinguished by the race and language of those who lived in them : Akkad, in the north, was predominantly Semitic ; Sumer, in the south, was more mixed, but the Semitic element here was swamped by the Sumerians, who had imposed on it their language and their civilization, and had the land called after their own name.[2]

It was only later that the Semitic peoples supplanted the Sumerians in Sumer as the ruling race, about the 27th century B.C., under Sargon of Akkad, but the Sumerians had the cultural victory, for Sumerian genius evolved a civilization which persisted for nearly 1500 years after its authors had vanished.[3]

> 'Not only did the Semites [says Woolley] adopt ready-made those stories of the Creation and the Flood which viewed as history or as parable had affected the Christian even more than the Jewish Church ; the Jewish religion, as it owed not a little of its origin to the Sumerian, so also was throughout the period of the Kings and the Captivity brought into close contact with Babylonian worship which was taken over from Sumer, and partly by its precept and partly in opposition to it attained to higher growth. The laws of Moses were largely based on

[1] Cf. *C.A.H.* i. 184–5. 'The term " Semite " is more convenient than accurate, and is derived from Shem, a son of Noah.' The whole scheme, in which in an elaborate genealogical table in Genesis many divisions of the world are traced back to Noah's three sons, is broadly geographical, and recognizes three zones, Japheth in the north, Ham in the south, and Shem in the centre. The table is not strictly linguistic—e.g., the Phoenicians, whose language differs only dialectically from Hebrew, and is related to Assyrian, are ascribed to Ham ; Lydian and Elamite, too, though linguistically different (from each other and) from Semitic, are ascribed to Shem. Yet the Semites belong essentially to Asia, and have been influenced from the north.

[2] C. L. Woolley, *The Sumerians*, Oxford, 1930, pp. 1 seq. Woolley believes (i) that the northern part of the Syrian desert and the upper Euphrates valley were inhabited by a people of Semitic speech, known as the Amurru (Amorites), (ii) that, coming from a comparatively civilized homeland and knowing city-life, these Semites next settled in Akkad ; (iii) that into Sumer itself there came a Semitic element of nomads from the Central Arabian plateau which was quite distinct from the Semitic population of Akkad, had little in common with it (except language), and had certainly not attained anything like the same degree of civilization ; and (iv) that the last of the incomers were the Sumerians themselves, a dark-haired people speaking an agglutinative language somewhat resembling ancient Turkish (Turanian) in its formation, though not in its etymology.

[3] C. L. Woolley, ibid., p. 189.

Sumerian codes, these came codes which lay at the bottom of the great Code of Hammurabi, and so from the Sumerians the Hebrews derived the ideals of social life and justice which informed all their history and have by Christian races been regarded in theory if not in practice as criteria for their own customs and enactments.' [1]

The Hebrews were all originally men of the Arabian desert, wandering with their flocks and herds, and slowly drifting over into their final home in Palestine, as described in the Pentateuch. It seems that about the 20th century B.C. peoples of the same origin as the Canaanites, but of a different culture, of whom the most famous were the Arameans, came from the East, and settled down in the territory of the original Semitic population of Canaan. This invasion doubtless caused the migration of the Hebrews.[2]

Biblical tradition gives us the place of origin of Abraham's clan Ur of the Kasdim,[3] which was situated in Sumer, by the 20th century B.C. the centre of power of the Aramean Semites, a city whose connexion with the Sumerians goes far back into the distant past. Yet Abraham and his people were not city-dwellers, but wandering shepherds.[4]

From the earliest historic times Semitic tribes are found concentrated upon the banks of the Persian Gulf. Their caravans crossed Arabia towards the Red Sea, passing over into northern Egypt under the 12th Dynasty. These migrations were in all likelihood caused

---

[1] C. L. Woolley, *The Sumerians*, p. 192.
[2] Cf. A. S. Cook in *C.A.H.* i. 192-3. ' The attempt has sometimes been made to view the entire history of the Semitic area as the result of successive waves of nomad Semites migrating from a " home " in the deserts of Arabia owing to overcrowding, dessication or some other natural cause.'
In this way five epochs have been distinguished

   (i) the first invasion, c. 4th millennium B.C., occupying Mesopotamia and North Syria ;
   (ii) c. middle of 3rd millennium came the Canaanites and an Amorite modification of the Semitic element in Mesopotamia ;
   (iii) 1000 years later the Aramaean wave, a vast movement, brings the Hebrew and related peoples and fills the north as far as the Taurus Mountains ;
   (iv) after another millennium come the Nabataeans and later settlers, and lastly,
   (v) the Mohammedan movement of the 7th century A.D.

Cook, however, states that all theories of this sort, though in accordance with many facts, give too schematic a view of the movements. Cf. ibid. pp. 230-1 : ' Amor holds a place in the Babylonian period which resembles that of Aram in the Assyrian Age,' and p. 234, ' It is difficult to distinguish between Hebrews and Aramaeans because Abram has Aramaean relatives and Jacob (Israel) has Aramaean wives and is actually regarded as once a nomad Aramaean. (Deut. xxxvi. 5).'
[3] Gen. xii. 28. Cf. S. L. Caiger, *Bible and Spade*, Oxford Univ. Press, 1936, pp. 35-7.
[4] Cf. Woolley in *Ur of the Chaldees*, E. Benn, Ltd., 1931, p. 168 : ' We must revise considerably our ideas of the Hebrew patriarch, when we learn that his earlier years were spent in such sophisticated surroundings : he was the citizen of a great city and inherited the traditions of an ancient and highly organized civilization.' Perhaps Abraham was like many a nomad chieftain in the East to-day, in touch with city-life, but not of it.

by the Elamite invasion of Babylonia. Other Semitic peoples, bringing along with them a part of the peoples whom they met on their way, came as far as the Jordan valley, and some of their tribes came into Egypt just at the time when the 14th Dynasty was disappearing in the midst of civil strife. These invaders killed or enslaved the population, and founded a new dynasty, the Hyksos. They made their capital Tanis, and established a fortified base at Hawaru (Avaris) in the Delta.[1] They then settled down to a peaceful mode of life.

The earliest contact of the Hebrews with Egypt is that described in the Biblical books of Genesis and Exodus, which refer to the patriarchs and the stories of Joseph, the Sojourn and the Exodus. There seems to be no valid reason to discredit these stories, although, in the words of Robertson-Smith,[2] the Biblical narrative cannot be regarded as history, but forms the material for history, a criticism which is applicable to a much greater extent to parts of Herodotus. The story of Joseph shows many a contact with Egypt, and for the first time we see the religion, customs, and culture of the Egyptians and another race, the early Hebrews, contrasted.

There are many details in the Pentateuch and other portions of the Old Testament which show a good knowledge of Egyptian conditions. The name Moses is Egyptian, and appears in 'Thutmose (' the god Thut is born ').[3] The story of Joseph—who married an Egyptian wife—has several Egyptian traits. Yet

'close examination of the Biblical narrative reveals throughout serious discrepancies of historical background, range of interest and religious spirit, such that the constituent elements cannot be due to one age or one circle. Briefly, the ' critical theory ' amounts to this, that the highly-developed history, law, and ritual are, in their present form, of post-exilic date, that is, after the 6th century B.C., and that the Pentateuch (together with the book of Joshua) consists of much that is of exilic or post-exilic data, together with much that is earlier.' [4]

A. S. Yahuda takes up a point of view which though opposed to many of the conclusions of the ' Higher Criticism ' of the Bible, possesses a remarkable appeal in some quarters. From among all Egyptologists, he says,[5] none has gone so far in his efforts to challenge the Biblical accuracy and genuineness as Wilhelm Spiegelberg, in spite of his admitting that he did not feel competent in Hebrew and that he had to seek guidance and enlightenment from a Biblical scholar,

---

[1] For the Hyksos see Breasted, *A History of Egypt*, London, Hodder & Stoughton, 1924, pp. 214–27.
[2] *C.A.H.* ii. 352.   [3] Ibid.
[4] Ibid. pp. 355–6.   Cf. A. S. Yahuda, *The Accuracy of the Bible*, Oxford Univ. Press, Heinemann, 1934, pp. 65–6.   Yahuda believes Mu-Sheh (Moses) simply means ' the child of the Nile '.
[5] A. S. Yahuda, *The Accuracy of the Bible*, pp. xxiv, xxv.

who in his turn did not know a single word of Egyptian. Spiegelberg, for instance, says : [1]—

> ' What accounts of Egypt, not based upon personal observation, appear like, can be learnt from the Jahwistic and Elohistic writers [2] of the Old Testament. The author of the legends about Joseph and of the account of the Exodus, which are wonderful enough if viewed as literature, has given an Egyptian background to the stories in which the scene is laid in Egypt. But in comparison with Herodotus, how colourless and featureless this Egyptian background is ! The Egyptian king is never referred to by name (Pharaoh, " Great House ", is a general designation of the Egyptian sovereign), no definite building is mentioned ; and yet an opportunity for this was afforded the writer in the account of the forced labour of the Israelites, whom he could have made to take part in the construction, for example, of the Pyramids or royal tombs, as modern illustrators of the Bible are wont to do.   One feels certain that the Old Testament writer had never been in the Nile Valley ; what he knows of Egypt has been gained from books and hearsay.   But what Herodotus describes, he can only have seen and observed himself.'

Yet Herodotus' knowledge of Upper Egypt has been queried, some authorities even going so far as to assert, as Spiegelberg does in the case of the Old Testament writer, that he was dependent to a great extent on books (e.g., Hecataeus' previous travels) and hearsay (which Spiegelberg himself admits) and that he never visited Elephantine at all.[3]

Archaeology has cast some light on the Biblical narrative of the Sojourn and the Exodus.

> ' With regard to the main fact [says Peet] that at some time or other certain of the people who subsequently came to be known as the Hebrews dwelt in Egypt for a period, and afterwards entered or re-entered Canaan, there is hardly a dissentient voice.   The fact that the Egyptian records contain no reference to the Sojourn does not in the least affect the problem,

---

[1] W. Spiegelberg, *The Credibility of Herodotus' Account of Egypt*, translated by A. M. Blackman, Blackwell, Oxford, 1927, p. 38.   Cf. Yahuda, op. cit., pp. xxv and xxvi. ' It is almost an irony of fate that the books of those Egyptologists, who most obstinately reject substantial Biblical-Egyptian relations, are among those which provide the most valuable evidence in support of the astonishing acquaintance of the Biblical authors with the most intimate conditions of Egyptian life.'

[2] J, E, D, P in the Biblical references indicate the original documentary source of the Pentateuch according to the Higher Criticism, e.g. (Gen. 1. P) (Gen. 2. J). J = the ' Jehovistic or Jahwistic Source ' ; E = the ' Elohistic Source', 9th or 8th centuries B.C., whereas D = the Deuteronomic Reviser, 7th century B.C. and P = the late ' Priestly Editor ', dating from the Exile, 6th and following centuries B.C.

[3] Cf. Sayce, *The Egypt of the Hebrews and Herodotus*, Rivington, London, 1896, p. 201.

for in the first place our Egyptian records are far from complete : in the second, the Sojourn may well have been on so small a scale that the Egyptians never thought it worth recording : and in the third place, the Delta which was the scene of the events, is almost a closed book to us in early times.' [1]

Nearly every possible and impossible date for the Exodus, from 1580 B.C. to 1144 B.C., has been conjectured by one scholar or another during the past century.[2]   But towards the end of it opinion settled down upon a moderately late date, ascribing the oppression to Rameses the Great (1292–1225 B.C.), the Exodus to his successor, Merenptah (1225–1215 B.C.), and the Invasion of Canaan to the period of anarchy in Egypt preceding the establishment of the XXth Dynasty (1205–1200 B.C.), the era of the Conquest and Settlement being thus shortened to roughly two centuries (1200–1000 B.C.). According to this theory, the chronology given in the Bible itself had to be entirely rejected.

Towards the end of the 19th century a different view began to prevail, as the evidence of the recently discovered Tell el Amarna Tablets (1887), the Israel Stele of Merenptah (1896), and other records began to be assimilated.   The popular theory that Merenptah was the Pharaoh of the Exodus was routed by the discovery of the ' Israel Stele '.   This inscription, self-dated as ' the third year of Merenptah ' (i.e., 1223 B.C.), tells in poetical form the glorious victories of the Pharaoh in Canaan and contains the well-known passage ' Israel is desolated, her seed is not '.[3]

The identification of Israel on this inscription or the location of the tribe in Canaan is now generally admitted, so that we have here a very explicit indication for the presence of Israel in Canaan early in the 13th century B.C., and also the earliest appearance of the name Israel outside the Bible.[4]

[1] E. T. Peet, *Egypt and the Old Testament*, Liverpool Univ. Press, Liverpool, 1922, p. 21.
[2] Cf. *C.A.H.* i. 356, Note 2.   Four groups of theories have prevailed as to the Exodus.   They associate themselves with
    (i) the Hyksos (i.e. before the XVIIIth dynasty) ;
    (ii) the age of Thutmose III and Amenhotep III and IV (the ' Amarna Age ', XVIIIth Dynasty) ;
    (iii) the age of Rameses II and Merenptah (XIXth Dynasty) ; and
    (iv) a later period (XXth Dynasty).
Most can be said in favour of (ii) and (iii).
[3] The inscription reads more fully :—
Devastated is Tehennu ;
The Hittite land is pacified ;
Plundered is Canaan with every evil ;
Carried off is Ascalon ;
Seized upon is Gezer ;
Yenoam is made a thing of naught ;
Israel (Israilu) is desolated, her seed is not ;
Palestine has become a defenceless widow for Egypt ;
Everyone that is turbulent is bound by King Merenptah,
Giving life like the sun every day.
[4] S. L. Caiger, *Bible and Spade*, Oxford Univ. Press, 1936, pp. 111–12.

Thus it seems that the Hebrews had been gone from Egypt and settled in Canaan long before the days of Rameses [1] or Merenptah. They could not very well have left Egypt under Merenptah and been long settled in Palestine at one and the same time !

Previous to the discovery of the Israel Stele, the Tell el Amarna Tablets found in a rubbish-heap on the Upper Nile in 1887, and purporting to be letters and dispatches, nearly all written in Babylonian cuneiform, sent during the years 1380–1360 to the Court of Amenhotep III, and his successor Akhnaton, by the kings of Canaanite cities named in the Bible, by the king of Jerusalem itself, had revealed the first explicit mention of the Hebrew people and the first certain mention of the Holy City outside the Bible.

These letters reveal that the land of Canaan, while still ostensibly a province of the Egyptian empire, was being invaded from the North by the Hittites and the east by the Habiru, against whom the vassal kings were sending frenzied appeals to the Pharaohs for help, protesting that unless reinforcements arrived quickly, the country would be lost to Egypt for ever, for fortress after fortress was falling into the enemies' hands.   It is more than tempting to identify these Habiru with the Hebrews of Joshua's invasion, since the circumstances of the Habiru invasion, on the face of it, are precisely those of the Hebrew invasion, as regards the date (c. 1407 B.C.), the locality, the results, and the actual place-names concerned.   In this event, the Tell el Amarna tablets would paint from the Canaanite side the same picture which the historian of Joshua–Judges paints from the Hebrew side, thus not only fixing the date of the Conquest (c. 1400 B.C.), but also that of the Exodus forty years before. [2]

The equation of the Hebrews with the Habiru has been treated with some reserve in certain quarters, but what has made this identification more and more probable is one of the most important of recent archaeological discoveries, that made by Garstang at Jericho in 1928. The walls of Jericho here disclosed a secret which remained buried

---

[1] Readers of the Joseph story are frequently confused to find that in it Egypt is sometimes called the ' Land of Rameses ' (e.g. Gen. xlvii. 11), seeing that the name Rameses was unknown to fame (Ahmosis, however, had a son named Rameses, c. 1600 B.C. See *Proceedings of the Biblical Archaeological Society*, 1890, p. 157) many centuries after the date claimed for Joseph according to the New View (c. 1847 B.C.).   Most critics, however, now agree that the mention of Rameses is a late ' gloss '.   The Bible tells us that the Israelites ' built for Pharaoh store-cities Pithom and Raamses ' (Exod. i. 11).   The old view identified both sites as cities founded by Rameses the Great (1292–1225), and that therefore the oppression must have taken place under the XIXth dynasty and not, as the New View now holds, under the XVIIIth dynasty (1447 B.C.).   As regards the archaeological evidence, Caiger, op. cit., p. 65, states that Pithom was located at Tell el Muskuta by Naville in 1883, but the city had clearly been founded centuries earlier than the time of Rameses II, and the name Pitum might be used of any temple where Tum was worshipped.   Similarly, Raamses was located by Petrie at Tell el Retabeh, but the identification with the Biblical Raamses is uncorroborated by any inscriptional testimony whatever, and the city so discovered was not founded by Rameses, but had been in evidence since the remote VIth Dynasty.   In any case, modern critics of the text of Exodus suspect the names as later insertions in the Biblical narrative.

[2] Caiger, op. cit., pp. 101–2.

for over three thousand years—namely, that the fall of the walls, hitherto looked upon as a mere legend, was a real historical event, due to an earthquake having occurred just at the time when the Israelites were besieging that city. The excavations showed that some extraordinary catastrophe had overwhelmed the city about 1400 B.C.

At this date the outer wall had collapsed down the slope of the hill on which the city was built, dragging with it the inner wall. The ruined city had then been set on fire. After the destruction of the city there was a complete break in the pottery and other deposits, proving that the ruin of Jericho had been not only complete, but lasting.[1]

There is no trace of any repair of the city between 1400 and 860 B.C., when Hiel the Bethelite rebuilt it.[2]

Significantly enough, if Joshua, as the older view implied, had attacked Jericho as late as 1200 B.C., he would have found no walls to fall down flat, for Garstang's dating of the city's fall at about 1400 B.C. has been confirmed by other authorities, and his conclusions are supported by the evidence of nearly 100,000 potsherds and scores of scarabs. Excavations at Ai, Bethel, Hazor, etc., yielded similar results.[3]

In view of all the latest archaeological data, the New View now assumes that the chronology explicitly given in the Bible is correct in essentials :

The Exodus is thrown back to about 1447 B.C., Amenhotep II thus becoming the ' Pharaoh of the Exodus ', and his predecessor, Thothmes III, the ' Pharaoh of the Oppression '. The Wandering lasted, as the Bible says, for Forty Years (1447–1407 B.C.), thus dating the Invasion by Joshua at the time of Amenhotep III. And the full ' 480 years ' claimed by the Bible is allowed between the Exodus and the Founding of Solomon's Temple in 967 B.C.[4]

Thus the truth of the Biblical account in respect of the historicity of the Exodus seems amply vindicated. It now remains to consider the contact of Hebrew and Egyptian as shown by the stories of Joseph and the Sojourn, and incidentally it will be shown that there is an historical basis in fact for these, as well as for the Exodus, and that they are far from being legendary.

---

[1] Josh. vi. 26.   [2] 1 Kings xvi. 34.
[3] Cf. *Wonders of the Past*, edited by J. A. Hammerton, Amalgamated Press, 1934, p. 5.
[4] The date of the foundation of Solomon's temple has been scientifically fixed as 967 B.C. ; 480 years before this, as 1 Kings vi. 1 states, the Exodus took place—i.e., in 1447 B.C.

Schofield (*The Historical Background of the Bible*, Nelson & Sons London, 1938, pp. 79 ff., 107) mentions a third alternative for the date of the Exodus—the close of the 13th century B.C.—' which would agree with the general results obtained from digging in Palestine—with the possible exception of Jericho ', since Garstang, as has been seen, dates its destruction to 1400 B.C., whereas Albright dates it to the 13th century B.C. Cf. *A.J.A.* (1942), pp. 266–7 and *P.E.Q.* Oct. 1939 and Oct. 1941.

G

According to the Bible,[1] the Sojourn lasted 400 years, and ended
with the Exodus. This would give, according to the new view,
c. 1847 B.C. as the date of Jacob's arrival in Egypt and the beginning
of the Sojourn.

Caiger [2] believes that the Hyksos kings were the most likely hosts,
as of Abraham, so of Joseph and Jacob, for the hostility to the Asiatics
roused by the Hyksos domination was so great that it is almost
inconceivable that any king of the XVIIIth Dynasty which succeeded
the Hyksos should have welcomed a Semitic tribe for any reason
whatever.[3] Peet,[4] too, believes that the Sojourn somehow preserves
a reminiscence of the Hyksos invasion but probably goes too far in
holding that the Hebrews must have gone out with the Hyksos when
they were expelled c. 1580 B.C. Yahuda puts the descent into Egypt
much earlier than the Hyksos.

'Every touch in the Joseph story emphasizes the alien character of the Hebrews to the Egyptians, which can only be understood under a purely Egyptian ruler'.[5]

The whole question, as we now see it, seems to turn on the date
of the Hyksos and the acceptance of the Biblical data. The view
held by some scholars, based on Manetho's history (quoted in
Josephus, who identified the Hyksos with Joseph and his Brethren!),
that the Hyksos, or the Shepherd Kings as they are commonly called,
were over 500 years in Egypt, is now discarded, as it is established
that their rule began about 1780 [6] and ended 1580 B.C. As we have
indicated above, c. 1847 B.C., according to the Bible, is the date
of Jacob's arrival in Egypt. Thus Joseph's appointment and the
beginning of the Sojourn must have been long before the Hyksos
came to rule over Egypt.

The genuine Egyptian atmosphere of the Joseph story [7] is now
generally admitted, and has been examined in great detail by many
writers.[8]

[1] Gen. xv. 13 ; but according to Exod. xii. 40 (probably a late gloss), the Sojourn
lasted 430 years.
[2] Caiger, op. cit., p. 57.
[3] T. H. Robinson, History of Israel, i. (1932), 64.
[4] J.E.A. xvi. (1930), 159. See also his article 'Ancient Egypt', p. 443, in
Eyre, European Civilization : Its Origin and Development, vol. i. Oxford, 1935.
[5] Accuracy of the Bible (1934), p. 47.
[6] For the Hyksos generally see C.A.H. i. 310 seq. As regards the dating, C.A.H.
i. in Chronological Table, p. 664, gives c. 1800 B.C.–1580 B.C. for the Hyksos Period,
but How and Wells Commentary to Herodotus on i.–iv. 418, and W. G. Waddell,
Herodotus, Bk. II., Methuen, London, 1939, p. 14, give different dates, the one
c. 1680–1580, the other c. 1700–1580 B.C.
[7] A romance called 'The Tale of the Two Brothers', by one Anna, a scribe of
Seti II (1209–1205 B.C.), though much later than the time of Joseph, bears striking
resemblance to the story of Joseph and Potiphar's wife, proving, if it does nothing
else, that such an event as happened to Joseph was by no means strange in the
annals of Egyptian literature.
[8] E.g. C. A. F. Knight, Nile and Jordan, J. Clarke & Co., London, 1921, and
most elaborately in A. S. Yahuda, Language of the Pentateuch in its Relation to
Egyptian (1934) ; Accuracy of the Bible (1934), etc.

The selling of Joseph in slavery to Potiphar is paralleled by many records of Kanamu (Canaanite) slaves. The name Potiphar, Zaphenath Paneah,[1] and so on, are of genuine Egyptian formation, though their precise meaning is still in doubt. Ankle-length examples of the 'coat of many colours'[2] are found in pictures of Semitic visitors to Egypt. The magicians of the story are frequently mentioned on the monuments—on the Rosetta stone, for instance. The signet ring, the vesture of fine linen, the gold chain about Joseph's neck are all in accordance with custom.[3] The office of merper or major-domo to the Pharaoh, held by Joseph, is often honourably mentioned in the inscriptions. Instances of this deep acquaintanceship with Egyptian customs and life could be multiplied.[4]

Many details in the Joseph and Exodus stories point to an environment where the Hebrews lived for themselves, preserving their special characteristics in spite of mixing with the Egyptians. Thus we are told [5] that the Hebrews spent a long time in Egypt as a tribe apart,[6] with their own manners and specific customs,[7] with their own worship,[8] living in a separate area assigned to them in the Delta near the Asiatic border,[9] and with their own organization [10] as a self-contained entity in the midst of an Egyptian world. In the long period of their sojourn—much longer than that of the settlement of Greek traders and mercenaries in Saitic Egypt—the Hebrews cannot possibly have escaped the influence of Egyptian culture and Egyptian life, but must, on the contrary,[11] in spite of their segregation, have adapted themselves from the very start to Egyptian conditions, conceptions, and customs. The Semitic dialect which they brought with them from their Canaanite home could not but keep absorbing Egyptian elements in the course of this period.[12]

A very rapid survey of Egyptian influence on the Hebrews at this time gives us the following points.[13] The musical instruments mentioned in the Bible are all depicted on the Egyptian monuments. The Hebrew weights and measures are of Egyptian rather than

---

[1] *J.E.A.* xii. (1926), 16–18, E. Naville, *The Egyptian Name of Joseph*; Yahuda, *Accuracy of the Bible*, pp. 23 seq.

[2] Cf. Gen. xxxvii. 3. 'Coat of many colours' is really a mistranslation of the Hebrew. Chetoneth passim = a long garment with sleeves. But 'many coloured' was, nevertheless, a true description of such garments. Cf. Yahuda, *Accuracy of the Bible*, frontispiece and illustration facing p. 24.

[3] Yahuda, op. cit., pp. 10–18.   [4] Yahuda, op. cit., passim.
[5] Exod. xii. 40.   [6] Exod. i. 9, seq.
[7] Gen. xlvii. 32; Exod. viii. 22.   [8] Exod. v. 17; viii. 21 seq.
[9] Gen. xlvii. 6, 11; Exod. viii. 22; x. 23.   [10] Exod. iv. 29.
[11] Gen. l. 2 seq.; Exod. i. 16.
[12] Yahuda believes that the forefathers of the Hebrews arrived in Canaan speaking an Aramaic dialect strongly tinged with Akkadian elements. They then adopted the Canaanite dialect, which began to develop in the course of their Egyptian Sojourn into the literary language we know as Hebrew (*Accuracy of the Bible*, pp. xxxii–xxxiii and p. 218, note 4). Caiger, *Bible and Spade*, Oxford Univ. Press, 1936, p. 8, quotes Hommel (*Ancient Hebrew Tradition*, 1897) for the theory that if their aboriginal home must be sought in Arabia, then the Hebrews took with them a dialect of Arabic in their immigration into Babylonia, and on their further immigration into Canaan they adopted the Canaanitish tongue—i.e., Hebrew.
[13] C. A. F. Knight, *Nile and Jordan*, 1933, James Clarke & Co., pp. 171–90.

Babylonian origin. Biblical ceremonial and ritual show distinct affinities with Egypt. The tabernacle, for instance, is made of Egyptian shittim wood (instead of Palestinian cedar), and its details of gold, silver, colouring, priestly vesture, as well as the ritual use of oil and incense, may all be derived from Egyptian origins. The practice of circumcision was also common in Egypt.

The sacred boat, made in the form of a chest containing sacred emblems, was a familiar feature of Egyptian ceremonial, being carried in procession on the shoulders of the priests, and has been regarded by many as the prototype of the Hebrew Ark of the Covenant. The golden cherubs which adorned its lid have been likened to the Egyptian winged figures, especially the figure of Maat, goddess of Truth, often seen within the Egyptian ark covering with her wings the sacred dish. Many other coincidences have been pointed out : most remarkable of all, the High Priest of Memphis wore as his distinctive badge of office a breastplate and appendages practically identical with those worn by Aaron. Such coincidence can scarcely be accidental.

'When we turn to the lists of *clean and unclean animals* enumerated in Leviticus [1] and Deuteronomy [2] it is remarkable to observe not only that the Egyptians had similar distinctions between what was pure and impure but that the great majority of the creatures named had their habitat in Egypt where the Hebrews would be perfectly familiar with them.' [3]

Further :—

'We see that the sons of Jacob went down to Egypt a people of simple pastoral habits, *keepers of cattle*, but that after their residence in the Nile lands they emerged an agricultural race, whose shepherd habits had largely been laid aside. It was the agricultural science of Egypt which the Israelites revealed when they were at last settled in Canaan.' [4]

According to Yahuda, the influence of Egypt over the early Hebrews has been much under-estimated by scholars obsessed by the Babylonian discoveries. It was in the Nile Valley (he claims) that Hebrew as a literary language was evolved, that most of the early Biblical legends took their final colouring, that Paradise must be located, and that the Book of Genesis was thrown into its present shape. He certainly succeeds in showing an extensive and hitherto unsuspected vein of Egyptianisms within the language of the Pentateuch, together with a surprising absence of Chaldaean linguistic traits.[5]

---

[1] Lev. ii. 1–47.   [2] Deut. xiv. 1–20.
[3] Knight, op. cit., p. 182.   [4] Knight, op. cit., p. 188.
[5] A. S. Yahuda, *Accuracy of the Bible*, Heinemann, London, 1934, p. xxxi ; cf. *J.E.A.* xvi. (1939), 159–60 : Peet believes that the narratives concerning Egypt were not written down in Egypt at the actual time of the Sojourn, but in the 9th century B.C. He finds ' no Egyptianisms which could not adequately be explained

Yet, in spite of having adapted themselves to the Egyptian environment, the Hebrews still retained some typical habits of their homeland.[1] Just as the Egyptians abstained from feeding with the
Hebrews,[2] so the Hebrews preserved their own language, their habits,
worship, and cult, which was an abomination to the Egyptians. As
such, the Hebrew settlement in Egypt at this time bears interesting
comparison with that of the Greeks in the Saite period, and Egyptian
influence on the Hebrew language and customs may have been, and
probably was, much greater than on those of the Greeks in Saite
times, but both peoples preserved their national individuality as
distinct from that of the Egyptians.

To the ordinary reader of the Bible nothing seems clearer than the
stern resistance which the early Hebrews set up against the ' reproach of Egypt ', against Egyptian idolatry, against city-dwelling,
luxury, art, and particularly against that exaggerated interest in the
bodies of the dead which was so characteristic of the Nile-dweller.
There is nothing in the Bible to correspond with the Egyptian
Pyramids, food and treasure for the dead, Book of the Dead, or (save
in one or two cases) mummies of the dead. In fact, nothing could
show a greater contrast than the Hebrew and Egyptian attitude
towards the future life.[3]

The subsequent history of the Hebrews till their next appearance
in Egypt many centuries later, under the name they are later known
by, can for our purpose be summed up briefly. The Hebrews
recorded that under Pharaoh (most probably Amenhotep III, 1411–
1375 B.C.) they had been conscripted to restore (build) the towns of
Pithom and Raamses, the supposed sites of which, we have seen,
go much farther back in time than the reign of Rameses II. The
tribes of Israel revolted against the task, Moses becoming the soul of
the opposition. According to Biblical tradition, a succession of
miracles enabled Moses to lead his brethren out of Egypt into the
desert of Sinai to form them into a people and give them a code of
religious, moral, and civil laws in the name of Yahweh (Jehovah),

---

as due to the same authors who in the 9th century and later committed the story to
writing and gave to it its anachronistic geography and its pseudo-archaeological
setting '.   He passes a very adverse criticism on ' Yahuda's *Language of the Bible,
and its Relation to Egyptian* ' on the ground that the evidence he relies on is purely
philological, that he goes too far in its application, and that in almost every case
the weakness arises from his insufficient knowledge of the finer points of Egyptian.

[1] See A. S. Yahuda, *Accuracy of the Bible*, Heinemann, London, 1934, pp. 35 seq.

[2] Gen. xliii. 32, we noticed a similar antipathy to Greek customs (see Part I,
Chapter 3, of this work and Herod. ii. 41. 7).

[3] Cf. Knight, op. cit., p. 184 : ' As an indirect rebuke of, and a silent protest
against, the fantastic realism of the Egyptian creed as regards the future life, the
Hebrew oracles on the question of the immortality of the soul remained dumb.'

[4] What may have been the original meaning or root of this mysterious name is
still in doubt.   It appears on the 15th-century Minaean inscriptions as YAH, and
as YA or YAU on Babylonian tablets of 2000 B.C. and later, always as a Semitic
deity.   It is found in name compounds among the Ras Shamra tablets, found (in
1929) in North Syria and contemporary with those of Tell el Amarna—i.e. 15th
and 14th centuries B.C. Daiches (quoted by Driver, *Exodus, Cambridge Bible*)
remarks, ' The question is not where the Name came from, but what Moses put

their national god, and the only true one, which were to distinguish them from all the other people of the earth. When, some generations afterwards, the Israelites entered Canaan, they absorbed the culture of the earlier inhabitants, and under Canaanite influence exchanged the habits of the nomad for a settled agricultural life. The struggle with the non-Semitic Philistines brought about the institution of kingship under Saul, and later, after a period of warfare by David, under Solomon, the Hebrews came into renewed contact with Egypt. Palestine was divided into two monarchies on Solomon's death—the notable event of whose reign was the building of the Temple. These were conquered, after being the pawn in the game of politics between Assyria and Egypt, Israel in 721 by the Assyrians and Judah in 586 by Babylon. As a result, the Hebrews as a political entity disappeared till the time of the Maccabees, c. 140 B.C.

The people of the southern kingdom of Judah were exiled [1] to Babylon, but were allowed to return to Judea when Cyrus the Persian conquered the Babylonian Empire in 538 B.C.[2] It is the Return from Exile that constituted the Jews as the People of the Book, and that established a theocratic state, with set rules of ritual and conduct in Palestine, with the rebuilt temple at Jerusalem as its centre, that left its mark on the Jews for all time.[3] ' It has been said that they went into captivity a political society and returned a church,' says Peet.[4]

This new stage in the religious development of Israel has often been carried back and ascribed to the beginning of the tribal history, before the Davidic monarchy. The assumption is incorrect, for it is the Persian age which is the vantage-ground from which the Old Testament, viewed in the light of modern research, becomes more intelligible. It is in this period that the differences between the Jews and other peoples became accentuated and received the cachet of legalism.

From this epoch dates that extreme emphasis [5] on the Sabbath and on Circumcision which made them the distinguishing badge of Judaism to the whole world, and that extreme carefulness of observance which henceforth characterizes Jewish piety.

Without going into a detailed account of a time the history of which is very obscure—the exact relation of the Jewish reformers

---

into it. For into that vessel a long line of Prophets from Moses onwards poured such a flood of attributes as never a priest in all Western Asia, from Babylon to the Sea, ever dreamed of in his highest moments of spiritual insight.' As to the name, cf. *C.A.H.* ii. 353. Note ' Jehovah ' would be incorrect because the vowels of Àdonày (lord) have been applied to the consonants (YHWH) of the ineffable name, the original pronunciation of which may have been YAHWEH.

[1] The Jewish dispersion—the Diaspora—all over the ancient world dates from this time.

[2] The Jews, as the people of Judah are now known, became inured to exile, and many of them refused to return to their fatherland when the edict granting them their freedom (Ezra i. 1–4) was issued, but they were inconsolable at first (cf. Psalm cxxxvii).

[3] Cf. *C.A.H.* vi. Ch. 7 : ' The Inauguration of Judaism '.

[4] T. E. Peet, *Egypt and the Old Testament*, Univ. of Liverpool Press, 1922, p. 209.

[5] Ezek. xx. 12, 20 ; xxxi. 18.

Ezra and Nehemiah to one another, for instance, is notoriously difficult to decide—certain facts can be clearly recognized: the fortification of Jerusalem, the re-organization of the Temple, its personnel and cult, the importance attached to the Sabbath; the introduction of the Law, the divorce of foreign wives and the separation from strangers, and the formation of an exclusive Judean community, almost an ecclesiastical community.[1]

That this process of reorganization seemed necessary is seen from the fact that in many of the towns of Palestine at this time the population had become mixed.[2] Outside Palestine this seems to have been even more the case—at Elephantine in Egypt the ' Judeans ', or ' Arameans ', as they are more widely called, mingle with Babylonians, Persians, and Egyptians.[3]

' The actual conditions in the towns and the inevitable inter-marriages would be detrimental to the growth of Jewish exclusiveness, and the keen bitterness provoked in such circumstances by the forcible acts of separation that mark the inauguration of Judaism can be readily imagined.' [4]

It is in the sphere of religion that the greatest difference between the Jews and other peoples, particularly the Greeks, is shown. The main characteristics of this religion as it evolved up to and including this period are well summed up by Jean.[5]

' Israel is monotheistical in principle. It is true that the people attach too much importance to external forms, and that their hearts are capable of harbouring at one and the same time feelings of adoration for YAHWEH and of veneration and piety for the gods of the Canaanite Bamoth, but there is among the Jews an élite, very small at times, which is faithful to monotheism both in theory and practice and hands down the torch from generation to generation; and this ' chosen few ' see not in the past, but in the future, a golden age, a kingdom of God whose King shall be the Messiah. They proclaim this belief, or rather this certainty, both in adversity and prosperity.'

This is a criticism which is applicable to the Jews even when the tide of Hellenism after the conquests of Alexander threatened to engulf them, not only in Palestine under the Greek Seleucid kings of Syria, when there were many Hellenizers in their midst, but also in the various countries of the Diaspora.

Monotheism and Messianism are thus the two dominating ideas of the ' chosen people ', and it is these which give to Israel its special

---

[1] The books of Ezra and Nehemiah are our main sources. The term theocracy has been coined by Josephus, c. *Ap.* 11 : 165 to describe this form of state. ὁ δ' ἡμέτερος νομοθέτης εἰς μὲν τούτων οὐδοτιοῦν ἀπεῖδεν, ὡς δ' ἄν τις εἴποι βιασάμενος τὸν λόγον, θεοκρατίαν ἀπέδειξε τὸ πολίτευμα, θεῷ τὴν ἀρχὴν καὶ τὸ κράτος ἀναθείς.
[2] For Samaria see Ezra iv. 9.   [3] See next chapter of the present work.
[4] S. A. Cook in *C.A.H.* vii. 179.
[5] In *European Civilization, its Origin and Development*, Oxford, 1935, p. 433.

character, which make it a people apart. There are two other points in the Jewish religious outlook which follow from monotheism and need emphasis.

The gods of the East had admitted foreign divinities to their pantheon. Ammon had reached Canaan, Ishtar and Teshub were venerated in Egypt. Syncretism had become customary : as a political factor it signified the relationships established between one people and another and, consequently, between the gods of the different peoples. Yahweh, on the other hand, allowed of no compromise, for he was the sole God of Israel and the only true God of the Universe.[1]

The gods of the ' Gentiles ', moreover, were satisfied once they had received the sacrifice of their worshippers, but Yahweh demanded from his followers the homage of a moral life in addition to sacrifices.[2]

It will be seen from these preliminary remarks how far different from the nations it came into contact with was the religion of the Jews at this period. Yet it was not their religion, as a religion, so much as its implications, that was to render the differences between them and another gifted race of the Ancient World, the Greeks, so acute when the two races were destined to meet eventually in Egypt.

During the whole of this period from 538 to 320 B.C., about which we have but little information, the Jews were vassals of a heathen empire, Persia. Alexander of Macedon broke the Persian empire, and after his death Palestine again became the pawn of contending nations, this time Egypt and Syria, and at first fell to the lot of Ptolemy I, to whom Egypt was assigned. It remained under Egypt until, in 198 B.C., Seleucid Syria, which had coveted this province for a century, wrested it from Egypt. The Syrian persecution—which was characterized by the worst offences against the Mosaic code— provoked a Jewish revolt which, after many vicissitudes, led to the establishment of Jewish independence in 140 B.C. by the Maccabees ; and this independence lasted till 63 B.C., when Pompey annexed the land to the Roman Empire. In the trail of the Roman power came the rise of the Herodian dynasty in Palestine, as vassal kings under Roman suzerainty. With the death of Herod the Great the kingdom was split up among his descendants as tetrarchies, Judea eventually becoming a Roman province under a procurator.[3] A rebellion against Roman authority which broke out in 66 A.D., and which Josephus described in his *Antiquities and Jewish War*, ended in the destruction not only of the Jewish state, but also of its religious centre, the Temple, in A.D. 70.

---

[1] Jer. x. 12–16.   [2] Amos v. 21–24 ; Isa. i. 11, 14, 16, 17 ; Jer. vi. 19, 20.
[3] Agrippa I, who played so prominent a part in the elevation of Claudius to the principate, had succeeded for a short time in reconstituting the kingdom of his grandfather ; but when he died in A.D. 44, Claudius once more placed Judaea under the direct rule of a procurator. Agrippa II, too, though he was able to secure the title of king and no inconsiderable territory, never reigned in Jerusalem, although he was trustee for the Temple treasures, and was permitted to nominate the high priest. Cf. *The Roman Empire*, by H. Stuart Jones, Fisher Unwin, London, 1908, pp. 106–7.

CHAPTER II

THE JEWS IN EGYPT IN LATER TIMES

AS has been shown, the stories of Joseph and the Exodus show the earliest definite contact between the people of Egypt and the Hebrews. The dispersion began as early as the Saite period (563–525 B.C.), and gathered force after the destruction of Jerusalem (586 B.C.).

Deuteronomy [1] suggests that in the 7th century the kings of Israel were exchanging soldiers for horses with Pharaoh. There were probably Jewish soldiers in the army which Psammetichus II (594–589 B.C.) led into Ethiopia.[2] A mass of Jews had emigrated into Egypt at the time of the capture of Jerusalem by Nebuchadnezzar in 586 B.C.[3] and after the Persian conquest of 525 B.C.[4] During the Persian period a very queer little Jewish colony existed at Elephantine, an island in the middle of the Nile near the present Assuan Dam. An analysis of the Aramaic papyri found there [5] and other outside evidence shows that between the 6th and 4th centuries B.C. this island was occupied by a sort of military colony composed of Judaeo-Arameans intermingled with a certain number of Babylonians and Persians. This colony had been established near the First Cataract as an outpost for the defence of the country against Ethiopian attacks.

The Judean origin of the colony is rendered doubtful by its consistent use of Aramaic, confined at this time to Syria and Mesopotamia.

The Elephantine Jews formed a striking contrast to the Palestinian Jews. Mixed marriages seem to have met with no opposition; the foreign element, Babylonian, was relatively large, probably accounting for the fact that its matrimonial law was similar to Babylon's. Woman's legal status was widely different from that of the Old Testament. The principal object of worship is Yahu (Yahweh), venerated in a real temple, but foreign gods were also worshipped, Ashan, Anath, Bethel. Most probably these people were mostly descended from the inhabitants of Samaria, whose religion was syncretic, and who had gone to Egypt before Zerubbabel had refused

[1] Deut. xvii. 16.
[2] Cf. *Epistle of Aristeas*, 13 ; and *Corp. Inscript. Sem.*, i. 1, No. 112 C.
[3] Jer. xxiv 8 ; xliii–xliv. ; Isa. xi. 11. Although most of the Jews were transported to Babylonia, some of them (including Jeremiah) fled to Egypt and settled in Tahpanhes (Daphnae) under the Pharaoh Hophra, afterwards dispersing to other Egyptian cities, such as Migdol and Noph (Memphis). Of these colonies in Egypt we know hardly anything but the little the Bible tells us.
[4] Epistle of Aristeas, 13 (*c.* 100 B.C.) ; cf. Caiger, *Bible and Spade*, p. 184.
[5] A. Cowley : *Aramaic Papyri of the Vth Century*, 1923, Oxford Univ. Press.

the aid of the Samaritans to restore the temple at Jerusalem. In spite of the extraordinary degree of tolerance they enjoyed, towards the end of the 5th century the jealousy of the priests of the god Khnum, and the national feeling that later caused the Egyptians to rise against the Persians, gave rise to acts of hostility. In 410, in the absence of the governor at Susa, the temple was ruined with the connivance of a Persian commandant. A counter-revolt followed, and some years later permission was given to rebuild the temple, but whether it was is unknown.[1]

Yet, however interesting are the Elephantine Papyri, the little community it reveals ' was but an eccentric deviation from the broad path of Hebrew history : it led nowhere, and had no influence on the development even of Egyptian Judaism '.[2]

Real Jewish settlement in Egypt began with Alexander, and the largest foreign element after the Greeks was the Jewish. At the time of the Christian era the Jews in Egypt had come to number about a million out of a total population of about $7\frac{1}{2}$ million. We think of the Jews to-day as pre-eminently financiers and traders. But in those days they had not yet any special reputation in that line. Josephus[3] says :—

> ' Ours is not a maritime country ; neither commerce nor the intercourse which it promotes with the outside world has any attraction for us. Our cities are built inland, remote from the sea ; and we devote ourselves to the cultivation of the productive country with which we are blessed. . . . If to these reasons one adds the peculiarity of our mode of life, there was clearly nothing in ancient times to bring us into contact with the Greeks, as the Egyptians were brought by their exports and imports, and the inhabitants of the sea-board of Phoenicia by their mercenary devotion to trade and commerce.'

The Jews of Alexandria were no doubt, like the Greeks of Alexandria, engaged in various kinds of trade and industry, but large numbers of the Jews in Egypt had been imported as soldiers.

The Maccabean revolt and the wars of the Hasmonean Jewish kings proved how formidable the Jews could be as fighters. The Elephantine Aramaic papyri have shown us Jewish soldiers, or soldiers of closely-related stocks, of the Persian king established near the 1st cataract long before Alexander came to Egypt. Perhaps semi-paganized Jewish communities of this type had been absorbed, and ceased to exist as a separate people before the end of the Persian period, but it seems likely that Ptolemy I found a Jewish element still existing in Egypt when he took over the country.

In any case, when Palestine had been united to their kingdom by the Ptolemies, a fresh stream of immigration from Judaea to Egypt

---

[1] Cf. Jean in Eyre's *History of European Civilization*, p. 427 ; Breasted, *Ancient Times*, p. 215 ; Caiger, *Bible and Spade*, pp. 183 seq.
[2] Caiger, ibid., p. 188.   [3] *Contra Apionem* i. Par. 60.

naturally followed. It was not only voluntary immigration. Regarding the Jews as good material for his army, Ptolemy I had transported masses of them to Egypt, 100,000 according to Pseudo-Aristeas, who says that he put 30,000 of them ' in the garrisons '—settled them, we may perhaps understand, like the Greeks and Macedonians in the land.[1]

Inscriptions and papyri give us traces of this Jewish population in the country towns of Egypt throughout the Ptolemaic period.[2]

All through the 3rd century Jews came to Egypt, generally settling in Alexandria, but sometimes in the country, where, under Ptolemy III, they already had two synagogues; to the one at Leontopolis Ptolemy III gave the right of asylum. They took up land, and were often employed as tax-collectors, but seldom did banking or money-lending, and hardly ever occur as traders: one Jewish horse-dealer named Daniel is mentioned.

In the 2nd century B.C. their settlements in Egypt were numerous; synagogues were built in several places, and the village authorities distinguished sharply between Greeks and Jews: one case of Jewish–Egyptian marriage is known. Under Ptolemy VI, Onias, son of the High-Priest Onias III, driven out by the Maccabees, came to Egypt, and was presented with a ruined temple in Leontopolis, where about 160 he built a smaller model of the Temple in Jerusalem as a religious centre for the Jews of Egypt, and copied the Temple service;[3] it lasted till A.D. 73, but the more pious Jews still looked to Jerusalem. It is related that both Ptolemy VI and subsequently Cleopatra III employed Jewish generals; and a Jewish mercenary, Abram, appears as member of a Graeco-Egyptian military association. In the civil war between Cleopatra III and her son Ptolemy Lathyrus the Jews supported her, the beginning of tension in Alexandria between Jew and Greek, for the Greeks favoured the victorious Lathyrus; but the tension, which was primarily political, only showed itself in words; Anti-Semitism accompanied by violence was unknown in Egypt before the Roman Empire.

The language of the Egyptian Jews was Greek: after a generation or two immigrants from Palestine forgot their Semitic speech. Yet there were Jews at Thebes c. 200 B.C., whose transactions with each other were drawn up in Aramaic.[4] Their Hebrew scriptures they

---

[1] Cf. Josephus, c. Apion. ii. 4.

[2] Synagogue at Athribis, O.G.I. No. 96; cf. No. 101; at Magdola, Lille, ii. No. 35; at Schedia, O.G.I. ii. No. 726; at Zenephyris in the Fayum, Preisigke, No. 5862; at Kerkeosiris (Tebtunis, No. 86); Jews at Psenyris in the Fayum, Chrest. No. 55; Jews who pay land-tax (i.e. are agriculturists) or pay money into the bank (i.e. are tax-payers); Wilcken, Griechische Ostraka aus Agypten und Nubien (Leipzig and Berlin, 1899), pp. 523 ff; ' Jewish Soldiers in the Ptolemaic Army ', Breccia, Bull. Alex., 1902, pp. 48 ff.; Hibeh, No. 96; Petrie, iii. No. 21 g., I. 12; an officer ' École Francaise d'Athénes; Bulletin de Correspondance Hellenique (Paris) xxvi. (1902) p. 454; a general, Archiv, i. 48 ff; Jewish inscriptions on the temple of Pan in Thebaid, O.G.I. Nos. 73, 74.

[3] Jos. Antiq. xii. 9, 7; xiii. 3, Jewish War, ii. 1. 1.; vii. 10. 2–3.

[4] ' An Aramaic Papyrus from Egypt ', Proceedings of the Society of Biblical Archaeology, xxix. (1907), 260 f.

knew only in the Greek translation which we call the Septuagint
because, according to the legend, the translation had been made by
the Seventy Translators under Ptolemy II. Since the Seventy
Translators were held to have been themselves miraculously inspired,
there was no need for the Egyptian Jews to concern themselves with
the original Hebrew. As a matter of fact, the translation of the Old
Testament was made, bit by bit, in Egypt during the last three centuries before the Christian era. According to the first form of the
legend it was not the Old Testament as a whole, but only the five
books of the Law which were translated by the Seventy, and it is
likely that a Greek version of the Law really was required by the
Egyptian Jews as early as the reign of Ptolemy II. In the later times
of the dynasty it made an important difference to anyone who ruled
Egypt, or aspired to rule it, if he had the Jews on his side.

The Jewish quarter, Delta, adjoined the palace quarter of Alexandria
on the north-east and reached down to the sea. In so far as it lay
beyond the harbour, it might be spoken of by enemies of the Jews
contemptuously as an out-of-the-way, wretched sort of place, whilst
the Jews might retort that the sea-front and its proximity to the royal
palace made it pleasant and honourable.[1]   It was not a ghetto,
inasmuch as there was no compulsion upon the Jews to live in the
Delta quarter; many, as a matter of fact, lived in other parts of the
city. But the Delta quarter was mainly inhabited by Jews, who had
gathered by choice, as they do in certain districts of London to-day.

We have in Ptolemaic times the mention of synagogues at Alexandria—one built on behalf of the famous Cleopatra and Ptolemy
Caesar ' to the Great God who heareth ' by a certain Alypus—a
rich member, no doubt, of the Jewish community.[2]   There were
a large number of synagogues in Alexandria. The principal one
was in Roman times one of the most impressive in the Empire, which
is described with pride in the Talmud.

---

[1] Joseph, c. Apion, ii. 33 ff.   [2] O.G.I. ii. No. 742.

CHAPTER III

THE QUESTION OF JEWISH CITIZENSHIP
AT ALEXANDRIA

THERE has been a long controversy as to whether the Jews were or were not citizens of the chief city of Egypt, Alexandria. This question has not been finally decided to the satisfaction of all parties, and it may be worth while to consider the matter before passing on to the theme of Anti-Semitism in Egypt, with which it is closely connected. In the first place, a review of what citizenship in Hellenistic times meant must be made, and then the question how far the Jews fitted into this scheme should be determined.

Democracy in the Hellenistic Age was universally recognized as the proper constitution of a Greek city, and as the institutions of the Greek city spread over barbarian lands it was the democratic type of constitution which was accepted as the norm. The people were in almost every city divided into a number of tribes, often of great antiquity, though in the majority of cases the tribal division seems to have been artificial and of relatively recent date ; at Athens, for instance, the ten tribes had been created by Cleisthenes. In the royal foundations of the Hellenistic age and in the cities which during that period adopted Greek constitutions the tribes seem almost invariably to have been purely artificial, and were usually named after gods, heroes of local fame, kings and queens of the dynasty, and their reputed divine and heroic ancestors. A tribe generally corresponded to a block of the city territory or to a ward of the town ; the five tribes of Alexandria were probably identical with the five wards.[1] The tribes were regularly subdivided into smaller units— demes—which in the old cities were either villages or family groups ; in the new they were as artificial as the tribes, bearing the names of gods, kings, and heroes. Demes of this type are recorded at Alexandria and Ptolemais.[2]

A primary rule of any democratic institution is that all citizens, irrespective of their birth or wealth, should have equal political rights, but there are indications that the Ptolemies favoured restriction of citizen rights in Africa, whatever their policy in Greece. Elsewhere in the Greek world there is no trace of any limitations of political rights.[3] In the 3rd century B.C. Ptolemais of the Thebaid passed a decree that in future members of the council and of the jury-courts should be chosen from a select list, and by the end of the

---

[1] Jones, *The Greek City from Alexander to Justinian*, Oxford, 1940, p. 158.
[2] Alexandria : *Archiv für Pap.* v. 82 seq. Ptolemais : Plaumann, *Ptolemais in Oberägypten*, p. 13.
[3] Jones, op. cit., p. 159.

Ptolemaic period there was at Alexandria a distinction between those citizens who were enrolled in the demes and the rest who were merely Alexandrians. The significance of the distinction is not known, but it has been conjectured that full political rights were confined to the former class. This distinction did not exist in the 3rd century B.C., and was perhaps the result of the troubles in the reign of Euergetes II.[1]

Though all citizens seem as a rule to have possessed equal rights, the citizenship might itself be limited to a relatively restricted number of the inhabitants, being determined by birth, and not by residence. Citizenship, however, was frequently granted by special decree to foreigners who had been benefactors to the city, and it also became increasingly common for pairs or groups of cities to make their citizenship interchangeable. There were, moreover, in every city a number of domiciled aliens (usually called κάτοικοι, not as at Athens μέτοικοι), many of whom had lived there for generations. Slaves did not as a rule acquire citizenship on manumission, as they did in Roman law, but freedmen and their descendants remained a separate class, forming in some cities a substantial element in the population. Apart from immigrants and freedmen and their descendants there was in some cities a portion of the native population excluded from the citizenship. In the new colonies planted by the kings it seems highly probable that only the Greek colonists were citizens, and that the natives, not only those that inhabited the surrounding territory but those that had been moved into the new town, remained outside the pale; at Alexandria the citizens were certainly a very small percentage of the population and are sharply distinguished from the Egyptian residents of the city.[2] Egyptians probably were still too alien to be accepted as fellow-citizens, since not all Greek cities adopted so exclusive an attitude. Rhodes, in fact, incorporated the Carian communities on her mainland territory as demes of the republic, granting their members Rhodian citizenship.[3]

The key institution in any Greek democracy was the Council, which had not only very considerable executive functions, but also important deliberative ones. No measure might be brought before the Assembly of citizens which had not been considered and approved by the Council, for all Greek cities, however democratic, recognized that the primary Assembly could be a dangerously irresponsible body. As regards the magistracies, there was a tacit convention whereby the people elected rich men, and they, as magistrates, contributed freely to the public services under their

---

[1] Ptolemais: *O.G.I.* No. 48. Alexandria: Schubart, *Archiv für Pap.* v. 114 seq; contrast *P. Hal.*, i. col. XI.
[2] A. H. M. Jones, *The Cities of the Eastern Roman Provinces*, Oxford, 1937, pp. 303–4; the fact that the tribes of Alexandria and Antioch corresponded to the wards of the town and not, so far as it is known, to regions of the territory, suggests that citizenship was limited to the urban population.
[3] Ibid., p. 383, note 6.

charge. A consequence of this was that the old distinction between magistracies and liturgies became blurred, with what result we have seen in a previous chapter.

Democracy was thus in the Hellenistic age tempered by the convention that the rich should have a virtual monopoly of offices, provided that they paid for it liberally.

The privilege of citizenship was a complex of rights to which were attached certain very definite obligations. At Athens they included voting in the Assembly, the holding of public offices, service on the jury, and a claim for certain personal privileges, such as admission to the dramatic performances at the Dionysaic festivals. The obligations were payment of taxes and military service. The State was in the habit of remitting from time to time certain or all of these taxes and other compulsory services.

Alexandria was in externals a city of the type described. Actually the position was rendered more complicated by the fact that Alexandria was the site of the king's palace and capital of the country, as well as being a free city in name. As has been mentioned before, Alexandria and the few other cities there were, were, in Egypt, a concession to the past. We can safely assume that what was originally a free city with its own rights and institutions became gradually more and more a municipality whose rights, if we conceive them from the point of view of a Greek city-state, had slowly been watered down in the face of the autocratic rule that ruled Egypt.

Therefore, in any discussion on citizen-rights at Alexandria we must beware of drawing an exact parallel with a Greek city elsewhere. While admitting that, at the outset of Ptolemaic rule in Egypt, Alexandria was to all appearances a typical Greek city, and was probably meant to be such by its founder as a centre of the Hellenic spirit, yet the force of circumstances, the uniqueness of its position in a country where the mass of the population was not Greek—where many foreign elements had been absorbed—brought about inevitable changes. As has been mentioned, Alexandria with its territory was not considered as being in Egypt, but as adjacent to Egypt ' Alexandria ad Aegyptum '. Yet Ptolemaic rule necessarily made it part of the country during the reign of the dynasty, and, as such, the policy of the kings was to make gradual encroachments on the institutions of the city. What was left then was simply the privileges of a municipality with the forms to some extent of a typical Greek state.

It is only when we bear these facts in mind that we can understand why Alexandria had no Senate at the time of Augustus and what citizenship at Alexandria really meant. Furthermore, we must be on our guard against identifying citizenship at Alexandria with modern citizenship. A person who did not have Alexandrian citizenship was not necessarily without certain privileges and rights at Alexandria, nor was he consequently regarded as an alien in Egypt. It seems that what could in the beginning be described as rights of citizenship in a city that had originally very little to do theoretically with Egypt and was not at first the capital of the country, became eventually certain privileges in a municipality, the chief city of Egypt—privileges which applied only to that city, and not to Egypt. Yet under the Roman Empire the Alexandrian citizenship acquired a new and special value, since it was the practice of the Emperors not to bestow the Roman *civitas* directly upon an Egyptian unless he was first admitted to citizen rights at Alexandria. As the necessary avenue to full citizen rights at Alexandria was the *ephebia*, it is not surprising to find natives of the νομοί in Egypt attempting to procure by questionable means admission to the ephebic training.

It is advantageous at this point to consider somewhat more fully what were the different classes of people at Alexandria itself and in Egypt.

(i) There were Macedonians who at a later date certainly, and possibly from the first, were not a part of the regular citizen-body, but formed a special class of the population with their own privileges.[1] Their recognition of a new king was at least formally necessary, and their residence was probably by no means confined to Alexandria. Certain people resident at Alexandria describe themselves in our documents (under Augustus) as ' Macedonians ', not as ' Alexandrians ', with no deme name.

Hence Schubart and Wilcken believe that all through Ptolemaic times there was a distinct class of ' Macedonians ' at Alexandria, who served largely in the army and at Court and originally held themselves superior to ' Alexandrines ' of the citizen body.[2]

(ii) Then there were the ' Alexandreis ' or Alexandrines. This name was apparently applicable both to those who possessed full rights of citizenship who were enrolled in a given tribe or deme and to those who were not so enrolled.

It is probable that by the ' Alexandreis ' we are to understand all resident Greeks of Alexandria, not members of the citizen-body only. Certain privileges belonged to all Greeks, as such, in distinction from natives. Polybius[3] seems to include the whole free Greek civil population under the term Ἀλεξανδρεῖς, whether they belonged to the citizen body or not.

(iii) Besides these, there were other men whose legal right to residence was unquestioned. They were variously designated.

They were, as we find, qualified with the phrase τῆς ἐπιγονῆς. The essential point in this term was the contrast of non-Egyptian

---

[1] H. I. Bell, in *J.E.A.* xiii. (1927), 173.
[2] Bevan, *A History of Egypt under the Ptolemaic Dynasty*, Methuen, London, 1927, p. 100.
[3] Polybius, xxiv. 14, 2–5.

with native. The term ' of the epigone ' is translated in Egyptian ' born in Egypt amongst the descendants of στρατιῶται '—i.e., the children and descendants of soldiers, settled in Egypt, not of Egyptian race :—Greeks, Persians, Thracians, etc. When a man who had been ' of the epigone ' entered the army, he became himself a soldier, and ceased to be ' of the epigone '. ' Epigone ' is not to be confused with ' epigonoi ', which was a corps of a military character under the command of the army authorities. In later times one of these classes ' of the epigone ', ' Persian of the Epigone ', was used indiscriminately to signify a certain legal status.[1]

(iv) Native Egyptians were present at Alexandria paying a special poll-tax, and no doubt a very large number of metics, foreign merchants, and slaves. All the native Egyptian element in Alexandria, strangers and metics, were definitely excluded from the citizen body.

How far, then, did the Jews fit into this population scheme ? The papyri show us that there were Jews in all the four main classes just mentioned.

(i) Those who assisted in the founding of Alexandria were undoubtedly classified either as ' Makedones ' or ' Alexandreis '. The Papyri make mention of Jewish Μακεδόνες.[2] Yet what the privileges of the ' Macedonians ' were—whether they entailed citizenship of Alexandria merely or something else—there is far from sufficient evidence to help us. If, as Schubart and Wilcken [3] hold, the Macedonians were a distinct class and held themselves superior to ' Alexandrines ' of the citizen-body, Josephus' statement [4] that the Jews at Alexandria counted as ' Macedonians ' might be taken to prove that the Jews did not belong to the citizen body. Many Jews served in the army, and the chief commands were sometimes held by Jews. Bevan [5] holds that some assimilation of the Jewish soldiers to the Macedonian soldiers is behind the statement of Josephus. Tarn, however, believes that, as their numbers increased, the Jews in Alexandria were organized separately, and that the Jew who under Augustus called himself a Macedonian was either a proselyte or an antiquary.[6]

(ii) Of the two classes of Alexandrians, those enrolled in demes and those not so enrolled, the Jewish ' Alexandreis ' may have belonged to the latter class. These Jews may have secured exemption on religious grounds from the performance of certain district duties,

[1] Loeb Library, *Select Papyri*, ii. 448.
[2] Jewish Μακεδόνες, *B.G.U.* iv. 1068; *B.G.U.* No. 1151 (cf. No. 1132). Two men who are apparently Jews, because their legal transactions are drawn before the ' archeion ' (bureau) of the Jews, describe themselves as ' Macedonians '.
[3] Wilcken, *Grundzüge*, p. 63.
[4] Josephus, *Cont. Ap.* 2. 35–37 ; *Jewish War*, ii. 487–8.
[5] E. Bevan, *A History of Egypt under the Ptolemaic Dynasty*, Methuen, London, 1927, p. 100.
[6] W. W. Tarn, *Hellenistic Civilization*, Arnold, London, 1927, p. 173.

H

religious in their nature or of police character, which the first class had to undertake, and may have thus been classed as Ἀλεξανδρεῖς without the deme.[1] Whereas the Egyptians might be punished by bastinado, Philo[2] tells us that the Alexandrines might be beaten only with flat sticks, *spathai*. The Jews in this matter were classed with the ' Alexandrines '. Josephus[3] says that the Jews of Alexandria were called Ἀλεξανδρεῖς, just as those of Antioch were called Ἀντιοχεῖς. Polybius,[4] while including the whole Greek population under the term Ἀλεξανδρεῖς, does not mention the Jews : possibly, as they were Hellenized in speech and dress, he did not distinguish them from the Greeks.

(iii) But there were also thousands of Jews in Egypt who were not Ἀλεξανδρεῖς. Like the Greeks, they had settled not only in Alexandria, but all over Egypt in the nomes. Beside the mass of the native population, the peasant serfs, in the villages and towns there lived in Greek times motley groups of men, whose legal determination, we have seen, was determined in certain ways.[5] The military and other settlers whom the Greeks found in Egypt, whether they were Persians, Jews, Syrians, or Babylonians, retained their status—i.e., they paid taxes and performed services differing from those of the native Egyptian population in part, although probably certain taxes were levied on all. The foreigners whom Ptolemy invited or brought to Egypt must have been settled either in the cities or nomes, and were given a definite fiscal status.

(iv) Moreover, there must have been Jews among the metics—a term which may have included emancipated slaves. The manumission of a Jewish house-slave is even mentioned in the papyri.[6]

Thus Jews were to be found in all elements of the population in Egypt.

We come next to the debated question of their citizenship. Josephus expressly asserts that the Jews possessed the citizenship at Alexandria, and according to some scholars it is implied by Philo. Schürer, Juster, and Momigliano maintain the affirmative point of view, while many modern writers, such as Willrich, Bludau, Wilcken, Schubart, and Reinach, adopt a negative standpoint.

It may be worth while to consider what Josephus and Philo have to say on this question before considering the negative point of view. Josephus asserts that

' Alexander, having received from the Jews very active support against the Egyptians, granted them as a reward for their assis-

---

[1] M. Radin, *The Jews among the Greeks and Romans*, Philadelphia, 1915, p. 110.
[2] Philo, *In Flacc.*, 78.   [3] Josephus, *Cont. Ap.* 2. 38–39.
[4] Polybius, xxiv. 14, 2–5.
[5] Cf. *P. Gurob*, 8 (210 B.C.) ' Three Jews of the Epigone ', οἱ τρεῖς Ἰουδαῖοι τῆς ἐπιγονῆς are mentioned in a village of the Fayum ; *P. Gurob.* 2 (226 B.C.) mentions at Crocidolopolis in the Arsinoite nome : Dositheus son . . . Ἰουδαῖος τῆς ἐπιγονῆς ; Aristeides, son of Proteas, Ἀθηναῖος τῆς ἐπιγονῆς ; Zophyres, son of Symmachos, Πέρσης τῆς ἐπιγονῆς.
[6] *P. Oxyr.* ix. 1205.

tance, permission to reside in the city on terms of equality with the Greeks (μετοικεῖν κατὰ τὴν πόλιν ἐξ ἰσομοιρίας πρὸς τοὺς Ἕλληνας).'

' This privilege was confirmed by his successors, who, moreover, assigned them a quarter of their own, in order that, through mixing less with aliens, they might be free to observe their rules more strictly ; and they were also permitted to take the title of Macedonians. Again, when the Romans took possession of Egypt neither the first Caesar nor any of his successors would consent to any diminution of the honours conferred on the Jews since the time of Alexander.' [1]

Josephus mentions the favour shown to the Jews by the successors of Alexander, telling us that Seleucus Nicator thought them worthy of citizenship (πολιτεία) in the cities of his foundation, and especially in Antioch, where they had equal rights with the Macedonians and Greeks, which πολιτεία, he says, still subsists ; and goes on to say that Vespasian and Titus refused to deprive the Jews of these ' privileges of citizens ' [2] (τὰ δίκαια τὰ τῆς πολιτείας) at the request of the people of Alexandria and Antioch, clearly implying that their position in both cities was the same.[3]

Josephus cites two authorities for his contention that the Jews were citizens. In the first place, he declares : ' Julius Caesar made a pillar of brass for the Jews at Alexandria, and declared publicly that they were citizens of Alexandria '.[4] In another place he speaks more vaguely of this stele, ' the slab which stands in Alexandria, recording the rights bestowed upon the Jews by Caesar the Great '. [5] In the next place Josephus quotes in full, to support his contention, an edict of Claudius [6] sent at the request of King Agrippa and King Herod, both to Alexandria and to Syria the content of which was as follows :—

[1] Joseph. *Bell. Iud.* ii. 487–8 (Loeb trans.), *c. Ap.* ii. 35 ff.
[2] Joseph. *Antiq.* xii. 121.
[3] Joseph, *cont. Ap.* ii. 38–9. Josephus here, too, claims ' All persons invited to join a colony, however different their nationality, take the name of the founders ' ; cf. *cont. Ap.* ii. 40 : ' Have not the Romans imparted their name to well-nigh all mankind, not to individuals only, but to great nations as a whole ? '
[4] Joseph. *Antiq.*, xiv. 188 : Καῖσαρ Ἰούλιος τοῖς ἐν Ἀλεξανδρείᾳ Ἰουδαίοις ποιήσας χαλκῆν στήλην ἐδήλωσεν ὅτι Ἀλεξανδρέων πολῖται εἰσιν.
[5] Joseph. *cont. Ap.* ii. 37 : τὴν στήλην τὴν ἑστῶσαν ἐν Ἀλεξανδρείᾳ καὶ τὰ δικαιώματα περιέχουσαν ἃ Καῖσαρ ὁ μέγας τοῖς Ἰουδαίοις ἔδωκεν. Bell (*Jews and Christians in Egypt*, London, 1925, p. 14) holds this stele is not very strong evidence, ' particularly as it is difficult to see what right Caesar *had* to give a decision concerning the Alexandrian citizenship '.
[6] Joseph. *Antiq.* xix. 281–5 (Whiston's trans.). The important words are : ἐπιγνοὺς ἀνέκαθεν τοὺς ἐν Ἀλεξανδρείᾳ Ἰουδαίους, Ἀλεξανδρεῖς λεγομένους, συγκατοικισθέντας τοῖς πρώτοις εὐθὺς καιροῖς Ἀλεξανδρεῦσι καὶ ἴσης πολιτείας παρὰ τῶν βασιλέων τετευχότας, καθὼς φανερὸν ἐγένετο ἐκ τῶν γραμμάτων τῶν παρ' αὐτοῖς καὶ τῶν διαταγμάτων, καὶ μετὰ τὸ τῇ ἡμετέρᾳ ἡγεμονίᾳ Ἀλεξανδρείαν ὑπὸ τοῦ Σεβαστοῦ ὑποταχθῆναι, πεφυλάχθαι αὐτοῖς τὰ δίκαια ὑπὸ τῶν πεμφθέντων ἐπάρχων . . . . Ἀλεξανδρεῖς δὲ ἐπαρθῆναι κατὰ τῶν παρ' αὐτοῖς Ἰουδαίων . . . . βούλομαι μηδὲν διὰ τὴν Γαΐου παραφροσύνην τῶν δικαίων τῷ Ἰουδαίων ἔθνει παραπεπτωκέναι, φυλάσσεσθαι δὲ αὐτοῖς καὶ τὰ πρότερον δικαιώματα·

(281). ' Since I am assured that the Jews of Alexandria, called Alexandrians, have been joint inhabitants in the earliest times with the Alexandrians, and have obtained from their kings equal privileges with them, as is evident by the public records that are in their possession, and the edicts themselves ; (282) and that after Alexandria had been subjected to our empire by Augustus, their rights and privileges have been preserved by those presidents who have at diverse times been sent thither : and that no dispute had been raised about those rights and privileges, (283) even when Aquila was governor of Alexandria ; and that when the Jewish ethnarch was dead Augustus did not prohibit the making such ethnarchs, as willing that all men should be so subject to the Romans, as to continue in the observa- tions of their own customs and not be forced to transgress the rules of their own country religion ; but that in the time of Gaius, (284) the Alexandrians became insolent towards the Jews that were among them, which Gaius, out of his great madness and want of understanding, reduced the nation of the Jews very low, because they would not transgress the religious worship of their country, and call him a god.   (285) I will therefore, that the nation of the Jews be not deprived of their rights and privi- leges, on account of the madness of Gaius ; but that those rights and privileges which they formerly enjoyed be preserved to them and that they may continue in their own customs.   And I charge both parties to take very great care that no troubles may arise after the promulgation of this edict.'

Bell [1] admits that this letter has been almost universally inter- preted as implying that the Jews possessed the citizenship, and is therefore totally opposed to the conclusions that they did not, which he draws from the famous London Papyrus No. 1912, which is also a letter of Claudius to the Alexandrians, the authenticity of which cannot be questioned.   Either, then, he says, Josephus' letter is a forgery—which he admits is unlikely, since the concluding lines, with its exhortation to both parties, recalls Claudius' attitude in the Papyrus letter—or it does not mean what it is generally supposed to mean.   Bell is inclined to hold the latter alternative is the truth, on the grounds that in the letter which Josephus quotes, Claudius twice [2] distinguishes between the Jews and the Ἀλεξανδρεῖς, and that he refers to the Jews as ' called Ἀλεξανδρεῖς '.   Why ' called ', if they were Ἀλεξανδρεῖς in the technical sense ?   Moreover, he says they had ἴσης πολιτείας ; he does not definitely state they had the citizen- ship.   It is possible, however, that the Jews were called Ἀλεξανδρεῖς, and that Claudius, like Josephus, is merely stating a fact.

Philo [3] several times speaks of the Jews of Alexandria as Ἀλεξανδρεῖς,

---

[1] H. I. Bell, *Jews and Christians in Egypt*, London, 1924, p. 15.
[2] Joseph. *Antiq.* xix. 281, 284.
[3] Philo, *In Flac.*, 10, 80 (M. 528) : τῶν ἰδιωτῶν Ἀλεξανδρέων Ἰουδαίων. *Leg.* 28, 183 (M. 572-3) : ἀλλ᾽ ἔοικε (Gaius) τῇ τῶν ἄλλων Ἀλεξανδρέων μέριδι προοκεῖσθαι.

but this word, as has already been noticed, though technically it meant Alexandrian *citizens*, might also denote merely inhabitants of Alexandria. In the *Flaccus* he says that Flaccus aimed at ' the ἀναίρεσις of our πολιτεία, thus depriving us of our sheet anchor, μετουσία πολιτικῶν δικαίων '.[1]

And in the *Legatio*, speaking of his own embassy, he says he was sent to fight ' for the πολιτεία',[2] in a sense which his readers would understand and, what is more, which they would admit to be applicable to the rights possessed by the Jews and threatened by Flaccus. The whole question seems to turn on the implication of the term πολιτεία. What does it imply? It has been suggested that it might mean in this context ' the rights of those who form a πολίτευμα ' —a word frequently used in Hellenistic times to mean ' a corporation formed by the members of a race or community domiciled in a foreign state '. πολιτεία, of course, may mean ' citizenship ' (*ius civitatis*), but Strabo[3] shows it need not have the meaning of ' citizenship '.

Such corporations enjoyed certain privileges in the cities which harboured them. Some foreigners of uncertain origin formed such a corporation in the island of Cos,[4] and the Jews had a πολίτευμα at Berenice in Cyrenaica.[5]

In Alexandria itself the recent Phrygians formed a πολίτευμα,[6] and that was the form of organization adopted by the Jews in that city, as is shown by the use of the phrase οἱ ἀπὸ τοῦ πολιτεύματος in the letter of Pseudo-Aristeas. This body had as its president up to the time of Augustus an official called ἐθνάρχης, whose place Philo seems to imply was afterwards taken by a γερουσία or Council of Elders.[7]

Pseudo-Aristeas, reflecting conditions in the middle or late 2nd century B.C., refers to the Alexandrian Jewish community as a πολίτευμα governed by πρεσβύτεροι and ἡγούμενοι.[8]

The author is describing an assembly of the Alexandrian Jews

---

[1] Philo, *In Flac.*, 8, 53 : πάλιν ἐφ᾽ ἕτερον ἐτρέπετο, τὴν τῆς ἡμετέρας πολιτείας ἀναίρεσιν, ἵν᾽ ἀποκοπέντων οἷς μόνοις ἐφώρμει ὁ ἡμέτερος βίος ἐθῶν τε πατρίων καὶ μετουσίας πολιτικῶν δικαίων τὰς ἐσχάτας ὑπομένωμεν συμφοράς, οὐδένος ἐπειλημμένοι πείσματος εἰς ἀσφάλειαν. ὀλίγαις γὰρ ὕστερον ἡμέραις τίθησι πρόγραμμα, δι᾽ οὗ ξένους καὶ ἐπήλυδας ἡμᾶς ἀπεκάλει· κτλ.
[2] Philo, *Leg.* 44, 439 (M. 597) : μεταπεμφθέντες ἀγωνίσασθαι τὸν περὶ τῆς πολιτείας ἀγῶνα.
[3] Strabo *ap. Jos. Antiq.* xiv. 17 : καθίσταται δὲ καὶ ἐθνάρχης αὐτῶν, ὃς διοικεῖ τε τὸ ἔθνος καὶ διαιτᾷ κρίσεις καὶ συμβολαίων ἐπιμελεῖται καὶ προσταγμάτων, ὡς ἂν πολιτείας ἄρχων αὐτοτελοῦς. ' There is also an ethnarch allowed them, who governs the nation ; and distributes justice to them, and takes care of their contracts, and of the laws to them belonging, as if he were the ruler of a free republic.'—(Whiston's trans.).
[4] *O.G.I.* 192.   [5] Ibid. 5362.   [6] Ibid. 658.
[7] Philo, *In Flac.*, 10, 74 (M. 527–8) : τῆς γὰρ ἡμετέρας γερουσίας, ἣν ὁ σωτὴρ καὶ εὐεργέτης Σεβαστὸς ἐπιμελησομένην τῶν Ἰουδαϊκῶν εἵλετο μετὰ τὴν τοῦ γεναρχοῦ τελευτήν. But Claudius in the letter quoted by Josephus (*Ant.* xix. 283) says : τελευτήσαντος τοῦ τῶν Ἰουδαίων ἐθνάρχου τὸν Σεβαστὸν μὴ κεκωλυκέναι ἐθνάρχας γίγνεσθαι.
[8] Pseudo-Aristeas (Sect. 310) : στάντες οἱ ἱερεῖς καὶ τῶν ἑρμηνέων οἱ πρεσβύτεροι καὶ τῶν ἀπὸ τοῦ πολιτεύματος οἵ τε ἡγούμενοι τοῦ πλήθους εἶπον.

RACE-RELATIONS IN ANCIENT EGYPT

addressed by the priests and elders of the visiting delegation of scholars from Palestine and by the elders and magistrates of the local πολίτευμα. They propose formally that the recently executed Greek translation of the Jewish sacred writings stand without altera- tion. The assembled Jews voted their approval of the proposition. The passage suggests the familiar picture of Greek city-state organiza- tion with magistrates (ἡγούμενοι), councillors (πρεσβύτεροι), and popular assembly (τὸ πλῆθος).

It is interesting to note that in the recently edited βουλή Papyrus [1] πολίτευμα is applied to the city-state organization of Alexandria itself.

It would seem, then, judging from Philo, Pseudo-Aristeas, and Strabo, that the Jewish community in Alexandria was a self-governing state, existing as a political entity apart from the Greek citizen body, and conducting its own affairs without official interference from the πολίτευμα of the Alexandrians. Jewish autonomy would be recognized by the power that stood above both groups—in the early period the ruling Ptolemy, in the time of Philo the Roman emperor.

Tarn says [2] that, in spite of Josephus' claim that Jews as a body were full citizens in Alexandria, Antioch, and the cities of Ionia, it was always impossible, because full citizenship—i.e., participation in government and legal administration—entailed worship of the city gods, which to a Jew meant apostasy. Jews as a rule, Hellenizers or otherwise, held fast to their religion. Jews in a city call them- selves in inscriptions a racial unit only (laos) and never in his opinion an enfranchised people (demos). Both Tarn and Bell conclude from the recently discovered letter of the Emperor Claudius, already mentioned (London Papyrus No. 1912, A.D. 41), that the Jews as a body were never citizens of Alexandria.

And both Tarn and Professor de Sanctis [3] hold that isopolity is the key to the matter.

Where the kings had power—as they had in new foundations like Alexandria or Antioch or in cities where, like Ephesus, the Seleucids restored democracy and could make terms—they gave the Jewish settlers isopolity, potential citizenship ; [4] that is, a Jew could be- come a citizen on demand, provided he apostatized by worshipping the city gods. This would account for the insistence of Josephus on the 'equal honour' of the Jews and the terms 'Antiochenes' and 'Alexandrians'. When Aetolia, for example, gave Ceos isopolity, the Ceans called themselves Aetolians.[5]

---

[1] *P.S.I.* x. 1160 = *Archiv für Pap.* ix. 253 (Wilcken) ; English translation and commentary by Oliver in *Aegyptus* (April 1931), also published in *Bull. de La Soc. Royale d'Archéologie d'Alexandrie* (Suppl. of *Fasc.* 25, 1930).
[2] W. W. Tarn, *Hellenistic Civilization*, Arnold, London, 1927 p. 176.
[3] In *Riv. di Filologia*, 1924, p. 473.
[4] The isopolity of the Jews is thrice mentioned : 3 Maccabees ii. 30 ; Josephus, *Antiq.* xii. 8 ; and (the material passage) Claudius' edict *Antiq.* xix. 281 : ἴσης πολιτείας παρὰ τῶν βασιλέων τετευχότας. (This edict rightly calls the Jews συγκατοι- κισθέντας ᾿Αλεξανδρεῦσιν—i.e. a politeuma beside the Greek politeuma.) For Antioch, see Josephus, *Bell. Iud.* vii. 44 : ἐξ ἴσου τῆς πόλεως τοῖς ῞Ελλησι μετέχειν.
[5] Tarn, *Hellen. Civ.*, pp. 177, 64.

According to Tarn,[1] it was a physical impossibility for Alexandria to be a ' city ' in the strict Greek sense. What Alexander really founded was a city of a new mixed type. It was a collection of polit-eumata, based on nationalities, the Greek politeuma being much the most important; outside these stood a few privileged Macedonians at one end and the mass of Egyptians at the other. It was the Greek politeuma which approximated more closely to the polis type than any other actually known. The Greeks were called ' the citizens ', the Alexandrians, and were divided into tribes; they supplied the magistrates, of Greek type, who looked after buildings, public health, and so on, and also Greek courts which administered a law compounded of the ' city law '—the law of the Greek citizens—and royal rescripts and had jurisdiction over all the inhabitants except, after the 3rd century, the Jewish politeuma.

The land attached to Alexandria was the land ' of the Alexandrians ' —i.e., of the Greek politeuma—and if there was a Council, it must have been that politeuma's governing council. There were, how-ever, many Greek inhabitants who were not members of the Greek politeuma, and the whole population was subject to Ptolemy's governor; there were other royal officials, like the prefect of police— and possibly the exegetes, who was responsible for the food supply and can hardly have been a magistrate, for he wore the purple.

The Greeks themselves, scattered about Egypt, and unable to form cities, formed themselves into true politeumata; each might cover a considerable district—we get ' the Greeks in the Delta ', ' in the Thebaid ', ' in the Arsinoite nome '—and the members imitated what of autonomous Greek organisation they could.

As Jews filtered into a Greek city, their position was at first merely that of metics; but as soon as they were numerous enough, they set up a synagogue, and probably formed a private association for worship, as was the custom of other metics. Such an association would have its officials—the ' ruler of the synagogue ' and others— to whom the Jews submitted their disputes according to Jewish law, in preference to going to the Greek courts.

The Jews were next allowed to form a politeuma, which made them quasi-autonomous ' settlers ' with rights greater than those of metics. Jewish politeumata, like others, managed their own internal and religious affairs, but in one respect they were privileged beyond any other: they ultimately acquired (at Alexandria not until after the 3rd century) the right of being judged by their own magistrates according to their own law, which probably means that they were excepted from the jurisdiction of the Greek courts:[2] perhaps this, rather than religious exclusiveness, was the origin of the discontent Greeks began to feel later.

The existence of these Jewish politeumata is explicably attested

---

[1] Tarn, *Hellen. Civ.*, p. 147.
[2] Ibid. pp. 160, 175-6. Cf. Goodenough, *Jewish Courts in Egypt*, 1929.

for Alexandria and Berenice in the Cyrenaica, and seems certain in
many cities, notably Hierapolis in Asia Minor.[1]
According to Stuart Jones,[2] the members of a πολίτευμα called
each other πολῖται, and bestowed on a member when admitting him
their πολιτεία. But the city of their domicile did not recognize
them as its πολῖται, nor as possessing its πολιτεία.

He believes that in Alexandria there were : (i) ἀστοί, full citizens
of Alexandria ; (iii) πολῖται, entitled to the benefit of the πολιτικοὶ
νόμοι ; (iii) λαοί, ' the natives ' ; and that πολιτεία could be used
to denote the sum of the rights belonging to the intermediate class
which were organized in several πολιτεύματα. Thus Josephus,
according to him, might have twisted his documents so as to make
it appear that the Jews were citizens of Alexandria—i.e., that πολιτεία
and πολῖται referred to the first and not to the second class !

It is worth while to notice his arguments briefly : (i) The city of
Alexandria was a Greek πόλις with an assembly (if no Senate),
magistrates, and public religious worships. It had its athletic (if
not military) training, the ephebia, the necessary avenue to full
citizen rights. These rights belonged to the 'Αλεξανδρεῖς of the
old foundation, to their descendants, and to those to whom the
freedom of Alexandria had been granted. The city was properly
called ἄστυ, as opposed to ἡ χώρα ; its citizens were ἀστοί, and its
laws were known as ἀστικοὶ νόμοι.[3] (ii) Between this privileged
body and the mass of the native Egyptian population came various
categories of persons designated by ethnic names, some of which had
lost their original signification.

The Alexandrian papyri of the Augustan period show that Jews
might be described as ' Persians ' or ' Macedonians '.[4] The
members of the Jewish πολίτευμα kept their own register [5] and were,
like the Macedonians, Persians, and other ethnic groups, raised
above the λαοί, or native Egyptians, who were always a depressed
class, the badge of which was the λαογραφία or poll-tax.

Ptolemy Philadelphus is cited [6] as proposing to reduce the Jews
to this status. Josephus [7] tells of a persecution by Ptolemy Physcon
with almost similar details. The Jews, then, were one of the privileged orders, in that racial hierarchy which the Romans so strictly
maintained in Egypt.

Two documents, one of the 3rd [8] and the other of the 2nd century [9]

---

[1] W. W. Tarn, op. cit., p. 175.   [2] J.R.S. 16. 1926, pp. 28 ff.
[3] P. Oxy., 706, 9.   [4] B.G.U. 1134, 1151.
[5] ἀρχεῖον (B.G.U. 1131, 1151).
[6] III Macc. ii. 28–30. The writer of Macc. III states that Philopator degraded
the Jews, εἰς λαογραφίαν καὶ οἰκετικὴν διάθεσιν, but ordered ἐὰν δέ τινες ἐξ αὐτῶν
προαιρῶνται ἐν τοῖς κατὰ τελετὰς μεμυημένοις ἀναστρέφεσθαι, τούτους ἰσοπολίτας 'Αλεξ-
ανδρεῦσιν εἶναι. Bell holds it is very unlikely that an Alexandrian writer of the late
Ptolemaic or early Roman period would have implied that the Jews did not possess
the citizenship if, as Josephus asserts, they had always enjoyed it. The degrada-
tion εἰς λαογραφίαν, he says, does not imply loss of citizenship but merely loss of
privileges they possessed.
[7] Contr. Ap. 2, 51 ff.   [8] Mitteis, Chrest., 21.
[9] Mitteis, ibid., 31.

B.C., relating to lawsuits mention the πολιτικοὶ νόμοι. The earlier document relates to the suit brought in 226–5 B.C. by Dositheus an Ἰουδαῖος τῆς ἐπιγονῆς against Heraclea, a Jewess; the papyrus shows that the suit was tried according to the πολιτικοὶ νόμοι. πολιτικὸς νόμος, Stuart Jones admits, can mean simply the ' city law ', binding on all persons of Alexandrian domicile, yet in the case of these persons of Jewish race he holds it *must* mean the law applying to πολῖται of the πολίτευμα—i.e., to those possessing full civil rights in a sense which the λαοί did not.

Wilcken [1] adduces some further arguments against the citizenship, one of which we have already noticed—namely, that, though there were Jews classed with the Macedonians, they did not possess the citizenship, if Schubart is right in holding that the Macedonians did not belong to the citizen body. Wilcken, following Schubart, cites a papyrus [2] in which a Jewish petitioner is described as Ἀλεξανδρέω(s), but the word has been altered to Ἰουδαίου τῶν ἀπὸ Ἀλεξανδρεία(s).

From this he argues there must have been a difference between the Ἀλεξανδρεύς or citizen and the Ἰουδαῖος τῶν ἀπὸ Ἀλεξανδρείας. Schürer [3] and Juster [4] rightly dispute this inference. Furthermore, the mention in B.G.U. 1151, 7f. of τοῦ τῶν Ἰουδαίων ἀρχείου, as compared with the πολιτικὸν ἀρχεῖον of the citizen-body in B.G.U. 1131, 14, 22, shows that the Jews had a special notarial office distinct from that of the πόλις, and therefore points to their forming a πολίτευμα, not a part of the body of citizens.

Some authorities adduce the London Papyrus 1912 further to clinch the argument against citizenship.[5] It is an authentic letter of Claudius in reply to an address of congratulation presented (with certain petitions) by an embassy from the city of Alexandria. It deals first with the honours, divine or semi-divine, voted him by the Alexandrians, and also with certain requests made by them in connexion with municipal affairs, and then with the violent disagreements between the Jews and the Greek population of that city.

After deploring the στάσις between Jews and Alexandrians, Claudius calls upon both parties to amend their ways, Ἀλεξανδρεῖς μέν. . . . καὶ Ἰουδαίοις δέ (lines 82, 88). ' Could there be a clearer indication ', says Bell,[6] ' that in the eyes of Claudius the Jews were not Ἀλεξανδρεῖς—i.e., Alexandrian citizens ? ' In line 95 he speaks of the Jews as living in ἀλλοτρίᾳ πόλει.

Their enemies might speak of Jewish citizens as aliens and as living ἐν ἀλλοτρίᾳ πόλει, but is it conceivable that the impartial

---

[1] Wilcken, *Grundzüge*, p. 63. Schubart's theory, however, is not conclusive evidence.
[2] B.G.U. 1140 = Wilcken, *Chrest.*, 58.
[3] E. Schürer, *Geschichte des jüdischen Volkes im Zeitalter Jesu Christi*, 3rd–4th ed., 1898–1909, 111⁴, 718.
[4] J. Juster, *Les Juifs dans l'empire romain*, Paris, 1914, 11, pp. 9 f.
[5] This document has been admirably edited by H. I. Bell in his book *Jews and Christians in Egypt*, London, 1924, and has been discussed by Sir F. Kenyon, in an article in the *Edinburgh Review* for July 1925.
[6] Ibid.

Claudius should? Yet it seems possible, since Claudius was not on the scene and relied on hearsay information. In line 92f. Claudius bids the Jews μηδὲ ἐπισπαίρειν γυμνασιαρχικοῖς ἢ κοσμητικοῖς ἀγῶσι. The reference is to the athletic contests presided over by the civic magistrates called gymnasiarchs and cosmetae, and the conclusion drawn is that if the Jews were not entitled to take part, then they did not possess the coveted citizenship. (The gymnasiarch and cosmetes, significantly enough, were also the magistrates associated with the ephebia, the necessary preliminary to citizenship (line 53).) This conclusion would be true unless it were possible for the Jews to have possessed the citizenship without taking part in the athletic contests.

It is worth noticing that the reading and meaning of the most significant word in this passage is a matter of dispute. Bell [1] reads ἐπισπαίρειν, and holds that the meaning of ' to be in alarm ' given by Liddell and Scott [2] to the word ἐπέσπαιρεν in Plutarch [3] would not be very appropriate here.

If ἀγῶσι, he holds, refers to contests in the election to the gymnasiarchy and cosmeteia, a sense like ' to aspire to ' is needed, but it is strange to single out only these offices. On the other hand, if ἀγῶνες is taken in the ordinary sense of athletic contests, Bell prefers to take the meaning of ἐπισπαίρειν as ' to strive in ', and accordingly translates ' nor to strive in gymnasiarchic or cosmetic games '.

Hunt and Edgar [4] read ἐπισπαίειν instead of ἐπισπαίρειν, and translate ' force their way into gymnasiarchic or cosmetic games '. Radin [5] suggests a plausible interpretation of ἐπισπαίρειν.

The warning to the Jews was in the interest of general security, and the Alexandrine Jews ' were not all Platonizing philosophers nor shrinking and persecuted martyrs, but for the most part a violent and turbulent rabble as likely to institute a pogrom as to suffer under one. In at least one of the great riots they seem to have been the aggressors, and ἐπισπαίρειν may well have the sense of ' jeering ' or ' scoffing ', which at such a time could hardly fail to provoke a counter-demonstration.'

That, if the Jews did not, or were not entitled to, take part in the games, they did not possess the citizenship, is perhaps a fallacious argument.

The Jews may have been granted exemption, as has been mentioned before, from civic duties that conflicted with their religion.

The stadium had been regarded as one of the chief symbols of the Abomination from the time of the Maccabees,[6] and it was even

---

[1] *Jews and Christians in Egypt*, 1924, p. 37.
[2] Liddell and Scott, 8th ed., p. 553; but the recent 1940 addition of this work gives the meaning (p. 658) of ' pant, struggle ' for the same passage in Plutarch.
[3] Plutarch, *Moralia*, 327 C. τοῖς Φιλιππικοῖς πολέμοις ἐπέσπαιρεν ἡ Ἑλλάς.
[4] Loeb, *Select Papyri*, ii. 86–87.   [5] *Classical Philology*, xx. (1925), 370.
[6] Josephus gives an account of the action of Herod the Great in introducing such contests at Jerusalem (*Ant. Iud.* xv. 8) which was regarded as an impious violation of the national traditions. In II Macc. iv. the high priest Jason is unsparingly condemned for establishing a gymnasium in Jerusalem and encouraging the

forbidden the Jews to assist the heathen in building one.[1] Participation in the games was regarded by the Rabbis as sheer idolatry, and permission to be present was only grudgingly given.[2]

An orthodox Jew would have felt scruples about taking part in a course of training such as was to be had in the Greek γυμνάσια, involving an exhibition of the nude male form, and probably worship, or recognition, of the gods of the palaestra.

The circus was characterized, to use the words of the Psalmist,[3] as ' the seat of the scorners '. If Jewish ἐπισπαίροντες, ' mockers ', were answered by Greek ones, the designation would not be a bad one. Apart from the contempt for the games possibly felt by orthodox Jews, unorthodox ones may have desired access, and this may have aggravated the situation, but to deduce that non-participation or non-attendance at the games was incompatible with citizenship seems to be reading more into the matter than can be justified.

The present letter cannot be reconciled with that quoted by Josephus in full [4] which has already been discussed, unless we accept all the afore-mentioned opinions against citzenship and Bell's view that Josephus' letter has been misinterpreted. Only in this sense would Josephus' letter fit in with the negative standpoint, a procedure which seems to stretch the point somewhat! In a recent work [5] Momigliano appears to take the positive point of view. He mentions the two edicts recorded by Josephus, in one of which Claudius restores to the Jews of Alexandria the citizen rights of which Gaius, his predecessor, had deprived them (this is the letter of Claudius to the Alexandrians in Josephus which we have already discussed),[6] while in the other he restores throughout the Empire the freedom of Jewish worship which during Gaius' reign had been impaired.[7] Both these edicts are regarded as authentic, especially as they are presupposed in Claudius' other letter to the people of Alexandria (London Papyrus No. 1912).[8]

Momigliano assumes that the Jews possessed Alexandrian citizenship, that they were Ἀλεξανδρεῖς (not ἀστοί).[9] He holds that no one has yet seriously discredited the letter of Claudius in Josephus, which Bell, too, as we have seen, does not find easy to reconcile with Claudius' letter in the London Papyrus 1912, especially the explicit statement in Josephus:

ἐπιγνοὺς ἀνέκαθεν τοὺς ἐν Ἀλεξανδρείᾳ Ἰουδαίοις Ἀλεξανδρεῖς λεγομένους, συγκατοικισθέντας τοῖς πρώτοις εὐθὺς καιροῖς Ἀλεξανδρεῦσι, καὶ ἴσης πολιτείας παρὰ τῶν βασιλέων τετυχότας.

---

priests to neglect the temple sacrifices in order to take part in the unlawful displays of the palaestra. (Cf. I Macc. i. 14.)
[1] Mishnah, *Ab. Zar.* i. 7. [2] Bab. *Talmud, Aboda Zara*, 18b.
[3] Ps. i. 1. [4] *Antiq.* xix. 280–5.
[5] *Claudius, The Emperor and his Achievement*, Oxford, Clarendon Press 1934, pp. 30, 96.
[6] Joseph. *Ant. Iud.*, xix. 280 ff. [7] Joseph. ibid., pp. 287 ff.
[8] H. I. Bell, *Jews and Christians in Egypt*, London, 1924, p. 15.
[9] For the distinction cf. E. Bickermann, *Rev. Phil.* liii. (1927), 362 ff.

Philo's statement [1] about the right of the Jews to be punished with the rod, like the Alexandrians, instead of with the flat of the sword, like natives, would tend to confirm this. Moreover, Momigliano does not agree that the Jews must have formed a politeuma of their own in Alexandria. [2]

Not all the Jews in Egypt, obviously, were Alexandrians, and, with the exception of a few minor categories, the great majority of those who were not Alexandrians appeared in the census lists on the same footing as the native Egyptians. It was this fact, according to Momigliano, which gave rise to the continual protests against the Alexandrian citizenship of the Jews; [3] for the anti-Jewish party would naturally be eager to confound the Alexandrian Jews with the Jews appearing in the census-lists. This, he holds, gives the clue to the interpretation of the papyrus [4] in which an Alexandrian appears as inscribed in the census lists, although his father possessed the rights of an Alexandrian citizen.

The phrase in Claudius' letter (London Papyrus, No. 1912) line 90, μηδὲ ὥσπερ ἐν δυσὶ πόλεσι κατοικοῦντας δύο πρεσβείας ἐκπέμπειν τοῦ λοιποῦ, ὃ μὴ πρότερόν ποτε ἐπράχθη, has created some difficulty. If the Jews were Alexandrian citizens, there could have been no good reason for one Gentile embassy and one Jewish embassy. Actually the passage indicates there were two Jewish embassies, [5] not one Gentile and one Jewish, as Bell, and Hunt and Edgar, have it. [6] Momigliano inclines to a view that would tell in favour of the Alexandrian citizenship of the Jews [7]—that the two embassies came respectively from Jews with, and Jews without, Alexandrian citizenship; they would be divided from one another by rivalries and jealousies, and might well be called ' inhabitants of two different cities ', not only in a metaphorical but in a concrete sense, referring to the disparity between their political rights. Probably, too, the Jews possessing Alexandrian citizenship were more Hellenized than the others. There appears quite a good deal to be said for Momigliano's theory, especially when one considers the position of Jews in the modern world, and compares those who are assimilated to the country of their adoption and possess citizen rights with those who are late-comers, are unassimilated, and as such subject to odium.

What conclusions, then, can be drawn from the mass of conflicting evidence and the criticism of the critics. Some definite facts impress themselves on one when one considers the ancient authorities and sources.

[1] Philo, *In Flac.* 80.
[2] On the ' politeuma ', cf. W. Ruppel, *Philologus*, N.F. xxxvi. (1927), 268 ff.
[3] A specimen of this has recently been discovered in the ' Acts of Isidore and Lampon ' which Momigliano discusses on pp. 35, 100, of his work.
[4] *B.G.U.* iv. 1140 = Mitteis and Wilcken, *Chrestiomathie*, i. 58.
[5] H. Willrich, *Hermes*, ix. (1925); so, too, Stuart Jones in *J.R.S.* 1926, (16), p. 21.
[6] Bell, *Jews and Christians in Egypt*, London, 1924, p. 29, par. 14. Hunt and Edgar, *Select Papyri*, Loeb Library, Heinemann, ii. 87.
[7] Momigliano, op. cit., p. 97.

(1) Josephus claims the Jews were Μακεδόνες [1] and Ἀλεξανδρεῖς,[2] two words whose meaning is in doubt. The Papyri [3] confirm his claim. Moreover, he states they were citizens, πολῖται, of Alexandria.[4]

(ii) On the other hand, there is evidence both literary [5] and papyrological [6] to show that the Jews in the Ptolemaic period, and in the Roman as well, formed a community or organization of their own separate from that of the citizen-body. It is, however, not beyond the bounds of possibility for the Jews generally to have had their own separate organization and at the same time to have been citizens of Alexandria. Yet if the Jews possessed the full citizenship—such separate privileges as they had (their own organization, a genarch or ethnarch, a γερουσία, whereas Alexandria had no senate, and their own judicial organisation) would be inconvenient in practice, even if they were necessarily granted these privileges owing to their religious principles. The Jews, indeed, had always preserved a separate identity since their first sojourn in Egypt in Pharaonic times. In modern times they have generally possessed the full citizenship in the countries in which they have long been resident, and at the same time have preserved their own organization or community centred round the synagogue in most cases; but that the restricted constitution of the Greek city-state of ancient times allowed of such an arrangement with full citizen rights, we have no evidence to warrant. It seems that the contrary would have been the case; we cannot attribute to Alexandria what enlightened modern constitutions allow. Enfranchisement of a large mass of non-Greeks with their peculiar culture and organization would have meant, in a Greek state jealous of its rights, a revolutionary arrangement which would have left its mark on the literature and records of the time.

If we consider the historical development of Jewish settlement in Egypt, the evidence is not so conflicting as it appears. It seems more than likely that Jews formed part of the original city-state organization which Alexander founded and, as such, were citizens of it like the first Greeks who were incorporated and were called Ἀλεξανδρεῖς, but what their numbers were remains uncertain.

---

[1] Joseph. *Bell. Iud.* ii. 488 : καὶ χρηματίζειν ἐπέτρεψαν (the successors of Alexander) Μακεδόνας. Joseph. *cont. Ap.* ii. 35 : καὶ ἴσης παρὰ τοῖς Μακεδόσι τιμῆς ἐπέτυχον.

[2] Joseph. *cont. Ap.* ii. 38 : τὸ δὲ δὴ θαυμάζειν πῶς Ἰουδαῖοι ὄντες Ἀλεξανδρεῖς ἐκλήθησαν. Joseph. *Antiq.* xix. 281 : Ἰουδαίους Ἀλεξανδρεῖς λεγομένους.

[3] Cf. *B.G.U.* 1068, 1151 (cf. 1132) for Macedonians and *B.G.U.* 1140 for Alexandrians (cf. Juster, *Les Juifs dans l'Empire romain*, Paris 1914, ii. 9 f.).

[4] Joseph. *Antiq.* xiv. 188 : Καῖσαρ Ἰούλιος . . . . ἐδήλωσεν ὅτι Ἀλεξανδρέων πολῖται εἰσιν.

[5] *Pseudo Aristeas*, 310, refers to the Alexandrian Jewish organization as a πολίτευμα. Philo, *In Flac.* 74, refers to the ruler of the community in Roman times as *genarches* (whereas in Strabo apud Joseph. *Antiq.* xiv. 117, he is called *ethnarches*) and hints that in Roman times the government of the community was vested in a *gerusia*.

[6] Cf. the contrast already noticed between τὸ τῶν Ἰουδαίων ἀρχεῖον (Jewish notarial office) in *B.G.U.* 1151, 7 f. and the πολιτικὸν ἀρχεῖον (that of the πόλις) in 1131, 14, 32.

This would not be in conflict, but in agreement, with Alexander's ideals, as far as we can gauge them. Furthermore, some of the Jews must, like their Greek compatriots, have been enrolled as Μακεδόνες, a military or social hierarchy with uncertain rights, from the earliest days of the conquest of the country.[1] Jews are known to have assisted Alexander, and there were Jews in the armies of the Ptolemies. Later there was a great influx of newcomers, both Greeks and Jews, into Egypt, several of whom were styled 'Αθηναῖος . . . etc., τῆς ἐπιγονῆς or 'Ιουδαῖος τῆς ἐπιγονῆς. If they settled at Alexandria for any length of time, they were styled οἱ ἀπὸ 'Αλεξανδρείας or, more briefly, 'Αλεξανδρεῖς. These people were not citizens or foundation members of the city of Alexandria, and the term 'Αλεξανδρεῖς, applied to them, was merely a geographical expression. In this case 'Αλεξανδρεῖς, denoting as a general term 'inhabitants of Alexandria', could be confused, and was so with 'Αλεξανδρεῖς, denoting 'citizens of Alexandria'.

The Jews belonging to this class in course of time found it convenient, and a protection for themselves in order to preserve their own culture and individuality, to form themselves into a separate body from the Greeks, described, by the term then in vogue in the Hellenistic Age to denote a racial unit, as a πολίτευμα.

In the same way, all over Egypt Greeks who did not belong to one of the three Greek cities in Egypt formed themselves into πολιτεύματα.

Moreover, it was even possible for the Greeks of the citizen-body at Alexandria also to be described thus, as belonging to a πολίτευμα, though of course a much more important one than the Jewish, especially as by this time Alexandria had become the centre of Ptolemaic autocracy, was filled with royal officials of the Egyptian territorial state, and had become a mere municipality : the Greek πολίτευμα, too, had lost its Council (βουλή).

The loss of the βουλή is significant—it probably meant that the kings had decided to curb the activities of the original city-state organization and to reduce its privileges to that of a municipality. The possession, on the other hand, of a γερουσία by the Jewish πολίτευμα was probably one of the causes of friction between Greek and Jew.

Josephus, while stating the privileges of the Jews μετοικεῖν κατὰ τὴν πόλιν ἐξ ἰσομοιρίας πρὸς τοὺς 'Ελληνας,[2] καὶ ἴσης πολιτείας παρὰ τῶν βασιλέων τετευχότας,[3] significantly mentions that the Successors of Alexander ' assigned them a quarter of their own, in order that, through mixing less with aliens, they might be free to observe their rules more strictly '.[4]

---

[1] Joseph. Bell. Iud. ii. 487–8 ; cont. Ap. ii. 35 ff.
[2] Idem, ibid. 487.   [3] Joseph. Antiq. xix. 281.
[4] Bell. Iud. ii. 488 : καὶ τόπον ἴδιον αὐτοῖς ἀφώρισαν ὅπως καθαρωτέραν ἔχοιεν τὴν δίαιταν, ἧττον ἐπιμισγομένον τῶν ἀλλοφύλλων. Cf. Bell. Iud. ii. 495 : τὸ καλούμενον Δέλτα, συνῳκιστο γὰρ ἐκεῖ τὸ 'Ιουδαϊκόν. The five quarters of Alexandria were called after the first five letters of the alphabet, two being later occupied by Jews (cf. Philo, In Flac. par. 55).

This statement which explicitly implies a separate organization does not conflict with the preceding statements of his on the equal rights of the Jews with the Greeks, if we understand it in the sense of the rights of one racial πολίτευμα as compared with those of another—both πολιτεύματα having equal rights of residence in the one city. It is in this sense that Seleucus Nicator must have made the Jews in the cities of his foundation, and especially in Antioch, ἰσοτίμους Μακεδόσιν καὶ Ἕλλησιν.[1]

Yet, for all that, however much the kings may have tried to modify the old forms of the city-state in the Greek cities within their kingdom to make room for another organization, the organization of the Greek section was deeply rooted in the past history of the Greeks, and it was thus to it that citizenship was ascribed.

At Alexandria the population at this time would be composed of a polyglot mixed mass of all races, with at one end a minority of Greeks, among whom must have been included some Jews, who had inherited or been rewarded with citizen rights dating back to the old form of the city's constitution from its foundation and, at the other end, a specific Jewish organization with its own laws applicable only to its members, and with privileges separate from those of the citizen Greeks. Yet, inasmuch as Alexandria was also the royal capital of a territorial state, the new thing in the ancient world, all these people, with the exception of the native Egyptians, were subject to the king, and had certain common privileges and duties.

What had caused the most trouble to the citizen Greeks of Alexandria and their supporters, Greek or otherwise, and in fact to modern critics, was the *laissez-faire* policy of the Ptolemies in not striving to bring, as it seems to us, some definite order into the varied grades of the population of Alexandria,[2] especially in clarifying the position of the Jews. They could belong to any of these classes :—

(i) Μακεδόνες, of (to us) uncertain privileges.
(ii) Ἀλεξανδρεῖς, citizens of the old foundation (some Jews).
(iii) Ἀλεξανδρεῖς inhabitants of Alexandria (most of the Greeks, and most of the Jews who formed a racial politeuma).

Josephus, according to this view, is right. There were Jewish citizens, not simply a few, but, in comparison with the vast multitude of later arrivals who were not citizens but belonged to a πολίτευμα, those Jews who had the citizenship must have been in the minority. It must have been the same with the later Greek arrivals : those who had the citizenship must have been fewer in number than those who had not.

It was the confusion of the Jews of those with, and those without,

---

[1] *Antiq.* xii. 119.
[2] Perhaps they did not look at them from the standpoint, prevalent in some modern states, of separate nationalities, though at first they did consider the Egyptians an inferior class, but from the standpoint of privileges, as is done in the enlightened modern states to-day.

the citizenship, as Momigliano has already shown, that led to trouble, for however low Alexandria had fallen as a city-state, citizenship still meant certain undoubted and jealously guarded privileges, and the Romans in their time made it the *sine qua non* for their own citizenship—unless, of course, one had become a Roman soldier, which of itself meant the Roman citizenship at the end of the period of service. That all Greeks in Alexandria were not citizens is now generally agreed, and it seems that general agreement can be reached as well when we say that not all Jews, but only some—how many is uncertain—were citizens, whereas the majority were not, but had an organization of their own comparable to that of the citizen-body.

The best interpretation of Josephus, who admittedly is apologetic, would be that it was not impossible or unknown for Jews at Alexandria (not the Jews, meaning all of them) to become citizens, as the historical instances he quotes prove.[1]

[1] His statement in *Antiq*. xiv. 188 : Καῖσαρ 'Ιούλιος . . . ἐδήλωσεν ὅτι 'Αλεξανδρέων πολῖταί εἰσι might create a difficulty.

    (i) It could be taken to refer to the minority of Jews who were actual citizens, and the papyrus *B.G.U.* 1140 proves there were actually Jewish citizens, or, less probably, as some critics have it—

    (ii) it refers to the majority of the Jews in their capacity as members of a πολίτευμα, the new organization in Hellenistic times, with almost equal rights to those of the citizen body.

CHAPTER IV

THE GREEK CONTACT WITH THE JEWS—ANTI-SEMITISM

W E have seen Greek and non-Greek sharply contrasted in the 5th and early 4th centuries, first the attitude of the Greeks towards foreigners, 'barbaroi', and then the breaking down of this policy of exclusiveness owing to the conquests of Alexander, which brought inevitably in their train a policy of assimilation. Though there were periods of reaction and a return to the old feeling of racial superiority, though a Greek city like Alexandria might be disposed to cling to old privileges acquired by a conquering race, the mass of the population as a whole in the Egyptian Chora, Greeks and Egyptians tended to assimilate and unite.

It was different with the Jews. The antipathy between the Greeks and the Jews which we see developing at Alexandria, and which was by no means unknown in other parts of the Hellenistic world, had not always existed. The first aspect which the Jews presented to the Greeks did not repel, but interested them. An exceedingly odd people, unlike all other peoples, holding fast to their peculiarities, cherishing them and separating themselves deliberately and persistently from the general body of mankind—that was the first impression the Jews made on the Greeks when they learnt of their existence. It seemed to the Greeks—and not without some truth—that their founder Moses, 'a man of extraordinary sagacity and courage', had deliberately made their customs unlike those of other peoples in order to keep them a nation apart, and that this Jewish exclusiveness was the answer to the intolerance of the Egyptians who had driven them out of Egypt in the days of old.[1]

Aristotle's disciples, Clearchus and Theophrastus, were the first Greek writers—so far as we know—to speak of them, at a time when the peoples of Nearer Asia had only just come under Macedonian rule. A community of 'philosophers'[2] was the way the Greeks put it, when the little Jewish state established under its High Priests on the uplands of Palestine first came to their notice, for here was a real community with a mass of peculiar ordinances which seemed to constitute a system of life regulated by some novel system of law—such as the Greek philosophers were fond of describing in their

---

[1] Hecataeus ap. *Diodorus Siculus*, xl. 3.
[2] From Theophrastus' unknown works quoted by the Neo-platonic philosopher Porphyrius *c.* A.D. 275: ἅτε φιλόσοφοι τὸ γένος ὄντες. Cf. Joseph. *cont. Ap.* i. 167; Eusebius, *P.E.* ix. 2, 404A: cf. Joseph. *cont. Ap.* ii. 220 seq.; cf. Radin, *The Jews among the Greeks and Romans*, Philadelphia, 1915, pp. 92 ff.

imaginary republics. ' Throughout the entire time ', wrote Theophrastus, ' inasmuch as they are philosophers by race, they discuss
the nature of the Deity among themselves, and spend the night in
observing the stars, looking up at them and invoking them as divine
in their prayers '. The peculiar intimacy of their relation with the
Divinity and the worship in a Jewish synagogue had nothing to
correspond in the worship of a Greek temple—the nearest thing
seemed to the Greeks to be the talk in a philosophic school. Hecataeus of Abdera, a Greek historical writer contemporary with Theophrastus, described the community in Jerusalem—the symmetry
and punctual discipline, the young men trained, as at Sparta, to
courage and endurance.[1]

But Jewish peculiarities and exclusiveness, however curious and
interesting when viewed in their own homeland, were quite another
matter when closer contact was made with them in the cities of the
Jewish Dispersion all over the Mediterranean world ; for then the
exclusiveness and the assumption of religious superiority began to
mean trouble.

It became a frequent source of complaint among Greek townsmen
that they had fixed themselves in their midst expecting to be treated
as neighbours, but held themselves apart from all the social amenities
of their cities, shunned their festivals, and avoided the gymnasium
and theatre. Such exclusiveness and obstinate unsociability in a
particular set of people could not fail to create resentment and hatred,
since the possible excuse that all the festivities and amusements in a
Greek city involved some offering of homage to gods which were
foul idols could only have exacerbated the position. Greek antipathy, moreover, was no different from that of other peoples before
and after them who failed to understand the Jews.

The anti-Semitism of the Pagan world sprang simply from the
resentment felt by Greek city populations at a set of people who
refused to share in their social interests and amusements, and
political causes accentuated them.

While the Jews were unpopular with the average Greek, they
found protectors in the kings, and later in the Roman emperors.
The Greek city-states, with their desire for independence and their
political passion, were apt to be troublesome to the ruler in whose
sphere of power they were situated. The Jews, on the other hand,
were loyal upholders of the supreme power, and generally had little
interest in the political rights of the cities wherein they sojourned,
as long as they were left in peace to practise their religion and follow
their business. In every city there would be this element on the
side of the dynasty.

The Jews made good soldiers, and were not in those days what
they afterwards became when Christian Europe had shut so many
walks of life for them—people spoken of as addicted peculiarly to

[1] Hecataeus *ap. Diod. Sic.* xl. 3 ; cf. Joseph. *cont. Ap.* i. 183–204.

finance and usury,[1] with little aptitude or opportunity for agriculture and war. As we have already seen, Josephus at the end of the 1st century A.D. could write of the Jews of Palestine, ' We are not a commercial people ; we live in a country without a seaboard and have no inclination to trade.' [2]

In Egypt large numbers of them were enrolled in the Ptolemaic army, and many of them were apparently granted, as military colonists, plots of land which they might cultivate in the intervals of active service.

Julius Caesar and the early Roman Emperors followed the policy of the Hellenistic kings in patronizing and protecting the Jews, in insisting that Alexandria and other Greek cities should grant the Jews in their midst liberty to follow their religion and their customs unmolested.

Till the mutual goodwill subsisting between the Imperial Government and the Jews gave place, in the course of the 1st century A.D., to that bitter enmity which led to the destruction of the Jewish state in Palestine, it was only occasionally, in consequence of the eccentricity of particular rulers and of some special circumstances, that kings or emperors showed hostility to the Jews.   After the last flare-up of Jewish nationalism, in the rebellion of Bar Kochba (A.D. 132–5), had been suppressed in Palestine, anti-Semitism expressed itself mainly in heavy taxation, till the Empire became Christian.   Judaism then appeared as a wicked perversity of its daughter religion.   The old Paganism in matters of religion had been comparatively easy-going, whereas the anti-Semitism of the Christian Empire took the form not of pogroms, but of the subjection of the Jews to various disabilities ;   honourable careers, open to them under the Pagan emperors, were henceforth closed to them—the army, for instance.

It was perhaps in Alexandria that anti-Semitism had its beginning, but although things did not come to actual pogroms till Roman times, anti-Semitism in literature began as early as the reigns of the first Ptolemies.   The first Greek book we know of in which the Jews were held up to odium was written not by a Greek, but, significantly enough, by an Egyptian, Manetho,[3] who in the early 3rd century B.C. wrote, under the patronage of the Ptolemaic court, a history of his people for the Greek public.   He gave currency to the story that the Jews were sprung from a pack of lepers who were expelled from Egypt because of their foul diseases.   The enmity between Jews and Egyptians was of old standing—the Hebrew scriptures represented the Egyptians in no favourable light—and was more bitter than the enmity between the Jews and Greeks.[4]   About a hundred years later (when Antiochus Epiphanes was trying to sup-

---

[1] There is only one instance in papyri of an imputation of usury against the Jews (Wilcken, *Chrest.* 60, A.D. 41) and this dates from a time when anti-Semitic feeling was peculiarly intense.
[2] Joseph., *cont. Ap.* i. 60.
[3] Idem, ibid. ii. 73–105, 227 seq.
[4] Cf. the destruction of the Jewish Temple at Elephantine.

press the Jewish religion in Palestine) a Greek, Mnaseas,[1] wrote against the Jews, and it was perhaps he who first set afloat the popular belief that the Jews kept the image of an ass's head in the Temple. In the last century before the Christian era the principal Greek men of letters, Posidonius and Apollonius Molon, were anti-Semitic, but not the historian Timagenes, although he was an Alexandrine. Literary anti-Semitism went on after Egypt had passed under the Romans, represented especially by the vain pedant Apion, who is chiefly remembered because Josephus' short apologetic work in defence of his people against the malevolent charges of Alexandrian anti-Semites up to that time came to be called ' Against Apion '. In the 1st century of the Christian era anti-Semitism passed at Alexandria from literature into violent action. There was no active anti-Semitism—in spite of the battle of the books—till the Roman conquest, when political causes brought it into the foreground.

During the Ptolemaic period, when the Jews served in the army and some of them played a prominent part as generals [2] in the civil wars of the 2nd and 1st centuries B.C., there is no trace of ' anti-Semitism ' in a religious or racial sense. The community more than once suffered in these wars, but the causes were political, not racial or religious.[3] Yet even in this period, as we have seen, some resentment must have been felt against residents of Alexandria, who by their religion were debarred from sharing in the religious, and therefore in much of the civic life of the city. But active anti-Semitism there was none till the Roman conquest, when the lurking dissatisfaction was accentuated by political causes and led to open hostilities.

The record of Alexandria under the late Ptolemies must have shown Augustus when he took over the country that it was the most dangerous centre of disturbance in Lower Egypt. Hence a substantial force of troops was kept close at hand to overawe the populace —the Greek inhabitants lost their senate and, although various titular magistracies, such as the gymnasiarchy, were allowed to continue, their main function was to spend their money for the pleasure of their fellow-citizens and enjoy a decorative position : they had no common administrative powers. This blow at the privileges of the Greeks was much resented, especially as the Jews were confirmed in all the rights and privileges they had previously enjoyed, and which

---

[1] Joseph. *cont. Ap.* i. 216–7 ; ii. 112 seq.
[2] Both Ptolemy VI, and subsequently Cleopatra III, employed Jewish generals ; Abram appears as a member of a Graeco-Egyptian military association. In the civil war between Cleopatra III and her son Ptolemy Lathyrus the Jews supported her ; the beginning of tension in Alexandria between Jew and Greek for the Greeks favoured the victorious Lathyrus, but the tension, which was primarily political, only showed itself in words ; anti-Semitism accompanied by violence was unknown in Egypt before the Roman Empire.
[3] See III Macc. v. 2, 28–30, for a persecution attributed to Philopator ; Bevan, *A History of Egypt under the Ptolemaic Dynasty*, Methuen, London, 1927, p. 307, mentions a better attested persecution by Euergetes II. These persecutions arose from Egyptian politics purely and simply as the Jews took sides.

included, as has been noticed, the regulation of their own affairs through an ethnarch and a council of elders : [1] Clearly, Augustus had no intention of founding his rule in Egypt on the goodwill of the Hellenic elements of the population, who were now relegated to the new position of conquered, instead of conquerors, forming a ruling class.[2]

The anti-Semitism of this period is rightly connected with the anger of the Greeks at finding themselves deprived of their privileged position in Egypt, while there had been no derogation from the standing of the Jews. The Alexandrines who saw their city degraded from a royal capital to a subordinate position under Imperial Rome were constantly hostile to the Emperors,[3] but, not daring to attack the Romans directly, vented their spleen on the Jews, whom they regarded as favourites of the Romans. It must be remembered that at this time there was still a Jewish state in existence in Judea allied to and under the suzerainty of Rome [4]—a fact which lent an added prestige to the position of the Jews in Egypt and Alexandria, and which forms a contrast to the position of the Jews all over the world later on, who had no real independent homeland to which to look up to. Thus the Alexandrines tended to identify the Jews with the Roman cause, and in their constant opposition to the Government found attacks on the Jews a convenient, because safer, method of showing their hostility to Rome.

Bell, on the supposition that the Jews were not citizens of Alexandria (a matter which, as we have seen, has not been decisively settled), inclines to the belief that what added fuel to the flames, and was perhaps the culminating feature in this explosive atmosphere, was the fact that the Jews, encouraged by the favours they had received, aimed at yet further privileges. In particular, they desired the full Alexandrian citizenship,[5] and even to be admitted to the public games, though orthodox Jews, as we have seen, regarded the athletic exercises of the Greeks, in which the competitors appeared naked, with abhorrence.

The mutual hostility grew during the early part of the first century,

---

[1] Joseph. *Antiq.* xiv. 7, 2 ; xix. 5, 2 ; Philo, *Leg. ad Gaium*, 10.

[2] J. G. Milne, *A History of Egypt under Roman Rule*, Methuen, London, 1924, p. 4.

[3] Cf. Mommsen, *Röm. Gesch.*[4] v. 582 f.

[4] ' Several descendants of Herod the Great were brought up at Rome together with the Imperial princes, and formed part of the coterie of which the centre was Antonia, the widow of Drusus, grandmother of Caligula and mother of Claudius. Such were the two Agrippas, father and son, and Herod of Chalcis the elder brother of the elder Agrippa. The Jews therefore had powerful friends at Court.' Stuart Jones, in *J.R.S.* (16), 1926.

[5] Bell, *Jews and Christians in Egypt*, p. 11. He infers this not only from the claims made by Josephus and perhaps from Philo, *Leg.*, 28, 178 (M. 572): γραμματεῖον . . . κεφαλαιώδη τύπον περιέχον ὧν τε ἐπάθομεν καὶ ὧν τυχεῖν ἠξιοῦμεν; 183 : τὸ δὲ δὴ καὶ προνομίας οἴεσθαι τυγχάνειν; and from Claudius' words, lines 88–95, in the *London Papyrus* 1912 : viz. Claudius' letter to the Alexandrians : καὶ Ἰουδέοις ἀντικρυς κελεύωι μηδὲν πλήωι ὧν πρότερον ἔσχον περιεργάζεσθαι, . . . μηδὲ ἐπισπαίρειν, γυμνασιαρχικοῖς ἢ κοσμητικοῖς ἀγῶσει, καρπουμένους μὲν τὰ οἰκία ἀπολάοντας δὲ ἐν ἀλλοτρίᾳ πόλει περιουσίας ἀπάντων ἀγαθῶν.

but there is no evidence of anti-Jewish disturbances under Augustus or Tiberius. Probably the strong hand of these emperors kept the seething discontent in check. However, on the accession of Caligula the results of a weakening in the central control of the empire were soon manifested, and the old smouldering enmity between the Greeks and Jews blazed into a flame.

The acute phase of the Jewish question of Alexandria dates from the year A.D. 38 and, so far as it falls within the reign of Caligula, it is graphically described in two works of Philo : the *In Flaccum*— the Invective against Flaccus—and the *Legatio ad Gaium*—the Embassy to Gaius—which are apparently chapters taken from a comprehensive work dealing with the relations of the Jews with the Roman Government. There is also a much briefer narrative in Josephus,[1] on which we have to rely for the events which took place after Claudius' accession.

A valuable source of evidence, though secondary only for this subject, is the so-called *Acta Alexandrinorum*, propagandist pamphlets which, while directed ultimately against the Roman Government, frequently conceal this purpose under the guise of hostility to the Jews.

On his accession Gaius released Agrippa the Elder,[2] who had been a protégé of Antonia, and who, after a chequered career ending with imprisonment under Tiberius, now became king of certain districts bordering on Judea. On the way to his kingdom in the following year (A.D. 38) he touched at Alexandria, which he had last visited a dozen or more years earlier as a bankrupt exile. His arrival was the signal for an outbreak by the Alexandrines. The Jewish account of what followed, as related by Philo and Josephus, throws the whole blame on the Greeks ; but it may be noticed that the visits of Agrippa and of his son to Alexandria were always coincident with riots.[3] The Jews of Alexandria made Agrippa's arrival the occasion for a parade in his honour, and the Alexandrians followed suit by marching a well-known imbecile through the streets in the guise of a mock king, to parody his sudden elevation from bankruptcy to a throne. However, once the mimicry was over, the Greeks, feeling sure that Agrippa would lay the Jewish case before his friend the Emperor, found a justification for their actions by pleading that the Jews had disregarded the order of Caligula for the erection of statues of himself in all temples, and so entered the Jewish synagogues to carry out this order.

They even induced the prefect Avillius Flaccus to withdraw from the Jews their special privileges. A pogrom followed in due course which is historically significant in setting a precedent for all later pogroms.

The wealthy Jews were driven into the Delta quarter, 400 of their houses were sacked, and many Jews suffered outrage—even death.

---

[1] *Antiq.* xviii. 257–9.   [2] See M. P. Charlesworth, *Five Men*, for his life.
[3] J. G. Milne, *A History of Egypt under Roman Rule*, p. 17.

Flaccus, so far from protecting them, laid the blame on their shoulders, and had a number of their elders publicly scourged. He then caused the Jewish Quarter to be searched for arms but, according to Philo, found none. The attempts of the Jewish community to lay a complaint before the Emperor were suppressed by Flaccus, until Agrippa took up their cause. In the autumn of A.D. 38 Flaccus was arrested, brought to Rome for trial and condemned. A colourable pretext was probably found in the facts that he had not been able to keep the peace in his province and had exceeded his powers in depriving the Jews of their privileges.[1] His principal accusers were Isidorus and Lampon, two of the leading anti-Semites in the Alexandrian community, so his treatment of the Jews could not have been the main count in the indictment the charges of which are not precisely known.[2] It seems that Isidorus, finding he had gained less influence than he hoped by his anti-Semitism, had staged a demonstration against Flaccus in the Gymnasium, and it is likely that Agrippa exerted what influence he could on the Emperor's decision. The Roman governor thus proved himself unpopular with both sections. The successor of Flaccus, Vitrasius Pollio, allowed both Jews and Alexandrians to send embassies to Gaius to present their respective cases. The Alexandrian delegation had at its head Apion; the Jews were represented by Philo, who graphically describes his experiences with the insane Emperor in the famous Legatio. The Jews got no satisfaction,[3] and their synagogues remained closed till the accession of Claudius, Gaius dismissing them with the words with which Philo's narrative breaks off, 'After all, those who don't believe in my divinity are more foolish than wicked.'

On 24 January, A.D. 41, Caligula was murdered, and in the negotiations with the Pretorian guards which set Claudius on the throne an important part was played by Agrippa, who had come post-haste to Rome to implore Caligula not to set up his statue in the temple at Jerusalem.[4] He had his reward, for Claudius made him king of Judea and his elder brother king of Chalcis on Mount Lebanon. The brothers then went eastwards, but not until they had secured for their co-religionists the promulgation of the two edicts [5] given in Josephus and already discussed. The first of these, to repeat, concerns Alexandria alone, and confirms the privileges enjoyed by the Jews there resident, while laying the blame for the occurrence under Gaius at the door of the Alexandrians, while the second extends the same liberty of worship to the Jews throughout the empire. This, Claudius tells us, he issued at the request of his dear friends

---

[1] Milne, *A History of Egypt under Roman Rule*, p. 18, ' neither of these arguments would be likely to have any great weight with Caligula as the riots had arisen over the question of his own deification.'
[2] *J.R.S.* 16 (1926), p. 23. [3] Joseph. *Antiq., Iud.* xviii. 8, 1.
[4] Jos. *Antiq., Iud.* xviii. 297. Agrippa had actually persuaded him to give up his project, but Caligula was shortly after assassinated. Josephus is our chief source for the details of the assassination and for the intrigues of Agrippa. See Book XIX of the Antiquities.
[5] Jos. *Antiq., Iud.* xix. 278 ff., 286 ff.

Agrippa and Herod.   According to Josephus, the Jews of Alexandria,
who had ever since the failure of their petition to Caligula been preparing for an appeal to force, had been ' up in arms ' [1] on hearing of
Caligula's murder, and Claudius instructed his Viceroy to quell the
disturbance, while at the same time dispatching the edicts above-
mentioned.   For what follows we are dependent on other sources
than Josephus, who says no more on Alexandria.

Until the discoveries of papyri in Egypt began we were practically
dependent for our knowledge of Claudius' dealings with the Jews on
the notice of their expulsion from Rome in A.D. 49, contained in the
Acts of the Apostles, [2] and the mysterious allusion in Suetonius, [3]
' Iudaeos impulsore Chresto assidue tumultuantes Roma expulit '—
which is generally interpreted as the earliest reference to the relations
of Christianity with the Imperial Government, and on the above-
mentioned passages in Josephus, which show the influence wielded
by the two Agrippas, father and son, and Herod, the elder brother of
Agrippa I, at the Court of Claudius and exerted by them on behalf
of their co-religionists.

The recently discovered letter of Claudius to the Alexandrines,
the famous London Papyrus 1912, mentioned so often in connexion
with the ' citizenship ' at Alexandria, throws still more light on this
matter.   It seems that both the Greeks and Jews had sent embassies
to Claudius to congratulate him on his accession, while asking various
favours—the Greeks for the confirmation or renewal of their old
privileges and a request for a Senate which Claudius shelved by
referring it to a royal commission ;   the Jews for the confirmation of
their rights and for further privileges, the chief of which, according
to Bell, was the citizenship.   Both parties, needless to say, excused
their own part in the disturbances.   Claudius' letter is a reply to the
two parties.   Claudius says that after hearing both sides he had
confirmed the religious liberties of the Jews.   Several scholars hold
that this refers to the edicts given in Josephus, but those edicts were
issued at the request of Agrippa and Herod, and not as the result of
an enquiry into the charges and counter-charges of Jews and Alexandrians, which probably took place after the restoration of order in
Alexandria.   The Emperor, while accepting from the Alexandrians
most of the honours proffered him, except those of divinity, and con-
firming certain rights of citizenship, was not disposed to favour the
Greek party in the quarrel of nationalities, and delivered a severe
admonition to both sides to desist from the feud, which had almost
reached the proportions of a war.

His decisions, which are a model of impartiality, were as follows :—

The Alexandrians are to live in amity with the Jews who have
for so long dwelt in the same city with them, and are to concede

---

[1] Jos. *Antiq.*, *Iud.* xix. 278.
[2] Acts xviii. 2 : διὰ τὸ διατεταχέναι Κλαύδιον χωρίζεσθαι πάντας τοὺς Ἰουδαίους ἀπὸ
τῆς Ῥώμης.
[3] Suet. 25 (Claudius).

to them the liberty of worship granted by Augustus and now confirmed.

The Jews are expressly enjoined :

   (i) to be content with their existing privileges, and not to agitate for an extension thereof ;

  (ii) not to send two embassies in future, as though they lived in two cities—a thing never done in past times ;

 (iii) they are not to intrude themselves into the athletic contests organized by the gymnasiarchs and cosmetae (ἀγῶνες γυμνασιαρχικοὶ ἢ κοσμητικοί),[1] but are to rest content with the enjoyment of peace and plenty in a city not their own (ἐν ἀλλοτρίᾳ πόλει) ;

 (iv) they are not to bring in Jews from Syria or Egypt—a practice which arouses suspicion in the Emperor's mind.

If they disobey these orders, he will punish them as persons ' fomenting a general plague for the whole world '.

Several of the interesting and difficult problems raised by these sections of Claudius' letter—for example, the question of Jewish citizenship and the theory that the Jews sent two embassies—not one—have been referred to in the previous chapter. It remains to consider one other point.

Stuart Jones refers to S. Reinach's and Professor de Sanctis' theory that ' the general plague of the whole world ', which the Jews are accused of stirring up is to be explained by the internal strife aroused in the Jewish communities of the Dispersion by the spread of Christianity and its reactions, but rejects it on the ground that the reinforcements introduced by the Jews (from Syria and Egypt) were brought in for the purpose of renewing the struggle with the Alexandrians.

The letter of Claudius is not the only document which throws light on anti-Semitic agitation in Alexandria.[1] The name ' Acts of the Heathen Martyrs ' has been given to a series of papyri—mostly very fragmentary—which contain what purport to be reports of trials in the Emperor's court, sometimes ending in the condemnation of prominent Alexandrians. These trials took place in the reigns of Claudius, Trajan, Hadrian, and Commodus : the papyri which describe them were nearly all written or copied in the early part of the 3rd century (except a parallel and slightly different version of the trial before Trajan, which was written not much later than the date of that event), and the reports have evidently been composed with a view to literary effect, so that it is possible to regard them as fragments of a single work.

The tone of this work is violently anti-Semitic.

It seems that Claudius' message had no lasting effect, for a few years later two of the former leaders of the Alexandrian embassy

---

[1] Momigliano, pp. 35–100 (Claudius, *The Emperor and his Achievement*).

to Claudius brought an action against the younger Agrippa, now a
king of Chalcis, before a court consisting of the Emperor and about
twenty-four senators.   The report of the proceedings is too fragmentary [1] to show what was the nature of the charge, but it appears
that Claudius definitely professed his friendship for Agrippa, that the
arguments degenerated into personal recriminations [2] between the
Emperor on the one side and Isidorus and Lampon on the other,
and that the two envoys of the Alexandrians were condemned to
death.   The Greek party at Alexandria elevated them to the rank
of martyrs in the cause of their country against Rome.   Over a
hundred years later allusion was made to them by another Alexandrian
nationalist leader when on his trial before Commodus, and the record
of their deeds and sayings seem to have been still circulated in Egypt
in the following century.

In the year following this trial (probably A.D. 53) Claudius ate the
mushroom, ' after which he ate nothing else ', and the unsolved
problem of Jew and Gentile was left to his successor.   What opinion
then can be passed of Claudius' handling of the situation ?

Bell [3] says : ' The character of Claudius was a curious mixture,
and included traits which made him, alike to contemporaries and to
posterity, somewhat " a figure of fun ".   His intentions as Emperor
were unquestionably good and his reign showed none of those
aberrations or that progress towards megalomania which have made
the names of Caligula and Nero infamous.'   His decisions ' betray
no trace whatever of any weakness of intellect ', but are ' reasonable
and well grounded ; in regard to the senate in particular he shows a
statesmanlike caution, neither acceding to the request nor rebuffing
the petitioners by a definite refusal '.   ' On the question of the Jews
he holds the scales even between the two parties and preserves
throughout a perfectly judicial attitude.'   From this letter to the
Alexandrians one would never suspect that Claudius was weak-
minded, as his critics have tried to make out.[4]   In the letter he
speaks as a judge who has heard both sides of a case ably presented
and has come to a decision according to his lights.[5]

It remains to deal with some further outbreaks of anti-Semitism

---

[1] Preserved partly in *B.G.U.* 511 and P. Cair. 10448 = Wilcken, *Chrest* 14.

[2] Ibid. : Claudius says to Isidorus, ' You slew many of my friends.'   Isidorus
replies, ' I obeyed the commands of the late Emperor and I will do the same for
you.   Name whom you will and I will accuse him.'   Claudius : ' You certainly
are the child of a chorus-girl, Isidorus.'   Isidorus : ' I am not a slave or the child
of a chorus-girl, but gymnasiarch of the famous city of Alexandria.   As for you, you
are the cast-off bastard of the Jewish Salome. . . . '   So Lampon said to Isidorus :
' Well, what can we do but give way to an insane monarch ? '

[3] Bell, *Jews and Christians in Egypt*, p. 22.

[4] Cf. Tacitus, *Ann.* xii. 3 : ' cui non iudicium, non odium erat nisi indita et
iussa '.

[5] Cf. Seneca, 'Αποκολοκύντωσις, 12.

> ' Deflete virum, quo non alius
> potuit citius discere causas,
> una tantum parte audita
> saepe nec utra.'

but briefly, since a full discussion of them would be outside the scope of this work.

When revolt against Roman rule broke out in Judea all the available troops were sent thither from Egypt as quickly as possible, and to the regular garrison was left the task of keeping order in Alexandria : the old feud between Greeks and Jews naturally revived on this occasion. A quarrel arose at a meeting in the amphitheatre, which developed into a general fight. The prefect, Tiberius Alexander, himself a Jew by birth, tried in vain to repress the leaders of the Jews, and finally had to call up troops and turn them into the Jewish quarter of the city, which they plundered with the help of the mob. It is said that 50,000 Jews were killed before the military were withdrawn, and the ravages of the mob went on still longer.[1]

An attempt by some of the Sicarii, who had fled to Alexandria after the fall of Jerusalem, to raise a fresh revolt was prevented by the Jews themselves, and after this there was quiet for some forty years.

We hear of a further conflict in the reign of Trajan in the so-called Acts of Hermaiscus,[2] in which Alexandrian and Jewish embassies appear before Trajan : the Empress Plotina is represented as having privately espoused the cause of the Jews—' godless ' Jews (ἀνόσιοι Ἰουδαῖοι), as they are called by Hermaiscus, the Alexandrian, and having won over the Emperor and the Senatorial members of his consilium.

Later in the same reign Alexandria passed through a still more terrible experience. The revolt of the Jews in the Cyrenaica in 115 spread to Egypt, a large part of which was for a time held by the Jews. There were great barbarities on both sides, but the revolt was not finally crushed till after the accession of Hadrian. In the course of it the Jewish quarter was so devastated that the community never recovered its former importance.

The last outbreak of anti-Jewish feeling in the Roman period occurred early in Hadrian's reign ; our knowledge of it comes from yet another, fragmentary text of the Acta. After this the Jewish community, shorn of much of its importance, does not seem again to have suffered from the hatred of its Greek neighbours till after the establishment of Christianity as the predominant religion of the Empire. In the Christians hostility to the Jews was reinforced by religious fanaticism. The final catastrophe occurred during the prefecture of Orestes (A.D. 412–15), when the Patriarch Cyril stirred up the city mob to attack the Jews,[3] who were expelled *en masse*. They seem to have returned later, for there were certainly Jews in Alexandria when the Arabs occupied the city in A.D. 612.

---

[1] Joseph. *B.J.* ii. 18, 7–8 ; iii. 1. 3.   [2] *P. Oxy.* 1242.

[3] Significantly enough, a few years later another Christian mob led by a lector, and at least not reprimanded by the Patriarch, murdered Hypatia, the woman philosopher, leader of the pagan school of philosophy. These movements mark the end of Alexandria as a centre of thought and learning.

CHAPTER V

THE GREEK CONTACT WITH THE JEWS— HELLENISM

IN the relationship established in Egypt between Greeks and Jews, anti-Semitism shows us only one side of the picture. There was another, and perhaps a more important aspect of the relationship between these two gifted peoples that was destined to leave its mark on the Western world. Hellenization of the Jewish population as well as of the Egyptians took place, and if there was no fusion of races, as between Greek and Jew (for the reasons we have seen), as there was between Greek and Egyptian in the Chora, there certainly was on the one hand an assimilation of Greek culture by the Jews, especially in Alexandria, and on the other an assimilation, though later on, of several aspects of Jewish culture via the daughter religion, Christianity.

The first direct contact with Hellenism as a culture in opposition to their own found the Jews strongly opposed to it.

Alexander's conquest of the Persian empire meant the incorporation of the Jewish state of Judea within his own, yet he allowed it to be governed as it was before, by its High Priests in the form of a theocracy. On his death, however, Ptolemy I acquired Judea, and down to 198 B.C. the country remained under Egyptian suzerainty, but there was little interference with its form of government or religious ritual.[1] When Judea changed masters in 198 B.C., Hellenism began to gain ground among the Jews under the new suzerain, Syria. Egyptian rule and the neighbouring Hellenistic cities had accustomed the Jews to the Greek language and civilization, and elements of the governing classes were favourable to Hellenism, and were willing to adopt the outward forms of this dominant civilization.[2] These elements, however, still claimed to be good Jews. It was only when Antiochus IV [3] attempted to suppress the Jewish religion

---

[1] If we except the persecution of Ptolemy IV, Philopator (in 217 B.C.) as related in III Maccabees. Some critics deny the historical character of this work. Others hold the Ptolemy in question was Euergetes II, as Josephus says.

[2] Maccabees, Book i, 1, 10–37; Book ii. 4, 7–19. 'The Hellenizers were accused of neglecting circumcision and of exhibiting all the moral shortcomings commonly attributed in the Old Testament to backsliders; it comes as an anti-climax when in 169 B.C. the two definite charges made against them were that they favoured Greek athletic exercises (which involved nudity) and wore Greek hats.' Tarn in *Hellenistic Civilization*, p. 169.

[3] Cf. I Maccabees—i. 32–51. Apparently Antiochus had no objection to the Jews as a race—his attempts forcibly to suppress the Jewish religion can by no means be called anti-Semitism, and it was really a form of Hellenization. He attempted to make of his empire a united people in culture and religion, which could only be Greek. Tarn (*Hellenistic Civilization*, p. 707) and Bevan believe that by this means he wished to strengthen his empire against Rome.

in Palestine that a tremendous reaction ensued both against Hellenism and Jewish Hellenizers which ended in the foundation of an independent state under the priestly Hasmonaean Dynasty[1] for seventy-nine years (142–63 B.C.).

> ' In the clash [says Bevan] between Hellenism and Hebraism at Jerusalem, as the books of the Maccabees represent it to us, Hellenism appears as something purely evil—the embodiment of the world principle at enmity with God, a matter of sensuous idolatrous pomps, impious gaieties, pride of power.'[2]

But there were other elements in Hellenism of whose value strict Jews had probably no conception. Men who spoke only Aramaic could judge Hellenism only by its outside—the difference in language was enough to cut them off from any possibility of appreciating those riches of human thought and feeling embodied in Greek literature and the Greek intellectual tradition.

It was different with the Jews dispersed throughout the cities of the Greek world, for Greek had become their mother tongue.

In Egypt, where the Jewish element was stronger than in any other Mediterranean country outside Palestine and Syria (their number in Egypt in the 1st century A.D. is given as a million), most of the Jews had become quite unable to read or understand their scripture in the original Hebrew, hence as early as the reign of Ptolemy II (283–246 B.C.)[3] the Law was translated into Greek in order that its content might be kept in their memory. In the course of the next century or two the rest of the Old Testament was translated into Greek, and this, with the Pentateuch, came to form that version of the Jewish scriptures known as the Septuagint.

This was the first open adoption of Greek as a medium of expression for their own literature, and is interesting as the Bible both of Paul and Philo.

There still remained the intellectual and spiritual heritage of Greece itself. Anti-Semitism at Alexandria may give one the impression that Greeks and Jews in Egypt never mixed, but this would be far from true at Alexandria. The Jews, at least in Philo's time, were not confined to the Jewish quarter, as some lived scattered throughout the other quarters, nor was that quarter itself exclusively peopled by Jews.[4]

The Jews had their own quarter, but that this was a ghetto is an interpretation which is far from true. Compulsory race-segregation for any length of time, both in theory and in fact, was a thing quite unknown in the Graeco-Roman world, and was an invention of the Middle Ages.

---

[1] Cf. Maccabees, Books i. and ii. [2] *Legacy of Israel*, Oxford, 1928, p. 39.
[3] Josephus, *cont. Ap*. ii. 45–7, represents the translation as being due to the second Ptolemy's ' keen desire to know our laws and to read the books of our sacred scriptures '. Cf. the more detailed account in *Antiq*. xii. 2. 1 seq.
[4] This may be inferred from Philo, in *Fl.*, 8, 55 (M. 525) : τούτων (i.e. the μοῖραι τῆς πόλεως) δύο Ἰουδαικαὶ λέγονται διὰ τὸ πλείστους Ἰουδαίους ἐν ταύταις κατοικεῖν.

At Alexandria were present two aspects of Hellenism—the part which consisted in idolatrous pomps and impious gaieties which had so enraged the strict Jews of Palestine in the time of Antiochus and had accentuated their desire to keep themselves a race apart, and the intellectual and spiritual sphere of Greece, for Alexandria was the city of the Museum, the greatest university of the Greek world for literature and science, royally endowed, the city with the world's largest library.

The fact that they were in a country which spoke Greek, read Greek, and wrote Greek, was penetrated by Greek culture and ideals, obliged many Jews in Egypt or elsewhere in the Greek East, whether there were orthodox elements among them or Hellenizers, to yield to the Greek influence. It seems that the Dispersion was much more open to Hellenistic influences than the Jewish homeland, where the strict Jews could control the situation. The Dispersion inevitably had a tendency to universalism, and was not averse to spreading the Jewish religion throughout the Hellenistic world, its propaganda thus preparing the way for Christianity.

Many Jews everywhere began to speak Greek and take Greek names. What made this easier was the fact that many of them had forgotten Hebrew and spoke Aramaic, the *lingua franca* of the East, which was now being replaced by Greek. Even the services in many synagogues were conducted in Greek, and, with Greek speech, naturally came Greek customs.

As regards the first aspect of Hellenism already mentioned we find that some Jews (but not the majority, who kept to the orthodox religion in spite of their outward assimilation to Greek language and everyday customs) went far beyond the imitation of Greek forms, and adopted Graeco-Oriental cults. But this was characteristic of Asia Minor and Syria.[1] In Egypt the synagogue at Athribis [2] was dedicated to Hypsistos by the local Jews, jointly with the prefect of police on behalf of Ptolemy V and his queen. In this case, and in those of the Judaeo-Pagan cults, the Jewish devotees may have believed they were still worshipping the god of their fathers, but under another name. The Jews could mean one thing by the term Hypsistos, and their pagan associates another.

These Jews seem to have been influenced by Hellenistic syncretism —the belief that different peoples really worshipped the same god under different names—and that names and cults could therefore be united.[3]

---

[1] A Jewish synagogue in Mysia worshipped Zeus Hypsistos. Cf. E. Zeller, *Outlines of the History of Greek Philosophy* (Eng. trans.), Kegan Paul, etc., London, 1931, p. 257. ' We find many traces of mutual influence. On the Greek side religious monstrosities such as the cult of " the Highest " or " the Lord " ($\H{v}\psi\iota\sigma\tau\sigma s$, $\kappa\acute{v}\rho\iota\sigma s$) in Asia Minor in which the Phrygian Sabazius and the Jewish " Lord Zebaoth " conflicted, while to many Greeks the Jewish religion with its image-free worship of God appeared as a religion of philosophic enlightenment ' (cf. e.g. Strabo, xvi. 35 ff.).

[2] *O.G.I.*, No. 96 ; cf. No. 101.

[3] We have seen this process already in being centuries earlier at Elephantine.

The majority of Jews, however, adopted only the outward forms of the dominant civilization.   The ideals of the Jew were not those of the Greek.   Though both desired political freedom, to the Greek it meant expression in a free self-governing community worshipping whatever gods it pleased ; to the Jew it meant complete freedom to worship a God beside whom there could be no other object of worship.   Yet Judaism, while its ideals conflicted with those of Hellenism, by no means closed its doors altogether to the second and nobler aspect of Hellenism—Greek thought.

Some Jews, if not the majority—the choice few, and it is the choice few who have moulded the thought of generations—began to take an interest in the utterances of Plato,[1] of Greek Stoic philosophy,[2] of the best of Greek literature and thought.   Plato, with his deep passion for justice and temperance, in his faith that behind the world movement there was a Power which cared for good, and the Greek Stoic, whose philosophy really governed his life, struck a kindred chord in the mind of the educated Jew.   Yet here was something, too, which, though far from as objectionable as the idolatrous cult to the orthodox, struck a dissonant note.

' We today [says Bevan] whether we are Jews or Christians, may regard the Hellenistic Jews of 2000 years ago as bearing the first brunt in a conflict in which we too are engaged.   For their problem is still in a way our problem.   In the civilization of the European peoples the Hebrew and Greek traditions have entered into combination, but their mutual adjustment still raises questions on which men are not agreed.   Both in the Jewish community and in the Christian community today there is an opposition between Traditionalist and Modernist, Orthodox and Liberal which really springs from the same old difficulty, how to harmonize the claims of the God of Israel with the claims of intellectual culture—an opposition, which exists not only between man and man, but often within the individual himself.' [3]

It was plain to an Alexandrine Jew that certain things in the Greek tradition he must firmly repel—the worship of the popular gods, or the practice of exposing infants,[4] or perversion of the sexual instinct.[5] Some of the Rabbis even condemned all attendance at a Greek theatre—it was the ' seat of the scorners '.[6] Yet Philo apparently went to see performances of the great Greek dramas.   Thus the line dividing Greek and Jewish society must in several respects have been very vague.

It was a problem how much one might admit of Hellenism and how

---

[1] Cf. Joseph. *cont. Ap.* ii. 220 seq., 255 seq.   [2] Cf. Joseph. ibid., 168 seq.
[3] *Legacy of Israel*, Oxford, 1928, p. 42.
[4] 'Εὰν ᾖ(ν) ἄρσενον, ἄφες, ἐὰν ᾖ(ν) θήλεα ἔκβαλε.   *Pap. Oxyrh.* iv. 744.
[5] Cf. Philo, *De Specialibus Legibus*, iii. 7 (305–6).
[6] Psalm i. 1. Rabbi Meir in *Yerushalmi Sanhedrin* 20c. applied to them the verse of the Psalmist, Psalm xxvi. 5.

much to retain of the Hebrew tradition. The difficulty to-day largely comes as a conflict between religion and science, but in those days it was the aesthetic,[1] rather than the scientific element in Greek culture which made the difficulty, for our modern civilization is scientific to a far greater degree than Hellenism. Many of the ritual and ceremonial practices of the Jews—e.g., circumcision, the dietary laws—seemed to the Greek view uncouth and barbarous. The line the Hellenistic Jews took to defend their peculiar practices was that they were figurative, and so useful as symbols, but it was not a line that appealed to the intellectual and philosophical among themselves or the Greeks, though it might appeal to the orthodox, the worshipper of tradition, and the unqestioning.

The problem of finding the right line was a difficult one for the Hellenistic Jews. In the sphere of religious thought, Philo's writings show us the most elaborate attempts at a synthesis which had a marked influence on Christian thought. Though much of his writing is taken from Plato or the Stoics, he is not a philosopher in the true sense of the word, but a religious preacher who uses philosophical terms and ideas for a homiletic purpose.

> ' The Jewish Greek philosophy as represented by Philo and his predecessors [says Zeller] exhibits a thorough-going eclecticism combined with a religious syncretism and a transition to mysticism [2] . . . this system is in reality a combination of Greek philosophy with Jewish theology, the scientific parts of which are derived predominantly from the former.' [3]

Like Plato, Philo gives a pre-eminent place in religion to the mystical experience—in this respect he is Greek, not Hebrew—for the mystical element in the Bible is slight, and Philo's language is clearly suggested by Plato's in the *Symposium* and *Phaedrus*. Yet his interest is not, like Plato's, to get a rational explanation of the universe.

> ' His attitude to God with which he rose to the mystical experience was essentially Hebrew and not Greek, but the God whom he desired to come into contact with was the God of Israel.' [4]

Philo had the Greek psychology ready to hand, and he could use it to frame rules for the systematic training of the soul to receive the vision of God. In Christianity we can trace the heritages of Judea and Greece as they were first combined by Philo—in instructions for the conduct and development of the spiritual life throughout the centuries. Further Greek influence is seen in his belief in a general way—in the way the Stoics believed—that the course of the world

---

[1] Cf. Plato, *Rep.* x.
[2] E. Zeller, *Outlines of the History of Greek Philosophy* (Eng. trans.), Kegan Paul, etc., London, 1931, p. 257.
[3] Ibid. p. 260.   [4] *Legacy of Israel*, Oxford, 1928, p. 48.

is governed by God's providence, as contrasted with the traditional Hebrew conception of a particular world-plan embodied in a Divine community. Thus any man of any nation ' who sees God ', who attains to the beatific vision, is to be taken as belonging to Israel. Philo insists it is not a question of race, and no Jew has ever spoken more warmly about the welcome to be given to proselytes. His large kindliness, embracing all the world, sets in strange relief the ' hatred of the human race ', moroseness, and gloom which were the charges commonly brought against the Jews in those days.

The two things which mainly make Philo's religion appear fantastic to us are his far-fetched method of allegorical interpretation applied to Scripture,[1] and his theories of intermediate beings between God and the world, especially the Logos.[2]

Here, too, we perceive unmistakable Greek influence, though among the Hebrews allegories and parables—for instance, those of the Prophets, e.g., Ezekiel, and the Song of Songs—were not unknown. Among the Greeks oracular utterances were commonly couched in figures and allegories—e.g., The Delphic Oracle—and to Philo the scriptures, as he read them in the Greek of the Septuagint, were an oracular utterance, with characteristics which the Greek habitually attributed to oracles. Since Alexandrine Jewish circles drew so largely from Greek philosophy, Greek suggestion may have counted for something in the application of the allegorical method to the Pentateuch. Yet Philo's method was not quite that of the Greeks. Intellectual Greeks generally tried to give an explanation of their myths as allegories, as symbols for physical processes—e.g., Poseidon was a symbol of water, Hephaistos of fire, etc. Philo, on the other hand, takes the Scriptural allegories as symbols of the inner life of the soul, of faculties, and virtues and vices, of God and the abiding powers of God, the Logos, Wisdom.

It seems possible that Philo derived his strange theory of inter-mediate beings between God and the world, especially the Logos, from Heraclitus, Plato, and the Stoics, though other suggestions have been made as to its origin. It is indeed strange to find it in the Hebrew monotheism of Philo. ' God cannot come into direct contact himself with the material world ' has been interpreted in this way : one cannot find God in the world, but only in the mystical elevation apart from the world. In the ordinary world there is an inferior revelation of God—the power and goodness there revealed are only a shadow of Him : this is what Philo means by the Logos—as compared with the Reality known directly in the moment of mystical contact. Philo's doctrine here seems strongly reminiscent of Plato's Theory of Ideas, and it will be noticed that his Logos is far removed from the Logos of Christian theology.[3]

---

[1] E.g. Philo, *Legum Allegoria* (*Allegorical Interpretation of Genesis*, ii. 111).
[2] E.g. Philo, *De Confusione Linguarum*, and *Quis Rerum Divinarum Heres*.
[3] C. A. F. Knight, *Nile and Jordan*, James Clarke & Co., London, 1921, p. 493 in chapter, ' The First Christian Century '.

K

Besides Philo, only two Jewish writers of the Graeco-Roman age have made a contribution of intrinsic value to world literature by works composed in Greek : the author of the Wisdom of Solomon, and the historian Josephus. Small original value is attached to the number of translations of Hebrew or Aramaic books which, however, have a considerable interest because the originals are lost—the First Book of Maccabees, the Psalms of Solomon, Judith, Tobit, the Fourth Book of Ezra (Ecclesiastes), etc. Even the Septuagint— the Bible of the early Christian Church—has no claim to be, as a Greek work, a great addition to Greek literature, in the way the English Bible was to English literature. Yet all these works have an importance of their own.

In the transmission of all that the Graeco-Roman world took over of the Hebrew tradition—the fundamental ideas and standards of value, the great body of religious literature—the part played by Hellenistic Judaism was of capital importance.

It was Hellenistic Judaism, and Alexandria was an important part of it, that did more eventually to break down the barriers between race and race than the conquest of an Alexander or the Empire of Rome.

The contact between Hellenism and Hebraism is of supreme importance as paving the way for the fusion of races from the spiritual point of view, as the first realization in the ancient world before the coming of Christianity that a synthesis of Greek and Hebrew cultures was at all possible. When the first Christian missionaries, themselves Hellenistic Jews, went out to preach, they found every-where in the cities of Asia Minor and Greece to which they came a body of Gentile proselytes, or semi-proselytes, attached more or less closely to the Jewish synagogues, so successful had Jewish propaganda hitherto been in the Hellenistic Age. Probably those forms of Hellenistic Judaism which disparaged the external observances and ritual ordinances had especially drawn proselytes. Moreover, the process which Josephus claims the second Ptolemy, Philadelphus, had begun ' in his keen desire to know our laws and to read the books of our sacred scriptures ',[1] had been responsible for spreading a better knowledge of Jewish culture and ideals in the Hellenistic world than the semi-prejudiced ideas about them that had been extant before. The Christian Church inherited the great problem of Hellenistic Judaism : how to find the right relation between Hebraic religion and Greek philosophy and culture. Dean Inge in a remarkable essay [2] traces back to Greece the religion and political philosophy of the Christian Church, and the Christian type of mysticism to Plato, and so to Greece. Hellenism, he asserts, is not the mind of a par-ticular ethnic type nor of a particular period. We are again reminded of the words of Isocrates :

---

[1] Joseph., cont. Ap. ii. 45. Loeb trans. : ἐπιθυμητὴς ἐγένετο τοῦ γνῶναι τοὺς ἡμετέρους νόμους καὶ ταῖς τῶν ἱερῶν γραφῶν βίβλοις ἐντυχεῖν.
[2] Legacy of Greece, Oxford, 1928, pp. 25–56.

' She (Athens) has brought it about that the name " Hellenes "
suggests no longer a race but a mental outlook, and that the
title " Hellenes " is applied rather to those who share our
culture than to those who share a common blood.' [1]

Hellenism was not destroyed, as some believe,[2] when comparing
the Hellenistic Age with the Great Age of the 5th century.

' Its philosophy was continuous from Thales to Proclus and
even further . . . its religion passed into Christian theology
and culture without any real break. The early church spoke in
Greek and thought in Greek.' [3]

Both the Stoic ethics and the Platonic metaphysics were taken
over by the Christian Church, which had as its essential kernel the
Gospels. This side of Christianity probably owed more to Hellen-
ized Judaism, which showed it the way, than is generally supposed.
The works of Philo exercised a great influence on the Christian
Church long after the Jewish community had forgotten them, for
Hellenistic Judaism had only been a passing phase in the history of
Judaism.

The exclusiveness which made the Jews a race apart, and which
was partly due to their strict religious tenets, prevailed. The
destruction of the Temple and the persecution forced them to close
their ranks, and the broader, wider, and less exclusive ideas of a
Philo of the Hellenistic Dispersion were given up. The Palestinian
Judaism which had Hebrew or Aramaic for its medium had no use
for the books written in Greek by the Hellenistic Jews. They were
preserved only by the Christian Church, which reaped the benefit
of Jewish Hellenism and became a world religion, advancing in the
steps of its predecessor, and opening its doors wider and wider to
receive the culture not only of Judea, but of Greece, in a synthesis
to embrace all mankind.

It is interesting to note that the anti-Semites of the 1st century
used to make it a reproach to the Jews that the Greek writers made
no mention of them, which proved that they were a mushroom
people.

Josephus, in refuting the attack, explains the absence of communi-
cation with Hellas, in the period that preceded Alexander's conquests,
by the self-contained character of the land.[4]

The isolated nature of Judea, whose inhabitants were essentially

---

[1] Isoc. *Panegyricus*, p. 50.
[2] Bentwich, in *Hellenism*, Jewish Publication Society of America, 1920, pp. 12–
13, remarks on the tendency to contrast the broad universalism of Hellenistic
Judaism with the narrow legalism of the Pharisees which eventually prevailed in
Palestine—a tendency he disapproves of. ' The fusion ', he says, ' at which the
universalists were aiming was not with the clear Hellenic reason, but with a lower
amalgam of Greek and oriental ideas which tended to debase Jewish monotheism.'
He would speak rather of Hellenisticism than Hellenism as the source of these
ideas.
[3] *Legacy of Greece*, Oxford, 1928, p. 27.   [4] Joseph., *cont. Ap.* i. 12.

engaged in agriculture and devoted to their own traditions, does much, in his opinion, to explain the national exclusiveness developed by the Jews in the ancient world. Again, he points out in his refutation of Apion, who charged the Jews with aloofness, that the Greek city-states in their prime were equally aloof, and that their culture was exclusively national. Plato ordained for his ideal Republic that it should not admit foreigners to intermix with its population, but should keep itself pure, and consist only of such as persevered in their own laws. And this was the standpoint of the Hellenes of the Classical Age, who regarded all foreigners as ' barbarians '.

Yet, whereas in the days of Greek freedom to be a Greek had meant to be a citizen of a Greek canton, after Alexander it meant to have Greek culture. Alexander in his empire sought to bring about a great fusion of ideas which, by a combination of racial excellences and national cultures in some larger expression of political life than the Greek city-state, should advance the work of humanity and give expansion to the Hellenic spirit. Hellenism was to be dominant, but it was to be brought into contact with Oriental systems. The fusion of cultures was prepared by the physical intermingling of the various elements, who were to build up together the new civilization. In the cosmopolitanism which ensued it was the Jews alone who refused to indulge in the free trade in ideas when national barriers were everywhere down and the old period of exclusiveness among the nations had ended. It was the refusal of the orthodox Jew generally to participate in this internationalism that aroused resentment. It was not really a question of religion—although, as we have seen, both the Jewish religion and the isolated geographic position of Judea tended to breed this exclusiveness.

To-day, on the other hand, what tends to arouse resentment is the opposite—the very fact that the Jews have become an international people among strongly national and exclusive states. Indeed, in this respect the parallel which some authorities find between the Jewish circumstances of the present day and those which existed in the Hellenistic period is not correct : it is true only in so far as the Jews of the Hellenistic Age, at Alexandria especially, tended to assimilate Greek culture, and though this process had its effect on the development of Christianity, it was a mere flash in the pan as far as orthodox Jewry was concerned.

PART III

CHAPTER I

THE ROMAN ATTITUDE TO RACE—THE REPUBLIC

WE have seen the two contrasting attitudes of mind prevailing in the Greek world : the race-exclusiveness of the Greek city-states before Alexander and the idea of Alexander which aimed at a unity of mankind.   How far the latter affected the subsequent history of the Ancient World in one particular corner of it has already been discussed.   Since Rome had relations with Egypt from the time of the Ptolemies, and later substituted her rule for theirs, thus bringing new political ideas to bear upon Greek and Egyptian alike in Egypt, the Roman attitude to race-relations needs some consideration : moreover, Rome was in a sense the heir to Alexander. Greece herself, through Alexander, had come very near to the attainment of the ideal of the unity of mankind.

In both Philip and Alexander the desire for empire was combined with the conviction that such an empire must be founded on a basis of Greek civilization.   Yet Alexander advanced a long way beyond his father in his idea of Hellenizing the world by means of cities and communications and in regarding Hellenic civilization as the only existing cement capable of holding together the structure of a universal empire.   If it had been possible for Alexander or his successors to realize such an empire, the πόλις would have sunk into the position of a municipal town.   Yet, even though each state might have lost those conditions of life that had nurtured all that was most brilliant in the Greek character, the gain would have outweighed the loss—racial exclusiveness, for instance, would have stood a good chance of disappearing.   Even as it was, the Greeks left the mark of their genius in the lands to which Alexander had brought them. Nevertheless, the idea of a political system embracing all mankind perished for the time being with Alexander ; and it was left to Rome to reinstate it—but along different lines.

Unlike the Greeks, Rome had a successful political idea inherent in her own institutions with which eventually to unite the peoples of the ancient world in a wider and more comprehensive manner than was possible with Alexander.

In the one case the idea depended on the genius of one man, and the ability of his successors for fulfilment ; in the other on the political genius and character of a whole people.   The evolution, progress, and development of this idea can be traced in its successive phases. The apparently sharp break which exists between the race-exclusiveness of the old Greek city-states and Alexander finds no parallel in the development of Rome's attitude to other peoples.

' The Greeks lived in mountain-walled valleys or on islands, the Phoenicians on peninsulas, but the Romans in Latio—on a plain.' [1]

It was the geographic character of Latium that made it impossible for a state to develop internally and remain isolated in the fashion of the Greek city-states. The necessity for an understanding with other states in the same region became inevitable. The Seven Hills of Rome offered little protection to the dwellers in the fields and villages of the extensive Roman territory, once Rome became a great territorial state. In Macedonia an almost parallel evolution to that of Rome took place : the territorial state, with its less rigid attitude to other peoples and its unlimited capacity for the incorporation of other elements, forms a strong contrast to the isolation and exclusiveness of the city-states. How far the fact that Macedon was a territorial state with a more open outlook than, say, Athens, or Sparta, influenced Alexander is hard to say. [2] The important fact, however, in the case of Rome, is that, for a city which had originally been a small city-state, development along the lines of the Greek city-state, once the city grew, was impossible.

Different geographical conditions, as has been indicated, may have been the reason for the great and important difference early on between Greek and Roman mentality, politically. Yet the conception of a citizenship wider than any territorial or ancestral unity which Rome was destined to reach, though it might be ascribed to many motives, presupposes, according to Momigliano, [3] ' an original ethical inspiration—the *intelligible arcanum* of every spiritual achievement '. Apart from this, the origin and development of the Roman tribes, the distinction between patricians and plebeians, the part played by the Etruscans in the shaping of the Roman state, the development of clientship, the passage from the tribal to the civic organization, and the religious bond of the Roman ' civitas ' must have fundamentally affected the development of this conception. It is noteworthy that the Romans regarded themselves as having a complex [4] origin—a sentiment which permanently accompanied the

---

[1] A. N. Sherwin-White, *The Roman Citizenship*, Oxford, 1939, p. 6.

[2] Cf. Hogarth, *Philip and Alexander*, John Murray, 1897, pp. 2, 3, 50. Philip was the creator of Macedonian political unity, and even had the conception by 358 of the unification of all Hellas. ' Twelve years later again his son, rising to a conception of world-wide empire on the stepping stone of his father's pan-Hellenic kingdom, dreamed of effacing the distinction of Macedonian, Hellene, and Asiatic.' Yet the invention of a professional, national army—the new thing in Greek history—though it made the Macedonians—who, like the Romans, were of mixed origin—one people, was, as we have noticed, one of the chief barriers in Alexander's way when he dreamed of a wider union. On the other hand, in Rome's case the army was one of the avenues to citizenship for non-Romans.

[3] *J.R.S.* xxx. (1941) 160 ; cf. *C.A.H.* xi. 435.

[4] The tradition of the mixed origin of the Roman tribes is very ancient. Cf. Ennius *ap. Varro, De Lingua Latina*, v. 55 ; cf. Cary, *A History of Rome*, Macmillan, London, 1935, pp. 38, 39 : ' The derivation of Rome from Alba Longa and the tale of an intermarriage with Sabines from the Quirinal reflect, however hazily, the

evolution of Roman citizenship—while the Greeks took the opposite way. Citizenship, moreover, in the Greek polis, required much more detailed participation in public life than did Rome. The failure of Athens to build an empire must have had some connexion with the refinements of Athenian democracy : the principle of elasticity [1] —of varying degrees or steps to citizenship—was absent in Greece. It was this potent factor that made the Roman Empire a success, so that citizenship could be granted eventually to all when they were ready for it.

The various stages by means of which Rome developed a citizenship capable of embracing the whole world may, in a sense, seem outside the scope of this work. Yet to understand more fully the attitude of Rome to Greek, Egyptian, and Jew, about which something has been said in the previous chapters, some treatment of the origins of Roman policy which attained its complete fulfilment in the Roman Empire is necessary.

In the progress of Rome from a small city-state in Latium to virtual leader of the League of Latin towns, and to the conversion of the members of the League to subject allies and then to Roman citizens,[2] we see at work, as if from the very beginning almost, a process that, with comparatively unimportant variations, was to typify Rome's relations with other peoples.

At first the incorporation of the Latins only, without any intermediate stage, was rendered possible by the juridical and social situation ; for, of all peoples in Italy, they were the most akin culturally and politically to the Romans. Later, however, Rome changed her policy and began to incorporate non-Latins, after a probationary period, during which these peoples were brought under the influence of Romano-Latin discipline and culture. This change was most significant for the future history of Rome's attitude to peoples, both in Italy and outside it, who were in no way related to her, as the Latins had been racially, but were to become so, in the end, culturally and politically.

---

fact that it was essentially a Latin city with an admixture of central Apennine folk.' As regards the Etruscans, Rome never contained a considerable Etruscan population, but the Etruscans may have ruled, and certainly did influence its development for a time (ibid. p. 60). Cf. Haarhoff, *The Stranger at the Gate*, Longmans, 1938, pp. 155 seq.

[1] Cf. Haarhoff, *The Stranger at the Gate*, Macmillan, London, 1938, p. 122. The use of the federal principle in Italy and the gradual extension of the franchise are proofs of the Roman principle of elasticity.

[2] At the close of the 6th century we find Rome's relations with her Latin neighbours taking two main forms—specific agreements with particular communities and general treaties involving the Latins as a whole, and the admission of Rome to possibly the leading place in the Latin League. The Cassian treaty of 493 B.C. established a relationship between her and the Latin states on free and equal terms. A significant change, however, came about a century and a half later. By 338 B.C. the various Latin towns no longer formed a federation, but each was bound to Rome by a separate treaty, while preserving its own local administration. The next step was the incorporation of several of these states in the Roman state. The Latini became citizens either by ' deditio in arbitrium dicionemque populi Romani ', or more completely by 'expugnatio '. Cf. Livy, 26, 33 13.

' It was a new thing in statesmanship [says Haarhoff] [1] when after the Latin War, the Romans gave their defeated enemies a place in the state on equal terms with themselves. In contemporary Greece—and the victory of Philip at Chaeronea, which symbolized a new order of affairs in Hellas, falls, curiously, in the same year 338 B.C. as the defeat of the Latins and the beginning of the new order in Italy—such an act had never been heard of.'

It meant that the Latins and Italians were confronted with something elastic, a scheme by which their privileges might be extended. Outside those Latin towns that were early on incorporated into the Roman citizenship, Rome utilized the ' civitas sine suffragio ' or limited franchise for the urbanized areas of Italy. This status was granted to various towns [2] for services to the Roman state, and the term ' municipium ', so applied to the states possessing this status, contained both the element of partial incorporation in, and the apparently contradictory idea of alliance with, the Roman state.[3]

Complete citizenship could only be obtained by transference to Rome, but the acceptance of this status did not destroy the separate existence of the state concerned. Owing to the way in which ' civitas sine suffragio ' developed—with the gradual incorporation of the ' municipes ' into the Roman state as ' cives '—the Romans were able to conceive of the revolutionary idea that citizenship was not entirely incompatible with membership of another secondary community.

The ' municipes ' performed their ' munera ' for Rome, and also performed the ' munera ' and enjoyed the ' honores ' of their local ' respublica '. It is in this new idea that the reason lies for Rome's success and Greece's failure to solve the problem of an imperial citizenship.[4] The developed form of the ' civitas sine suffragio '

---

[1] Haarhoff, *The Stranger at the Gate*, Macmillan, London, 1938, p. 138.
[2] E.g. Cumae and Suessula, in *Campania and Fundi and Formiae*.
[3] Sherwin-White, *The Roman Citizenship*, Oxford, 1941, p. 40. The contracting parties possessed a community of social rights especially of ' connubium ', and a member of either could acquire the complete franchise of the other state by transference of domicile.
[4] Sherwin-White, *The Roman Citizenship*, Oxford, 1941, pp. 67 seq. It seems that Rome did not seek to abolish the local life of her new boroughs, ' the municipia ', though certain changes in the competence of municipal magistrates became necessary. Rome entered in this period on the road that led to the municipal system of the Empire, for the history of the ' civitas sine suffragio ' is closely related to that of the ' municipium civium Romanorum '. The special characteristics of the later Roman citizenship as a dual citizenship are due to the fact that Rome in the historic period did not obliterate the local traditions of those fully developed city-states which ' came into the Roman state '. A compromise was effected. In a sense the ' colonia civium Romanorum ' formed a contrast to the ' municipia '. These had no true ' respublica ': hence the ' coloni ' did not cease to be true Roman citizens. Later, however, came an important tendency to assimilate the ' coloniae ' to the ' municipia ' with a Romanized type of constitution and magistrates.

came to be regarded as a half-way stage in the incorporation of non-Latin peoples in the Roman state.[1]

Another and more significant method by means of which Rome was to extend her influence still further was the institution of ' Latin rights '.

At the close of the Republic and under the early Empire ' Latin rights ' played an important role.   This institution was due to the settlement with those Latin states (' prisci Latini ') which in 338 had not been directly incorporated in the Roman state and included the ' coloniae Latinae ' of almost similar status.   The ' nomen Latinum ' became an instrument of Romanization without the implication of any idea of race or nationality, owing to the nature of the tie established between Rome and the remaining unincorporated Latin peoples.[2]

The separation of the geographic and political meanings of the term ' Latium ' took place when ' Latin ' colonies were planted all over Italy, and the development of the ' ius Latii ' into a juristic concept was fairly rapid.   It was the first political institution of the Roman state to be transplanted beyond the confines of Italy, and was most suitable because of the lack of any territorial connexion in the term, such as bound the community of ' cives Romani ' to a specific area of Roman territory.

Latin rights implied, however, a close bond between Latin or Roman citizens.   ' Latini ' had the ' commercium ', the ' connubium ' with Roman citizens, and the peculiar right of ' migratio ' to Rome which meant the acquisition of full citizenship there.[3] Thus Latin rights meant a specially privileged status second only to the Roman citizenship, and the Ius Latii eventually became one of the favourite methods for the gradual elevation of provincial communities to a parity with Rome herself, as happened in the case of Spain and Gaul.

Besides ' Cives ' and ' Latini ' stood the ' Socii ' proper, or ' foederati ', who were true ' foreigners ' racially and geographically.   The chief instrument in the formation of a federation of allies was the specially Roman institution of the ' foedus iniquum '.[4]   The ' socius ' was a member of a city-state of a tribal unit which had

---

[1] Cf. Velleius i. 14, 7.   The Sabines were the first ' municipes ' to be elevated to the status of full citizens (238 B.C.) by the grant of the ' ius suffragii ' and enrolment in a tribe within a generation of the original grant of ' civitas sine suffragio ' in 290 B.C.

[2] These states were ' free on certain terms ', such as the surrender of lands, and the suspension of social relationship—' connubia commerciaque et concilia inter se ', and the appointment of ' tresviri ' for the creation of a ' colonia Latina ' either by law or by a ' senatus consultum '.

[3] M. Cary, A History of Rome, Methuen, London, 1935, p. 128.   Cf. Sherwin-White, The Roman Citizenship, pp. 103–5.   The right of migratio had disappeared by the time of the Social War, very probably in the interests of the Latins themselves.   Acquisition of citizenship ' per magistratum ' probably replaced it, and by the last quarter of the 1st century B.C. the ius Latii was stabilized as an intermediate link between ' peregrinus ' and ' civis Romanus '.

[4] Sherwin-White, The Roman Citizenship, pp. 112–14.

agreed to ' respect the majesty of the Roman people ' (' maiestatem populi Romani comiter conservare '). It is to be noted that there is a certain continuity in this concept which links together by community of principle the ' civis Romanus ', the ' Latinus ', the ' civis sine suffragio ', and the ' socius iniquo foedere '.[1]

The influence of the Roman constitution among the allies was considerable, and they were always turning more and more towards Rome as their centre. At the time of the Social War the Roman Government was still contracting with foreign Powers treaties that differed in no essentials from those which were still in force between the Italian allies and herself. This probably made it difficult at first to incorporate all Italy within the Roman citizenship, but once this step was taken, the still more important one of the spread of Roman citizenship outside the territorial state which the whole of Italy was to comprise could be taken, and so citizenship could logically be extended to the whole world at a later date.

Of the Social War, Sherwin-White [2] says aptly enough :

> ' An accommodation of the two forms of ' civitas ', national and
> local, was being sought—just the renewal on a large scale of
> that accommodation which Rome had discovered two and a half
> centuries before—Rome was forced by the war to renew the
> practice of an earlier day that had been resting too long in disuse,
> and to adjust the Roman conception of the citizenship to the
> idea that her allies were forming about it.'

It is to be noted that the allies maintained the privileges of their separate states while asserting the sentiment of Italian unity. What they really wanted was not enfranchisement in the modern sense but social and political unity. They were eventually incorporated, as

---

[1] The ' socius ' enjoyed some share of the ' iura ' which the Latin name enjoyed, such as ' connubium ' and ' commercium '. Cf. Diodorus, 37, 15, 2, and Livy, 35, 7, 5. Sherwin-White, op. cit. p. 151. The ' civitas foederata ' and ' civitas libera '—the federated ally and the free state outside Italy—were converted into something like a type of subjection to Rome at the very time Rome refused opportunities for provincial annexation. Rome had at first learned to declare a community to be ' free ' from the Greeks, and applied it in a wider or more limited sense. Flamininus at Corinth declared the freedom of those Greek communities whose fate Rome could claim to decide by right of conquest—that is to say, the subjects or allies of Philip. The reason for Rome's avoiding a policy of provincial annexation at this period was that where Rome acquired sovereign powers over a community through the conquest of its overlord, the immediate possibility of a ' foedus ' with the subject state was absent. Actually, the notable treaties made by Rome in the East are with the great Powers or with small communities whose independence is either known or possible. The Roman adaptation of the declaration of freedom preserved the rights of conquest, without involving Rome in the encumbrance of provincial government. The Romans thus perfected a new political device which enabled them to secure the political control of large areas of the various communities and without the necessity of governing them directly. In its final form the system of ' libertas ' recalls the method used in the re-establishment of the Latin Name in 338 B.C. This benevolent protectorate however quickly changed to the control of a master and both ' civitates liberae ' and ' civitates foederatae ' became subject states.

[2] Sherwin-White, op. cit., p. 130.

communities under the various enabling laws,[1] but though they ceased to be independent states, they retained a great deal of their former character by becoming self-governing municipia.[2]

Cicero had emphasized the principle that no Roman citizen could hold the franchise of another state while retaining that of his own [3] and, from the history of the unification of Italy, he draws the conclusion that

> ' all members of boroughs have two fatherlands, one in nature, one in the state. . . . We must prefer in affection that one which is called the state and the whole community, for which we must be ready to die, and to which we must surrender our whole being and in which we must place all our hopes and to which we must consecrate all that is ours. But the fatherland which begot us is not much less beloved by us than that which adopted us.' [4]

This meant that while a man was a member of only one sovereign state, he was attached as municeps to a secondary community, his municipal patria,[5] which, though not on the same scale as the state, imposed its obligations and offered its honours to him.

All Italians south of the Po became Romans, and, to achieve uniformity, rural communities of various types were assimilated to ' municipia '. This municipalization of Italy meant that the city-state of Rome disappeared, while ' Rome ' came to mean either literally a town or to stand for an idea.[6] After 89 B.C. the municipium ceased to be exceptional and became the typical basis of the Roman citizenship.

---

[1] *Lex Iulia, Lex Plautia Papiria* and *Lex Calpurnia*.
[2] *I.L.S.* 8888.   [3] Balb. 28.   Cf. Nepos, *Atticus*, 3, 1.
[4] *De Legibus* ii. 2, 5 : Omnibus municipibus duas esse censeo patrias unam naturae alteram civitatis. . . . Sed necesse est caritate eam praestare qua reipublicae nomen universae civitatis est, pro qua mori et cui nos totos dedere et in qua nostra omnia ponere et quasi consecrare debemus.   Dulcis autem non multo secus est ea quae genuit quam illa quae excepit.
[5] Even in the areas of central Italy the new municipia are the old tribes.   The tribe of the Marrucini, for example, continued to exist thinly disguised as the ' municipium ' Teate—the central oppidum of the old tribe.
[6] Cf. Horace, *Ep.* i. x. xi. xiv, passim ; Carmen S. 11.

CHAPTER II

THE ROMAN ATTITUDE TO RACE—THE EMPIRE

IT is with the Empire, however, rather than the Republic that
we are more directly concerned when discussing the Roman
citizenship, since it is the Roman Empire that stands in direct
succession to Alexander's ideal. It is moreover the Roman attitude
to provincials in the Empire, especially Greeks, Egyptians, and Jews,
that is noteworthy from the point of view of this work.

The ' Pax Augusta ' and the establishment of a stable
government with a more consistent policy than had marked that of
the Republic made possible the unification of the Empire as a whole
and the reconciliation of the Greek Orient to the rule of Rome. We
find that the connexion with Latin culture is gradually loosened while
the franchise comes to mean a passive citizenship, the old privileges
and duties of ' civis Romanus ' being effaced. It is the ' Pax Augusta '
that rendered possible the extension of the citizenship over non-
Italian areas and areas not deeply Latinized, whereas in the Republic
some measure of Latinity had been the *sine qua non*. Loyalty to
Rome, to ' The City ', too, began to appear, and this was expressed
in terms of respect for the ruling house and in the adoption of Latin
or Roman ways by peregrine communities.

Under Caesar and Augustus came the first large-scale extension
of the Roman citizenship in the form of ' oppida civium Romanorum '
in provincial areas based upon Italian immigration, either of legion-
ary veterans or of farmers, merchants, and business men. Further,
in the more Romanized areas of Spain and Southern Gaul the ' ius
Latii ' was extensively granted. But the grant of the ' citizenship '
itself to a purely native community was rare: such communities
were given Latin rights rather than the citizenship.[1]

It was Caesar who extended the citizenship to the Transpadanes,
granted Latin rights to Sicily, and was responsible for the grant of
similar rights to Narbonensis and the civilized parts of Spain,[2] but
of the direct elevation (at this time) of non-Latin or non-Italianized
communities to the highest status there is no trace. Caesar's liberal-
ity to Greeks and freedmen is also remarkable.[3] He carried out on
a large scale beyond the geographic limits of Italy what was formerly
normal within those limits only and only exceptional and occasional
beyond them: for, once Gallia Cisalpina became ' togata ',[4] nothing
more than the true nation of Italy in the modern sense would have
been produced if the process had stopped with Italy. But even

[1] Sherwin-White, *The Roman Citizenship*, p. 170. [2] Ibid. p. 177.
[3] E.g. at Urso, Carthage, Corinth, *ILS* 6087, cv ; *CIL* x. 6104 ; Strabo 8, 381c.
[4] Phil. viii. 27.

before the Principate was established the Roman state had already burst its geographic bonds, and it was Caesar who extended it still farther, exporting Latin rights and the system of ' coloniae ' in bulk outside Italy. But whatever were Caesar's intentions, whether his imagination, like that of Alexander,[1] had outrun contemporary senti-ment, is uncertain. Yet it is not without some significance that his suc-cessor embarked upon a policy of slower and more conservative advance.

When Roman citizenship was bestowed—as it was through the ' ius Latii ' upon non-Italian peoples—the question arose as to whether it carried with it the full status of the older order of Roman citizens.   There is no sign in the Ciceronian age that any citizen was barred on the ground of foreign extraction from office or honours (the Italian peoples incorporated after the Social War, especially the Etruscans and Greeks, were as much foreigners to the elder Romans of the Ciceronian age as were the partly Romanized Spaniards and Gauls to the contemporaries of Augustus).   An ancestor of Velleius Paterculus was given the citizenship for services rendered in the Social War, and his sons reached the praetorship.   Even before the Social War Q. Varius was not prevented by a provincial origin from reaching the tribunate, though he was dubbed ' Hispanus '.   The obstacles that hindered ambitious Italian provincials from achieving a ' status dignitatis ' were political and social, rather than any exact legal disqualification : Sherwin-White [2] holds that the notion that there was such a thing as an official Ius Honorum, like the Ius Connubii, is due to a mistaken interpretation of the phraseology of Tacitus, who uses this term to describe the request made by the Gallic primores for admission to senatorial rank and office, privileges which depended on the grant of the ' latus clavus '.[3]   Provincials were for the most part not so much excluded from, as not yet em-ployed in, high office.   There was not any formal defect or flaw in the rights of such provincial citizens ; simply their names were not accepted by the magistrates at the elections, and later the ' latus clavus ' was not, in fact, given to them.   In this respect the Augustan Age ushered in the period in which the material importance of the citizenship began to decline.

During the reign of Tiberius the process of development slowed down a great deal : it is when we come to Claudius that we find a sudden spurt.   Yet Claudius himself did not carry out any revolu-tionary reforms or proposals, but reasserted the general principle of the traditional policy of Rome : he was not the magnificent innovator he is considered to be in some quarters.[4]   Actually Claudius pro-

[1] V. Chapot, in *The Roman World* (Eng. trans.), Kegan Pau[l] 1928, p. 37, says of him : ' There were traits in him that recall[ed] aspiration towards a universal monarchy which should abolish r[ ] and break down the barriers between the peoples, whom his n[ ] tended to bring together.'
[2] Sherwin-White, op. cit., p. 180.   [3] Tacitus, *Ann.*
[4] Cf. Sherwin-White, op. cit., p. 82 ; Rostovtzeff, *Social and[ ] the Roman Empire*, 82 f. ; A. Momigliano, *Claudius*, 36 f.

posed to make fuller use in the service of the state of those provincial citizens of Rome who were descendants of the new citizens of the Caesarean and Augustan periods, and seems to have favoured some further extension of the citizenship to peregrine communities. As regards the first point, he aimed at throwing the Senate open to the provincials : ' I think that not even the provincials are to be rejected provided they are an ornament to the Senate.'[1] There seems to have been some opposition to the recruiting of the Senate outside Italy, and this is Claudius' retort to it. The only qualifications that he considers necessary are significantly not those of domicile or origin, but of loyalty and wealth—together with a respectable degree of Latin culture.[2]

Claudius took the first step in challenging the Augustan idea of the essential primacy of Italy when he extended the recruiting ground for the senatorial service to Gallia Comata. It is characteristic of his high sense of statesmanship, which has already been seen in his treatment of the Alexandrian–Jewish question, that in his extension of citizenship and of Latin rights he reaffirmed the belief that Rome's greatness depended on a policy the opposite to that of the Greek city-states.

' What else was the ruin of the Spartans and the Athenians but that, strong though they were in arms, they barred their subject peoples from their polity as foreigners.'[3]

Yet, according to Sherwin-White,[4] the available evidence provides no support to the sarcastic phrases of the Apocolocyntosis, or to any modern view that Claudius showered the citizenship broadcast upon peregrine communities.[5] The ' Oratio Lugdunensis ' itself, according to him, if pressed, means that Claudius saw the possibility that a day would come when the ' Urbs ' would comprise the ' Orbis Terrarum '. There is more definite and suggestive evidence of viritane donations of citizenship in connexion with Claudius than with any other emperor. The gift of honorary citizenship to individuals in return for services rendered was a long-established practice among the Romans, but it is only with the establishment of the Roman world-power, and more especially of the direct government of the provinces, that this honorary and individual citizenship began to acquire a positive importance outside Italy—i.e., to assure

[1] *Tabula Lugdunensis*, col. ii. 6–8 : ' Sed ne provinciales quidem si modo ornare curiam poterint reiciendos puto '.

[2] Ibid., col ii. 3–4, and 35 : ' immobilem fidem obsequiumque '; cf. *Ann*. xi. 24 : ' iam moribus artibus adfinitatibus nostris mixti aurum et opes suas inferant potius quam separati habeant '.

[3] Tac. *An*. xi. 24 : ' Quid aliud exitio Lacedaemoniis et Atheniensibus fuit, quamquam armis pollerent nisi quod victos pro alienigenis arcebant.'

[4] Sherwin-White, op. cit., p. 185.

[5] Apocolocyntosis.[3] ' Ego mehercules pusillum temporis adicere illi volebam dum hos pauculos qui supersunt civitate donaret. Constituerat enim omnes Graecos Gallos Hispanos Britannos togatos videre : sed quoniam placet aliquos regrinos in semen relinqui, et tu iubes fieri, fiat.'

its holder of certain privileges in his own country, such as exemption from the ultimate jurisdiction of the Roman governor. It was not, however, till the imperial period that it became normal for a man of peregrine origin to make a real use of his citizen status without surrendering his connexion with his original home, since till then the Ciceronian principle was valid : ' duarum civitatium civis noster esse iure civili nemo potest '.

Early in the Principate numbers of Roman citizens appear who enter the imperial service, and even hold important posts, without being attached to any ' municipium ' or ' colonia ', and it is especially through service in the auxiliary forces of the army that the number of unattached citizens increased.[1] The charge brought against Claudius is that he was lavish with such grants in the wrong part of the Empire, that he planted citizenship in unfertile soil—for instance, in Achaea there are numerous instances of Greek ' cives Romani ' who bear the Claudian nomina, Claudius Lysias in the Acts and in Egypt a man and his sons who were apparently, contrary to the rule, not even citizens of Alexandria.[2]

Actually Claudius did not grant citizenship to ' whole groups ' in the eastern provinces, for there are no municipia Claudia in the Orient. He held some view about the unity of the Roman Empire, for he admitted Greeks to the equestrian order, and, after military service, to the imperial procuratorships,[3] and he regarded the two languages of Latin and Greek as ' uterque sermo noster '.[4] There is, however, apparently no evidence of any large gift of citizenship to any ' Galli '—at least of the ' Tres Galliae '—or to any ' Britanni '.

It is tempting to assign to Claudius the credit for first regularizing and systematizing the practice of presenting auxiliary veterans with the citizenship on discharge. In return for the civilian services of the Graeci, provided always they had imbibed some understanding of Latinity, he was prepared to distribute the citizenship as a reward.[5] This is the correct interpretation of the ' Apocolocyntosis '.

There was a pause under Nero, but activity was renewed under the Flavians. It was this period that was the greatest age of the municipalization of the Roman world. The Flavians completed the work of centuries in Spain. ' Universae Hispaniae Vespasianus imperator . . . Latium tribuit.'[6]

' The impression [says Sherwin-White][7] is as though now a great machine were at work to stamp with the seal of a formal

---

[1] Cf. *ILS* 8888 for an early instance in 89 B.C. when a group of Spanish cavalrymen received the citizenship ' virtutis causa '.
[2] *P.S.I.*, 1183, A Papyrus written in Latin ' Idem professus se et filios civitate donatos esse a Ti. Claudio Caesare . . . domo Aegypto nomo Oxyrhincho '. A.D. 45.
[3] Cf. Ti. Julius Alexander, *OGIS* 663 ; C. Stertinius Xenophon *SIG* [3] II, 804 ; C. Julius Dionysius, P. Lond. 1912.
[4] Suet., *Claudius*, 42, 1.   [5] Cf. Dio. 60, ii. 7 ; Tac. *Ann.* xi. 38 ; xii. 53.
[6] Pliny, *Nat. Hist.* 3, 30.   [7] Sherwin-White, *The Roman Citizenship*, p. 194.

recognition all that had been done or is being achieved in the
way of what is called Romanization '.

' Oppidum . . . Caesarea . . . a divo Claudio coloniae iure
donata : eiusdem iussu deductis veteranis oppidum Novum et
Latio dato Tipasa, itemque a Vespasiano imperatore eodem
munere donatum Icosium.' [1]

The new historical feature of this period was the elevation of the
provinces to the same level as Italy and the widening of the ' fines
imperii '. The panegyric of Aelius Aristides on Rome reveals how
far the Empire had already travelled away from the conceptions of
the Augustan Age towards the thought and ideas of the late Empire.
In one famous passage of this panegyric the former division of
Hellenes and Barbarians is replaced by that of Romans and non-
Romans. [2] It is interesting to note here that the Romans never thought
of themselves as the chosen people and did not call the many various
races with whom they came into contact ' barbarians ', but were
always inclined to think of the distinction in terms of culture, rather
than in terms of race, and mostly it was certain races, like the Ger-
mani or the Britons—people widely separated from Graeco-Roman
civilization—who were commonly referred to as ' barbari '. Yet in
practice the Romans realized that the Barbarian could make a positive
contribution : he was given a place in the Civil Service and in the
Army which led to citizenship. Even in the hour of her decay the
' alienigenae '—the men of other race, whom the Greeks excluded,
Claudius Claudianus of Egypt and Rutilius Namatianus of Gaul—
are proud to be part of the achievement of Rome. All this says much
for Roman political theory, which was not only non-racial, but elastic
in practice. [3]

The speech of Aristides is not only an expression of sincere admiration for the greatness of the Roman Empire, but also a master-
piece of thoughtful and sound political analysis.

To Aristides, the Roman Empire is a world-state, and Rome the
centre of the world. By world Aristides means, of course, the
civilized world (οἰκουμένη), the Mediterranean lands. The Roman
Empire succeeded in building up and achieving the unity of the
civilized world—a task in which both the Oriental monarchies and
the Greek cities had failed. In this united world there are no Greeks
and barbarians, natives and foreigners. All, we may say, are men.
Yet there is a distinction between the best men who are Roman
citizens, though not necessarily natives of Rome or of Italy, and the
masses who are ruled by them.

[1] Pliny, *Nat. Hist.* 5, 20.   [2] Aelius Aristides, *Orationes* (ed. Keil), 26, 63.
[3] Haarhoff, *The Stranger at the Gate*, pp. 218, 219 ; cf. p. 216. There are four
main uses of the word ' barbarus ' and its cognates in Latin. ' The words are
applied in the 5th century Greek fashion to all non-Greeks, including the Romans.
They are applied to those outside the Graeco-Roman world. The Christians sometimes use them of the pagans, those who are outside the Church. And they are
used metaphorically, as in Greek, of anything rude and uncivilized.'

Sherwin-White remarks that even the distinction between citizens and non-citizens is being effaced in this Orbis Romanus.[1] Many of Aristides' ideas are clearly Roman. His ἄστυ κοινόν is simply ' communis patria ', and even the principle which Claudius re-established can be recognized in its Greek form ξένος οὐδεὶς ὅστις ἄξιος, i.e., ὠφέλιμος—' no one is a foreigner, who is worthy '.[2] In this viewpoint of a provincial which gives expression to what may be called the official policy of the Roman Government, Italy had no place, and the city is less the material Rome than an idea : the provinces are raised to the level of Italy, and her primacy disappears.

The increasing recruiting of the Senate, and in particular of the personnel, of those branches of the civil and military administration which were reserved for Senators, from the most able of the provincial nobility, especially from the Spanish provinces, provides the clearest evidence of this.   Under Trajan the aristocracy of the Greek Orient began to feel the necessity of somehow bringing the Greeks within the orbit of the Roman state.

Moreover, when Trajan forbade the levy of troops from Italy,[3] it meant a further loosening of the connexion of Rome from that of Italy, which became merely the land in which Rome happened to be situated.[4] The Hellenic revival under Hadrian and his philhellenism testify to a growing consciousness of the unity of the Roman world. Tacitus speaks of that ' urbs quam victi victoresque eodem iure obtinemus '. [5]

Under Severus the complete balance, equalization, and even fusion of the Greek and Latin elements of the Roman world took place. The next important step was the severance of the connexion between Latin culture and Roman status. This had long been prepared by such means as the increasing adlection of Oriental senators or the continual bestowal of the franchise on auxiliary troops drawn from the less civilized parts of the Empire. Severus is credited with a momentous innovation.

The Roman colonies in the eastern provinces had been, without exception, based upon veteran settlements, and any other form of city-building had been after the fashion and law of Hellenic city-states. He bestowed the ' ius coloniae ' and the ' ius Italicum ' on city-states and principalities, some of which were not so much Greek in their life and thought as Semitic—e.g., the old town centres of Mesopotamia, like Nisibis, are given the titles of a Roman colony. No one had done such a thing before.

In the Severan period there is thus an extension to the Greek-speaking provinces of what formerly had been confined to the Latin provinces which is a finger-post to the ' Constitutio Antoniniana '.

---

[1] Sherwin-White, op. cit., p. 201.
[2] Aelius Aristides, *Orationes* (ed. Keil), pp. 26, 60, 74 ; cf. Tabula Lugdunensis, col. ii. 6–8. ' Sed ne provinciales quidem si modo ornare curiam poterint reiciendos puto ', and passim.
[3] S.H.A., *Marcus*, ii. 7 ; Dio 74 (75) 2, 4.
[4] Cf. S.H.A. *Severus*, 4 5.   Cf. Dio 76 (77), 2, 1.   [5] Tac. *Hist*. iv. 74.
  L

The encouragement which Severus appears to have given to the development of municipal or quasi-municipal life in Egypt [1] suggests that there was an attempt to set the provincial peoples in a position where the Roman franchise would have some meaning for them and where at least they would be something better than serfs. The decentralization of the governmental system under the Romans seems to have prepared the way for a kind of municipal life in the capitals of the Nomes [2] and, to a smaller degree, in the villages.[3]

The important change brought about by the introduction under Severus of urban councils, βουλαί, to the ' metropoleis ' of the Nomes has already been discussed : [4] in fact, in this period the process had begun whereby the Nomes became the ' civitates ' of the late Empire. The assimilation of the three cities of Egypt to the normal type also took place at this time.

The rigid separation of Egypt from the rest of the Empire, and of the classes within Egypt from one another, was already slackened.[5] Evidence of this is seen in the right of intermarriage with the native Egyptians which Hadrian granted to the citizens of his new city Antinoopolis, in this respect deliberately departing from the charter of Naucratis, which he had otherwise followed in his new creation.[6]

In Caracalla's edict ' De Reditu ', dated a few years after the great ' Constitutio ',[7] there is an explicit indication of such a policy of educating the Aegyptii in something like city life.

Special exemption is granted to such Aegyptii as visit Alexandria, among other causes, ' for the sake of a more civilized life ',[8] and special attention is called to the difference between country folk and those that have had the benefit of living in a city.[9] In the Chora, moreover, the Egyptians seem to have been prepared for the ' civitas ', but through the spread of Greek rather than Latin culture. The grant of a Council to Alexandria—a petition so long and perhaps so often refused—was one of the wisest acts of Severus in a country where the capital city seemed to be permanently opposed to any devotion to the Roman Empire.

All these details seem to fall in place as part of a scheme which in turn was part of the vast process, through which the Orbis Terrarum had been passing for two and a half centuries. The final act itself—the ' Constitutio Antoniniana '—can be summed up in the three words of the writer of the *Vita Severi*, ' civitatem omnibus datam '.

P. Giessen 40, containing a document which has been taken for a Greek text of the ' Constitutio ' itself, has added little, according to Sherwin-White, to the understanding of this act of Caracalla, and has somewhat unnecessarily complicated its discussion.

The old divisions of ' peregrini ', ' cives Romani ', and communi-

[1] P. Jouguet, La Vie municipale d'Égypte, pp. 269 f., 345 ff. A. H. M. Jones, Cities of the Eastern Roman Provinces, pp. 329 ff.
[2] P. Jouguet, La Vie municipale d'Égypte, pp. 454 f.   [3] Ibid. pp. 221, 271.
[4] See p. 64 of this work.   [5] P. Jouguet, La Vie municipale d'Égypte, pp. 454 ff.
[6] Ibid. p. 184 (Wilcken, Chrestomathie, n. 27 ; cf. C.A.H. xl. 650).
[7] Ibid. n. 193 (Wilcken, op. cit. n. 22).   [8] Ibid. p. 25.   [9] Ibid. ad fin.

ties of ' Latini iuris ' were now swept away, and the world that had long been regarded as the ' orbis Romanus ', first in the sense that it was subject to Roman government and Roman laws, now became such in a real sense, even from the aspect of constitutional law, because its inhabitants were all, with some possible exceptions, Roman citizens. Caracalla gave the franchise to all the free inhabitants of the Empire, and by his edict simplified the relationship of all the members of what a contemporary writer calls ' the world of Rome '.[1] It is to be noted that within the urban organization of the Empire the Roman citizenship was only supplementary to the local ' patria ' : so, too, in the rural areas the political status of, e.g., ' Aegyptii ' or imperial ' coloni ' remained the same as before. In Egypt, perhaps, the decree had the greatest numerical effect in creating new Romans.

Dio assigns as a motive for the measure a possible extension of the inheritance tax,[2] but in Egypt, at least, this tax had always existed, and under Trajan tax and citizenship had gone hand in hand.   Moreover, the citizenship was now extended throughout the rural non-urbanized areas.

' We shall probably do Caracalla no more than justice [says Cary] [3] in attributing to him the same statesmanlike motives as had guided the franchise policy of the long line of Roman emperors since Claudius. In any case, it is unlikely that Caracalla's measure entailed any notable addition to the number of Roman citizens, for the process of enfranchisement had already been carried very far by his predecessors. In 212 the long-standing distinction between Italians and provincials, between conquerors and conquered, was virtually obliterated, and the Roman empire was definitely converted into a commonwealth of equal partners.'

Sherwin-White,[4] too, states that Caracalla probably was not aiming at practical benefits, and this scheme of ' civitas omnibus data ' may have been connected with other vast conceptions of his—for instance, the enormous size of his buildings and the generality of his thoughts.

In the Giessen papyrus Caracalla stresses both the greatness of the gods who have preserved him, the necessity of a similarly great recompense, and the greatness of the Roman people. It is the ' maiestas populi Romani ', and not the ' magnitudo imperii ', with which Caracalla is concerned. The importance of Caracalla is that, by completing the process of a century, he set the ' maiestas populi Romani ' upon the widest possible basis. The unifying element that

---

[1] Dio, 78 (79), 26, 1 : ἡ οἰκουμένη αὐτῆς (i.e. Ῥωμῆς).
[2] Dio, 77 (78), 9, 3 ; cf. C.A.H. xii. 45 ; M. Cary, A History of Rome, Macmillan, 1935, p. 718, note 14.   Dio's statement overlooks the fact that the Emperor might easily have extended the tax without the franchise.
[3] M. Cary, A History of Rome, p. 713.
[4] Sherwin-White, The Roman Citizenship, p. 22.

held together the very diverse constituents of the Empire was their common interest in Rome, and Caracalla's edict identified the whole population of the Empire with Rome.

The restoration and meaning of the central sentence of Papyrus Giessen 40, have been disputed: δίδωμι τοί(ν)υν ἅπα(σιν ξένοις τοῖς κατὰ τ)ὴν οἰκουμένην π(ολιτ)είαν Ῥωμαίων [μ]ένοντος [παντὸς γένους πολιτευμ]άτων (or]ατως) χωρ(ὶς) τῶν (δεδ)ειτικίων. (' So I give to all foreigners in the world the Roman citizenship, provided that the status of all communities remains unchanged, except the " dediticii ".') A. H. M. Jones [1] holds that under the Principate the native inhabitants of Egypt, and possibly of Cappadocia, remained ' dediticii ' because they never had any civic organization conferred on them. In this status we find the reason why no Aegyptus was capable of becoming a Roman citizen directly. But, according to Sherwin-White,[2] the conferment of the citizenship—indeed, of any civic status or local autonomy, of ' leges et iura ', for instance—to the new nome cities would annul the condition of dediticius. The populations of the villages could hardly continue to be known as ' dediticii ' after the ' Constitutio Antoniniana '.[3] Bell is of the opinion that it seems clear that the Egyptians as a whole received the citizenship, but that the change probably made little practical difference, for the new citizens do not appear to have been exempt from the poll-tax. In fact, wide concessions were made to existing usage, and a hybrid law arose combining Roman and Graeco-Egyptian elements. Bell also holds that the Giessen papyrus is almost certainly the text of the ' Constitutio Antoniniana '.[4]

If the papyrus does contain the text of the ' Constitutio Antoniniana '—which Sherwin-White denies—then two views are possible: either the dediticii must be identified with the class of criminals

---

[1] A. H. M. Jones, *J.R.S.* 1936, ' Another Interpretation of the " Constitutio Antoniniana " ', pp. 229 f.; cf. *C.A.H.* xii. 45. The retention of the Latin term (dediticii) in a Greek version current in Egypt implies that it had a recognized technical meaning defining a political category not primarily Eastern.

[2] Sherwin-White, *The Roman Citizenship*, p. 223.

[3] Cf. Rostovtzeff, *A Social and Economic History of the Roman Empire*, Oxford, 1926, p. 273. Rostovtzeff, however, holds that since in Egypt, more than in any other land, the cities were a superstructure, the creation of a city bourgeoisie begun by Hadrian meant little to the mass of the Egyptian peasants and artisans, who continued to live the very same life as had been their lot from the dawn of Egyptian history. He holds (ibid. p. 369) that Caracalla's edict remains a puzzle and asks (i) How many of the ' peregrini ' were styled ' dediticii ' in the time of Caracalla? (ii) Were the free peasants of the villages included in this class? (iii) Were the rural population of the city territories included? (iv) Were all the tenants of the emperors ' dediticii ' or not? As long as these vital points remain undecided, the historical importance of the edict and Caracalla's purpose cannot be definitely understood.

[4] *C.A.H.* xi. 657–8. But cf. V. Chapot, *The Roman World*, Kegan Paul, etc., London, 1928, p. 254. Chapot holds the natives of the Nile valley were reckoned legally among the ' dediticii ', and were thus excluded from the grant of citizenship. He applies an indirect test. Most of the citizens created *en bloc* after 212, entered the ' gens ' of Caracalla and became ' Aurelii ', but for the first twenty years after the edict, among the Αὐρήλιοι of Egypt are found *only* citizens of the Greek towns, or, in the μητροπόλεις, ' the people of the gymnasium ' (οἱ ἀπὸ γυμνασίου).

' qui in dediticiorum sunt ', to whom it was but right and proper to
refuse the citizenship, or it must be identified, according to Bickerman,[1] with the large masses of conquered barbarians settled within
the Empire by Marcus Aurelius and his successors.   Bickerman
holds that Caracalla proposed to give the citizenship to barbarians
who were attracted to the Empire and ready to serve in the ' militia
armata ', but was not prepared to make Roman citizens of the rest
who had been forcibly settled there.

It is a moot point whether a measure capable of being described as
' civitas omnibus data ' can have been affected by the three lines in
dispute.

It is undisputed that Caracalla was thinking in terms of sentiment,
was even inspired by a grand boastfulness, rather than aiming at
some material change in the circumstances of his time, when he made
the world Roman.   At all events, he finally stripped the citizenship
of any specific content; the claim to it was based neither on Latin
nor on Greek culture, nor on any service done for the State, nor on
the existence of urban organization in some form.   Henceforth a
man was a Roman citizen simply because he was a free inhabitant of
the civilized world.

According to Rostovtzeff [2] the ' Constitutio ' marks the end of one
period and the beginning of another.

> ' It symbolises the death of the Roman state as founded on
> the Senatus Populusque Romanus. . . . Everybody was now
> a Roman citizen, and this meant in plain fact that nobody was
> such any more.   As soon as the Roman citizenship became a
> mere word and mere title, it lost every shred of importance.[3]
>
> ' Bestowed on all and sundry Roman citizenship was a mere
> name : it only meant that the bearer of the title lived in one of
> the cities of the Empire.   Later it became synonymous with an
> inhabitant of the Roman Empire in general, that is, a subject of

---

[1] E. Bickerman, *Das Edikt des Kaisers Caracalla* (Berlin, 1926), pp. 23 f.   Cf.
M. Cary, *A History of Rome*, Macmillan, 1935, p. 718, note 14 : ' They were
probably war captives on the European borderlands in a condition of " serfdom ".'

[2] Rostovtzeff, *Social and Economic History of the Roman Empire*, Oxford, 1926,
p. 370.

[3] Sherwin-White, op. cit., p. 211, gives the stages in this process.   The content
of the citizenship, as far as concerns public duties or public honours, had been
whittled down by the middle 2nd century A.D.   A man could be a Roman without
the exercise of the ' publica iura ' though they were a possible consequence of
citizenship.   (The right of appeal, ' ius provocationis ', however, remained a part
of the theoretical meaning of the citizenship.)   As a result there was some assimilation of the rights of non-Roman persons and communities to those of Roman
citizens and, by the increasing co-operation within a community, of Roman and
non-Roman elements of the population.   It became the normal thing to have
mixed groups of Roman citizens and of ' homines peregrini iuris ' living in the
same village or canton and exercising communal authority jointly.   Such a situation must have meant a considerable decline in the positive importance of the
citizenship, when it was seen that the possession of it left men in much the same
position as before, in relation to their neighbours, as far as power or privilege was
concerned.   The status of Roman citizen became a matter of honour and titular
distinction, and did not separate off its possessors from their fellows.

the Roman emperor, who was now the embodiment of the state. With the rise of the imperial power Roman citizenship had lost its political value. Now it lost its social importance as well.'

But if the citizenship no longer implied certain political and social rights, its bestowal on all the world, thus bringing everyone to the same level under Roman law, was a tremendous gain for civilization and a realization of the ideals of Alexander the Great and the Stoics. The citizenship now no longer implied certain rights and privileges restricted to one country or to a certain number of communities or individuals. A title common to all mankind—that is the important point, not the change in its value political or social. The idea of mankind as one great community had at last been realized—the Roman world had become the achievement of the Empire.

Rome ended by securing the allegiance of the East as firmly as that of the West. In the western provinces the task was easier, since a superior civilization had attractions for the Iberian, Celtic, Germanic, or Numidian peoples. But in the eastern provinces Rome lacked this glamour. Here she had to contend with loyalties and traditions, whether Greek or oriental, that were in most cases based on an older civilization than that of Rome herself.

In the Hellenized provinces the traditions of Alexander and the kings [1] were potent forces, yet these do not seem to have been inimical to Rome, except at Alexandria, for goodwill after the Augustan Age was not lacking to overcome the friction between Roman and Hellene ; moreover, Greek traditions were preserved within the Roman framework as Hadrian's foundation of Antinoopolis, the grant of citizenship to Greeks in Egypt as a preliminary to enlistment in the Roman legions,[2] and the possession of Alexandrian citizenship as an essential step, for natives of Egypt, to the Roman citizenship, bear witness.[3]

Yet, from the reign of Augustus, according to Bickerman,[4] all inhabitants of Egypt except the citizens of the Greek cities were to the Romans ' Egyptians '. Thus the prevailing view that the effect of the Roman conquest was to reinforce the Greek element in Egypt and correspondingly to depress the status of the Egyptians has been called into question. Nevertheless, the Romans recognized a difference between Hellenic and Egyptian culture, assessing the inhabitants of the nome-capitals who were regarded as more Hellenized at a lower rate than those of the villages, though both paid the poll-tax.[5]

It was, however, with the Alexandrians and the Jews that Rome found the greatest difficulty in effecting a reconciliation to her rule. The question of Rome's attitude to Alexandria can be dealt with briefly, since a good deal has been said on the subject in previous

---

[1] Livy, 9, 18, 6, and 9, 18, 3.   [2] C.A.H. xii. 286.   [3] Ibid. p. 296.
[4] E. Bickerman, in Arch. Pap. viii. 1927, 239 ; ix. 1928, 40–43.
[5] C.A.H. xii. 298.

chapters, but that of Rome's attitude to the Jews, generally, demands lengthier treatment, since this has hardly been touched on.

It has already been remarked that the citizens of Alexandria could not forget that their city had once been the capital of the richest and most powerful of the Hellenistic monarchies ; that their failure to obtain a Senate was the more galling because Augustus confirmed the rights of the Jews, with their council of elders ; that the militant nationalism of the Alexandrians, who were very disinclined to yield pride of place to Rome, found expression in hostility to the Jews, who were as yet favoured by the Romans, and that this evoked a literature that was hostile to Rome, though it had a strong anti-Semitic tone.

The troubles that arose with the reigns of Gaius and Claudius have been dealt with.

Claudius' attempt at pacification, however, was incomplete, for Vespasian, by his exactions and by laying hands upon the royal palace, seems to have provoked an anti-Roman outburst.[1] That Alexandria was eventually reconciled to the Roman dominion, and accepted the second place in the rank of cities, seems to be proved by the description in the Sibylline oracles, but it is probable that the conversion came late.[2] Aristides the Sophist, although in one passage he recognizes Alexandria as the second city of the Empire and con-trives to avoid almost any admission of imperfection in the Roman world,[3] makes an obscure reference to cities that cannot help dis-orderly behaviour because of their size. The breach was probably not completely healed till Severus restored the city's council and its self-respect by one and the same edict,[4] yet, inasmuch as the grant of a Senate was granted not merely to Alexandria but to the nome-capitals as well, the concession must have deprived it, for Alexandrian pride, of much of its value.

The outstanding features of the political technique devised by the Roman Republic, and which suffered but little change under the Empire, have been well summed up.[5] These were—

> ' respect for " libertas ", a sturdy belief that freedom could be preserved even in communities which were parts of a larger whole, and an ideal of inclusiveness which led to the absorption first of Italy and later of the Empire at large into the imperial citizenship of Rome '.

The chief weakness was the absence of a more ample Civil Service, which seems to have been remedied to some extent by Trajan and his successors, but to the end of the Antonine Age the character of the Roman control was still under the predominant influence of traditions inherited from the Republic.

> ' Lack of officiousness, reluctance to interfere, anxiety that Rome's share of the responsibility for detail should be small

---

[1] Suet. *Vespasian*, 19, 2 ; Dio Cassius, 65 (66) 8.
[2] *Or. Sib.* xxii. 48–9.   [3] Or. 26 (ed. Keil).
[4] Dio. 51, 17, 3.   [5] H. Last, in *C.A.H.* xi. p. 437.

and that of local authorities great—such were the most striking expressions of a policy which left the governed free and content if defence, imperial taxation, and the more serious judicial business were reserved for the imperial power.' [1]

According to Sherwin-White, Rome succeeded practically everywhere in securing co-operation but failed with the Jewish communities simply because the Jews were not prepared to co-operate, ' for the essence of the " Orbis Romanus " in the fullest sense is that it was produced by the willing co-operation of both sides—subject peoples and Rome alike '.[2]

But the situation was not as simple as all that. As has already been seen, especially in the case of Alexandria, the Jews were the *protégés* of Rome, and seem to have been in the Diaspora on the side of the ruling Power. One of the elements that aroused the enmity of the Alexandrians was, indeed, their very co-operation with and respect for Rome. The Roman Government itself helped to strengthen everywhere the position of the Jews by admitting their privileges.

' These privileges [says Chapot] [3] were maintained by Rome for various reasons : in many places they were already established and Rome made as few innovations as possible ; also, there were treaties of alliance with the petty kings of Palestine which sanctioned respect for their traditions, and the Roman government judged it more imprudent to put constraint upon the Jews than to supervise them. Moreover, chance favoured them : in the great riot of Alexandria Julius Caesar was helped by a Jew, the born enemy of the Alexandrians.'

In Palestine itself, as Momigliano has shown,[4] in spite of the wide difference in outlook between orthodox Jewry and Rome, there was some attempt at an understanding under the rule of Herod—an attempt which failed owing to his death and the incompetence of the succeeding provincial governors of the country. Moreover, it is to be remembered that the Jewish Rebellion, though it began before the Year of the Four Emperors, culminated at the same time as the revolts of Julius Civilis and his Germans and Julius Classicus and the Gauls.

It was thus to the interest of Rome to put down—though with unmitigated severity in the case of the Jews—rebellions which seemed to threaten the unity of the Empire. Actually a different and much more conciliatory policy might have been possible in Palestine if the times had not been fraught with such danger.

Roman relations with the Jews till the tragedy of A.D. 70 were, on

---

[1] H. Last, *C.A.H.* xi. p. 438.
[2] Sherwin-White, *The Roman Citizenship*, p. 255.
[3] Cf. V. Chapot, *The Roman World* (Eng. trans.), Kegan Paul, etc., London, 1928, p. 220.
[4] *C.A.H.* x. Chapter XI.

the whole, conciliatory, if not friendly.   It was the destruction of the Temple that really marked the turning point, though, as we shall see later, the anti-Semitic propaganda from Alexandria exercised no mean influence.   But till A.D. 70 Judaism, unlike Christianity, was a religion recognized by law, and was not likely to be deemed 'atheism'.[1]

The Romans first entered into political relations with the Jews in the course of the 2nd century B.C., when the Hasmoneans were instigating the revolt of their country from the hegemony of Syria. A treaty with the Jews was made, as it was clearly in the interests of Rome that an independent nation should separate the Syrian and Egyptian monarchies and form a barrier to any union of their forces hostile to the Republic.[2]   For nearly a hundred years this state of affairs remain unchanged, but when Syria became Roman, the motives that had won Roman support for the Jews barely existed, and with Pompey's entrance into Jerusalem, Palestine, too, became a Roman possession.

It was the internecine strife between the Hasmonean princes Hyrcanus and Aristobulus that had brought Pompey.   It is noteworthy, too, that while he was at Damascus, Pompey received a deputation [3] from Judea which made representations to him to the effect that the Hasmonean princes had changed the form of government under which their ancestors had lived, and desiring him to restore the order of things that had formerly existed in the land.   The suggestion accorded with Pompey's arrangements, and the kingship was abolished, after an existence of forty years, and the High Priesthood reinstated in full power, but under Roman suzerainty.

Roman relations with the newly revived theocratic state were on an amicable footing.   In fact, only a few weeks before his murder Caesar even allowed the High Priest Hyrcanus II and his Idumean minister Antipater to rebuild the walls of Jerusalem, and granted a remission in the amount of the tribute.[4]   Although the Jewish Government afforded Cassius and the Republicans help after Caesar's murder, they were supporting one Roman party against another, and, after Philippi, were clever enough to represent themselves as the victims of the Republican party.   With the rise of Antipater's son Herod, who had allied himself to the Hasmonean house by marrying Mariamne, relations with the Romans, this time with Antony, became even closer.   Yet here, too, the Jews were espousing the losing side, and it was only Herod's adroitness and his known hatred of Cleopatra that brought the friendship of Augustus after Actium. Indeed, even before Actium, owing to the loss of Syria and Palestine to the Parthian invaders, Herod had been made king instead of ethnarch, since his cause was too closely bound up with the restoration of Roman power in the East and since, as an Idumean, he could never become High Priest.[5]   Momigliano holds that the belief was

---

[1] C.A.H. xi. 255.   [2] I Macc. viii. 22 seq.   [3] Joseph. Ant. xiv. 3, 2.
[4] C.A.H. x. 316.   [5] Ibid. p. 320.

strong in Roman circles that Judea could not be kept quiet under the rule of pure-blooded Jews, hence they were ready to uphold the authority of the house of Antipater and smooth its path in succeeding to Hyrcanus.[1] Whatever were Herod's failings—and they are well known—he did attempt to reconcile two different worlds, Gentile and Jewish:

'He had to be a match for both and yet in neither of them did he feel at ease. . . . While he laboured to raise Judea to the rank of one of the greatest client-kingdoms of Rome, by secularizing it as far as possible and giving it a definitely Hellenistic structure on another side his policy bore a strong Jewish imprint.[2] . . . His true forerunners were the sons of Tobiah, who like him were Judaized rather than Jewish. Though he apparently succeeded better than they, because he had what they lacked in their struggles with Syria and Egypt, the solid support of Rome, his political failure was not far different. He could not transform the Jews, still less turn his kingdom into a stable element in the Roman system of client states. The Tobiads made the first, Herod the last, attempt to bring Judea within the circle of Hellenistic (and ultimately Roman) civilization: soon after began the tragedy which led to the total overthrow of the Jewish state.'[3]

All traces of the theocracy were systematically swept away, only to revive with very limited powers; only in Judea itself, on Herod's death, when his kingdom was split up into tetrarchies, and except for one brief interval under Archelaus in Judea, the whole country was put under direct Roman rule. It seems that with the death of the one strong man who kept Palestine together, and with the resultant dynastic quarrels of his descendants, Augustus believed it impossible to maintain the unity of Palestine as a strong client-kingdom in the East. Under Claudius, however, some semblance of union was again brought about when the Emperor made Agrippa I king of a large Jewish kingdom which absorbed several of the tetrarchies, but on Agrippa's death the kingdom again was split up, and Judea,

---

[1] C.A.H. x. p. 318.

[2] Cf. C.A.H. x. 326, 331. Herod's coinage no longer bore legends in Hebrew, but in Greek; his court assumed a Hellenistic character, many of the higher posts being held by non-Jews of Greek training; literary men with foreign modes of thought, like Nicolaus of Damascus, adviser and historian of the king, were specially favoured; the king's sons received a Greek training, several of them being sent to Rome to complete their education; theatres, amphitheatres, and hippodromes arose in Jerusalem and in other cities; the structure of the Army was Hellenistic and it was composed of mercenaries. On the other hand, Herod remained a Jew in religion, began rebuilding the Great Temple at Jerusalem, and intervened on behalf of the Jews of the Diaspora whenever their religious liberties or political rights were in danger. Indeed, in the Diaspora Herod enjoyed great popularity, which lasted long after his death. In the Diaspora men could better appreciate the advantage of Herod's prestige, since they cared less about scrupulous observance of the law.

[3] Momigliano in C.A.H. x. 321-2.

which contained the majority of the Jewish population, was administered by a procurator.   On the whole, Roman policy with regard to Palestine does not seem to have been very consistent—the procurators who administered Judea failed to understand the mood of the people, and made some serious mistakes, which brought Rome into great discredit.   Moreover, the lack of control at the centre of the Roman state itself, when an emperor like Gaius [1] could attempt to force the Jews against their will to worship him as a god, brought the Roman name into great discredit.   For once the Roman desire not to intervene overmuch in the affairs of the governed, especially in the sphere of religion, was forgotten.   There were many pinpricks of this nature due to the procurators [2] and their subordinates themselves, and it seems unfortunate that in a period of changing masters the Jews should have seen fit to lose all patience and embark on revolt.

Momigliano says :

> ' The complete lack of understanding and consequently of tolerance that most of the Jews evinced for the Romans was matched on the Roman side : indeed the Roman lack of sympathy was so great as to overpower their natural administrative sagacity which bade them respect the religious traditions of Judaism.   If the procurators could not hide their antipathy in their daily contacts with their subjects, far less could their underlings and the soldiers, drawn from the non-Jewish population of Palestine : hence arose numberless small fracas, rendered serious simply because the Romans, in conflicts between Jews and non-Jews, usually took (whether rightly or wrongly) the side of the latter.   But occasionally the provocation came direct from Rome, and produced not isolated outbreaks but an almost general uprising.' [3]

The one way of restoring some calm to Judea would have been to hand it back to a vassal king of the Jewish faith, for this would have given the Jews a feeling of greater autonomy, and would have put an end to the constant friction between governors and governed. Claudius had been wise enough to approve of this solution when the old kingdom of Herod the Great had been reconstructed for his friend Agrippa, but this reconstitution was only a passing phase, and the old pernicious system of procurators, as we have seen, came back on his death.

---

[1] Cf. *C.A.H.* x. 851.   Gaius' attempt to impose the imperial cult on the Jews marked the beginning of a series of disorders that was to culminate in the rebellion of 66.   Gaius' intention to set up his own image in the Temple itself greatly widened the gulf between Jews and Romans.

[2] Gessius Florus' confiscation of seventeen talents from the Temple treasury in 66 so shocked the religious sentiment of the people that a riot broke out.   Josephus makes the Jewish War against Rome begin from the stringent measures Florus took to put the riot down.

[3] *C.A.H.* x. 851.

Thus the Jews were not opposed to co-operation as some authorities insist, but failure on the part of the Romans to respect their religious principles and their desire for greater autonomy brought about the *débâcle* in Palestine. This was Rome's one great failure, and perhaps her only one, and in extenuation of it one may plead the troubled period when the Julio-Claudian dynasty was already tottering on the brink of the abyss. It seems that the only emperor after Augustus who really had some insight into the position was Claudius. With the failure of the rebellion and the destruction of Jerusalem, there were outbursts of anti-Semitic feeling here and there, as at Antioch, and Jewish disorders in Cyprus and Egypt, but the Roman Government succeeded in overcoming these. Apart from their desire to leave the Jews in the Diaspora in full possession of the rights they had always had, without being at all affected by the events in Palestine, the Romans left the status of Judea as before, as a separate province, though subordinating its equestrian procurator to a legatus of Senatorial rank, who commanded the Tenth Legion left there as a garrison. The Jews outside Palestine and those who had supported Rome naturally retained their status as ordinary provincials.

But by abolishing the Sanhedrin and the High Priesthood and by forbidding the resumption of the worship of the temple at Jerusalem, the Romans destroyed the political and religious centre of Judaism, and the poll-tax of two drachmae that the Jews had been accustomed to pay to the temple was diverted to the Temple of Capitoline Jupiter. But this did not mean that the existence of the Jewish nation was no longer recognized : the religious privileges that the Jews originally enjoyed were maintained ; further, the creation of the Fiscus Iudaicus, on the same lines as the fiscus Asiaticus and the fiscus Alexandrinus, implied the recognition of the Jews as a separate entity. The attitude of the Romans to the Jews from the political point of view in both the Diaspora and their own homeland, as well as the reaction of the Jews, has been outlined.

In the Diaspora the Jews were not regarded as a subversive element, but as a factor loyal to the imperial Government. The disturbances at Alexandria were not due, on the part of the Jews, to disaffection with the treatment meted out to them by Rome, but primarily to Alexandrian hostility to Rome. In Palestine itself, as we have seen, lack of understanding in a period of stress, and the failure to provide a greater measure of autonomy, besides the incapacity of the procurators, had brought about an unenviable situation, which left a heritage of ill-feeling and misunderstanding long after the national centre of the Jews had been destroyed.

It remains to consider the attitude of the Romans to the Jews as evidenced in literature. From the political standpoint the attitude of Rome to the Jews as a people had been no different from her attitude to the Greeks as a people. In either case if there was rebellion against Roman authority in Palestine or Greece, it was put down with great severity. The destruction of Corinth in 146 B.C.[1] shows us that the Roman treatment of the Greeks had not been much different from her treatment of Palestine.

In Roman literature, too, we find an attitude of mind that was applicable both to Greeks and Jews, though here the factor of religion entered, and the anti-Semitic literature of Alexandria, which had its origin in opposition to Rome, influenced the Romans, just as to-day a similar type of propaganda has used the Jews as a scapegoat. But it must be stressed that the Romans themselves recognized the Jewish religion as the lawful religion of the subjects of part of their Empire, though Christianity,[2] which was regarded as a subversive movement, was not till the time of Constantine granted legal recognition.

The break with Rome on the part of the Jews in Palestine may have been regarded by some orthodox elements as due to religious factors, but actually this is far from true. The situation in the first century A.D., when Rome was the suzerain Power, was quite different from that in the second century B.C., when Antiochus Epiphanes had done his best to undermine and overthrow the Jewish religion. Rome, on the contrary, had granted the fullest recognition and protection to the Jewish religion. When Pompey conquered Palestine in 63 B.C. he allowed the Jews complete freedom of worship, and the theocracy was maintained, though with limited powers. Augustus, too, while setting up Herod as king (who, as we have seen, relegated the High Priest and the theocracy into the background), exempted the Jews from the newly established cult of the Roman emperors.[3] In the last two centuries B.C. the Jews were widely diffused over the Near East and even formed a considerable colony at Rome in Pompey's day.[4] Their religion was carried into many Mediterranean countries. In spite of clashes between the more unruly elements of the Jewish and Gentile population in the East, the Roman emperors generally maintained a policy of religious toleration in regard to the Jews, though they set a ban on proselytizing.[5]

---

[1] Cary, *A History of Rome*, p. 210.   [2] *C.A.H.* xi. 255-7.

[3] Cf. The Jews, the Roman Empire, and Christianity, A.D. 50-180, in *Greece and Rome*, vi. no. 18, p. 170 ff. After the fall of the Republic, there was a revival under Augustus of the national religion ' but it failed to broaden ultimately or to deepen religious feeling . . .; the significant development came when the combination of the old gods and the new imperial family was regarded as one of the most important pillars of the principate.' A political was now added to a religious obligation with important consequences for Jews and from A.D. 50 for Christians. Cf. p. 173 : The Jews were allowed ' to meet on the Sabbath and feast days, to settle their private religious disputes, to be excused from appearance in court on the Sabbath, and from taking part in the imperial birthday ceremonies, provided that in their own synagogues they prayed for the Emperor's welfare '. (Cf. Joseph. *Antiq.* xiv. 10.)

[4] Philo, *Leg. ad Gaium*, p. 23, says it was not till the capture of Jerusalem by Pompey, that Jews were brought to Rome in large numbers, but the picture of the Jewish community at Rome in 59 B.C. given by the Pro Flacco, pp. 68 seq., presupposes a settlement there of Jews that was founded much earlier than 63. Four or five years could not have been sufficient to provide the Jews with an established position in the Roman capital. Cf. M. Radin, *The Jews among the Greeks and the Romans*, The Jewish Publication Society of America, 1915, pp. 227 seq.

[5] *C.A.H.* xi. 255.

Indeed, in regard to the rebellions in Palestine itself (A.D. 66–70 and 131–4), notwithstanding the mad antics of a Caligula and other acts which offended Jewish religious susceptibilities, the main issue at stake in the mind of the Romans was not the religion, but the attempt—for such they regarded it—of the Jews to overthrow Roman rule. The issue was thus political, and not religious.

The political attitude of the Romans towards the Jews should be distinguished and not confused with the disparaging attitude shown in literature. The poets and the orators may have had some influence, but their effect on Roman policy towards subject races, especially in the Empire, can be regarded as negligible. Roman political development in the Empire shows no trace of such influence, and we can regard the remarks made by such characters as simply symptomatic of certain classes or individuals. Nevertheless, their attitude is interesting by way of contrast to the spirit of development shown by the ever-widening circle of the Roman citizenship. There were three attitudes of mind among the Greeks to religion : (i) the popular frame of mind ; (ii) that of the poets ; (iii) that of the upper classes addicted to philosophic analysis.

At Rome there was a division on almost similar lines. The upper educated classes, imbued with Greek philosophy and thought, tended to look askance at any Oriental religion or cult. Failing to gain satisfaction from the State religion, they adopted the various forms of theism, pantheism, or agnosticism developed by the Greek philosophical schools, while their interest in the ceremonial of the State religion became simply an empty habit and a form of patriotism. It was these people who were the chief enemies of Judaism as a religion which they regarded as a rival to any philosophic doctrines they had adopted. The lower classes at Rome, the mass of the later plebs, a mixed multitude themselves could get little religious satisfaction out of the State-ritual. The same failings to satisfy the personal and emotional side of human nature were as evident in the Roman State religion as it was in the Greek city-state. The lower strata of the population thus turned to the various cults for satisfaction. It is therefore not surprising to understand the success of Christianity when it made its appearance among the varied cults that were destined to conquer Rome and which, with Judaism, had their votaries even among some of the upper classes.

The Stoics who aspired to establish a religious philosophy for all mankind, and pursued a vigorous missionary propaganda, particularly in the East, saw in the Jews not only obstinate opponents, but dangerous rivals, who carried on a competing mission with great success. They became the first professional Jew-haters. Inevitably, too, antipathy towards the Jews was influenced to a very great extent by the stories and tales emanating from Alexandria. Two Stoic writers of the first century B.C.—Posidonius and Molon [1]—charged the Jews with regarding other nations as their enemies, and accusing them of

---

[1] Josephus, *cont. Ap.* ii. 79.

atheism, misanthropy, cowardice, and stupidity, respectively. These
remained the stock charges for centuries, and they assumed an
added bitterness after the Roman conquest, when to the peculiarity
of Jewish customs was added the stigma of being a subject people.

The specific answers to the charges advanced by the anti-Jewish
scribblers are now to be found most fully stated in Josephus.   In
his day the literary campaign against the Jewish name was as remorse-
less as the military campaign that destroyed the political independence
of the Jews.   The Romans, tolerant themselves in religion, had long
been intolerant, as were the Greeks, of Jewish separation and national
exclusiveness.   A strict and unqualified monotheism usually made
an unfavourable impression upon polytheistic peoples, especially
when the conclusion had to be drawn from such monotheism that
their gods were false and ineffective.   We have seen, too, that the
practice of their religion compelled the Jews to abstain both from
public functions and from private gatherings at which sacrifices were
made to heathen deities.

Cicero,[1] shortly after the capture of Jerusalem by Pompey, had
denounced their ' barbarian superstition ' in language typical of the
outlook of the Roman upper classes.

> ' Even while Jerusalem was standing and the Jews were at
> peace with us, the practice of their sacred rites was at variance
> with the glory of our empire, the dignity of our name, the custom
> of our ancestors.   But now it is even more so, when that
> nation by its armed resistance has shown what it thinks of our
> rule : how dear it was to the immortal gods is shown by the
> fact that it has been conquered, reduced to a subject province,
> made a slave.'

Yet Cicero can be discounted, for notice what he says of the
Greeks : [2]

> ' I grant them literature, I grant them a knowledge of many
> arts, I do not deny the charm of their speech, the keenness of
> their intellects, the richness of their diction : . . . but truth
> and honour in giving testimony that nation has never cherished.'

This by an admitted Philhellene of the race that produced men
like Socrates, Plato, and Aristotle.   The only conclusion one can
draw is that Cicero does not really mean what he says.   In this
speech, in order to defend Flaccus on a charge of extortion while in

---

[1] Cicero, *Pro Flacco*, 69 : ' Stantibus Hierosolymis pacatisque Iudaeis tamen
istorum religio sacrorum a splendore huius imperii, gravitate nominis nostri,
maiorum institutis abhorrebat ; nunc vero magis, quod, illa gens quid de nostro
imperio sentiret ostendit armis : quam cara dis immortalibus esset docuit, quod
est victa, quod elocata, quod serva.'

[2] Cicero, ibid. 66 seq.   One of the numerous counts in the indictment was that
Flaccus had seized certain sacred funds, the money which Asiatic provincials, Jews
in origin, had, in accordance with the ancient custom, collected, and were about to
transfer to the temple of Jerusalem.

office as governor of Asia, he has recourse to arguments from probability. Thus to prove a man of Flaccus' character and achievements simply could not have committed the crimes he was charged
with, he denounces the Greeks as a nation utterly incapable of giving
honest testimony (the witnesses were Greeks and Asiatic Greeks at
that), and next passes to the Jews, who fare little better at his hands.
This criticism of both Jews and Greeks is an excellent example
of what the poets and orators could bring up to prove a case or drive
home a point. Yet those who were in actual charge of the political
administration of the provinces of the Republic and the Empire knew
better, and seem to have been, generally, uninfluenced by the idle
chatter and senseless prejudices of the day.

There is, however, another side of the picture. The same elements in Jewish customs which had impressed Greeks, such as Theophrastus and Clearchus, made some impression on philosophic
Romans. Polybius [1] the Greek historian who lived as an Achaean
hostage in Rome during the second century B.C. refers to the ' great
fame of the temple ' (ἡ περὶ τὸ ἱερὸν ἐπιφάνεια). Thus the fame
of the shrine at Jerusalem most probably reached Rome a century
earlier than Cicero's time. Cicero [2] himself jestingly refers to
Pompey as ' noster Hierosolymarius ' (' Our hero of Jerusalem ').

Moreover, as it was a constant habit of the Romans to find, in
those institutions of other peoples which could be called severe or
simple, the image of their own golden age of simplicity, we find
Varro [3] referring to the Jews, among others, as a people whose
imageless cult still maintains what the Romans had given up.

In the next generation after Cicero Jewish propaganda seems to
have been so wide and successful that it attracted adherents, especially
among the masses, and occasionally among men of education, but,
generally speaking, the upper classes tended to regard it as a foreign
cult—to be looked at askance, in the same light as for example the
cult of Isis, and as a threat to the national religion. It is not surprising, then, to find sketches of Jewish activities in Rome during
the following years drawn with a distinct lack of sympathy.

The later poets of the Augustan Age, Horace [4] and Ovid,[5] expressed
a supercilious disdain for the Jewish custom of Sabbath-keeping, their
proselytizing activities, and their credulous belief in miracles. Isis
and Judaism were the two oriental cults which at this time had the
greatest success in Rome.

The attitude of the Augustan statesmen towards foreign cults at
Rome itself can be seen in the last words of Maecenas : [6]

' Take active part in divine worship, in every way established
by our ancestral customs, and compel others to respect religion,

---

[1] Polybius xvi.   [2] Cicero ad Att. ii. 9.
[3] Quoted by St. Augustine, De Civ. Dei, iv. 31, 2.
[4] Horace, Sat. i. 9, 69 ; i. 4, 143 ; i. 5, 97.
[5] Ovid, Ars Amatoria, i. 55 seq., 413 seq. ; Remedia Amoris, 214 seq.
[6] Dio Cassius, lii. 36.

but avoid and punish those who attempt to introduce foreign elements into it . . . those who introduce new deities are by that very act persuading the masses to observe laws foreign to our own. Hence we have secret gatherings and assemblies of different sort, all of which are inconsistent with the monarchical principle.'

This is as regards the influence of extraneous cults on the Roman State religion. Yet Rome banned interference with the religion of others as well, and Augustus' commendation of Gaius' avoidance of sacrifice at Jerusalem [1] is in agreement with Roman policy. Seneca, although he hated the Jews with the double hatred of a Roman aristocrat and Stoic philosopher, yet admits that their religion is spread throughout the Empire.[2] The bitterest attacks on the Jews, however, were written after the destruction of Jerusalem, when the failure of Rome to break the stubborn spirit of her conquered foe became apparent. It is significant that neither Vespasian nor Titus held the title of ' Judaicus ' after their triumph.[3]

It is possible that such a title might have been taken to mean that they had Judaized: the term ' Iudaicus ' would suggest to the general public a ' convert to Judaism ', at a moment when, despite the fall of the temple, Judaism was still spreading throughout the Roman world. Titus, moreover, was himself suspected of Eastern proclivities.[4] To both Juvenal[5] and Martial[6] the spread of Jewish habits was amongst the surest signs of degeneracy, but these poets aimed rather at ridiculing the Jews and their converts than misrepresenting them.

The classical exponent of Roman anti-Semitism, however, is Tacitus, the historian who wrote in the time of Nerva and Trajan— i.e., just after Josephus—and who both in his *Annals* and *Histories* made mention of the Jews. He seems to have surpassed all his predecessors, Greek or Roman, in distortion and abuse, and he combined the charges invented by the jealousy and rancour of Greek sophists with the abuse of Jewish character. His account, like the remarks of the poets, cannot be taken seriously.

Tacitus[7] gives several alternative accounts of the origin of the Jews, such as that they were fugitives from Crete who settled on the

---

[1] Suet. *Aug.* 93.
[2] Seneca apud, Aug. *De Civ. Dei*, vi. 10 : ' Cum interim usque eo sceleratissime gentis consuetudo valet ut per omnes iam terras recepta sit : victi victoribus leges dederunt ', cf. Strabo apud Jos. *Antiq.*, XIV. vii. 2 : καὶ τόπον οὐκ ἔστι ῥᾳδίως εὑρεῖν τῆς οἰκουμένης ὃς οὐ παραδέδεκται τοῦτο τὸ φῦλον μηδ' ἐπικρατεῖται ὑπ' αὐτοῦ.
[3] Dio, lxv. 7, 2 ; cf. Radin, *The Jews among the Greeks and Romans*, Jewish Publication Society of America, Philadelphia, 1915, pp. 301-2. In Dio's own time the emperors assumed gentile cognomina—e.g., Septimius Severus is Parthicus, Arabicus, Britannicus—whereas in Vespasian's time it may not have been customary to have such a title. The name Germanicus used by Gaius, Claudius and Nero was, however, a hereditary cognomen.
[4] Suet. *Titus*, 5.
[5] Juvenal, *Sat.* xiv. 96 seq. ; iii. 10 seq., 296 ; vi. 156, 542.
[6] Martial, vii. 30 ; xi. 94.　　　　　　[7] Tac. *Hist.* v. 2 seq.

M

coast of Libya, or that they sprang from Egypt but were driven out
owing to a pestilential disease. This assertion was made before by
Manetho in his History, and Tacitus does nothing else but bow, as
did his Roman predecessors, to the bias of Alexandrian story-tellers.
His account of the Exodus is fanciful and tricked out with misrepresentations of Jewish observances which are ludicrously inconsistent with each other. Tacitus says that the Jews paid veneration
in the temple to the image of an ass,[1] but actually refutes this statement soon afterwards, saying that the Jews suffered no consecrated
statues or images to be erected either in their cities or their temples:
' nulla simulacra urbibus suis, nedum templis sinunt '.[2]

He tells us afterwards that when Pompey conquered Jerusalem
and made his entry into the temple he found neither statues nor
images but a void and empty tabernacle: ' nulla intus deum effigie
vacuam sedem et inania arcana '.[3]

It is interesting in this respect to note that the elder Pliny, as well,
described the Jews ' as a people notorious by their contempt of
divine images '.[4]

Tacitus' whole account is vitiated by hearsay and prejudice, and
shows how much a typical Roman aristocrat failed to understand
the Jews, but regarded their strange religion as a threat to Roman
or pagan institutions. He repeats, for example, the old Greek
prejudices and misrepresentations:

> ' The Jews are extremely loyal to one another, and always
> ready to show compassion, but toward every other people they
> feel only hate and enmity. They sit apart at meals, and they
> sleep apart . . . the earliest lesson their proselytes receive is
> to despise the gods, to disown their country. . . . The Egyptians
> worship many animals and monstrous images: the Jews con-
> ceive of one god only, and that with the mind alone: they
> regard as impious those who make from perishable materials
> representations of gods in man's image: that supreme and
> eternal being is to them incapable of representation and without
> end. . . . Liber established festive rites of joyous nature,
> while the ways of the Jews are preposterous and mean (absurdus
> sordidusque).' [5]

Tacitus emphasizes the national tenacity of the Jews (moriendi
contemptus), their ready charity—though he misrepresents it—
their freedom from infanticide, their conviction of the immortality
of the soul, their purely spiritual and monotheistic cult.[6] This
account of Tacitus, however disparaging, reveals the moral superiority of the conquered, and just as captive Greece took Rome captive in
the realm of literature, so was captive Judea, via her offspring
Christianity, destined to take Rome captive in the sphere of religion.

---

[1] Tac. *Hist.* v. 4.   [2] Ibid. 5.   [3] Ibid. 9.
[4] Pliny, *Nat. Hist.* xiii. 4, 46: ' gens contumelia numinum insignis '.
[5] Tac. *Hist.* v. 4 (Loeb translation).   [6] Ibid.

It is against the forerunners of Tacitus, whose theories Tacitus had swallowed—writers who were mainly Alexandrian Greeks— that Josephus, the historian, wrote his *Contra Apionem* in defence of his people. His aims were to uphold the antiquity of the Jews against those who denied their historical claims, and to disprove the charges levelled against the Jewish religious ideas and legislation and he does this with considerable success.

In the *Contra Apionem* [1] he makes the pointed contrast between the individual creative impulse of the Hellene and the respect for tradition of the Hebrew. He refutes those who say that the Jewish state is of late origin because the Greek authors are silent about it. One main cause of the silence (which we have already noted) was the isolation of Judea and the character of the Jewish people, who did not delight in merchandise and commerce, but devoted themselves to the cultivation of the soil. It was only in the writer's day that the Jews were beginning their mercantile development, and are to be compared with the Romans, who only entered into the Greek sphere of interest later in their history.

He quotes from Manetho, the anti-Jewish historian, giving extracts about the Hyksos tribes and kings, whom he identified with Joseph and his brethren. Modern historical criticism, however, while agreeing as to the early origin of the Jews, has rejected this identification. He even adduces passages from various Greek writers to show that the Jews were not entirely unknown to the Hellenes before Alexander's conquests.

> ' The libels upon us [says Josephus] originated with the Egyptians. To gratify them, certain authors undertook to distort the facts ; they misrepresented the circumstances of the entry of our ancestors into Egypt, and gave an equally false account of their departure. . . . Again the profound contrast between the two cults created bitter animosity since our religion is as far removed from that which is in vogue among them as is the nature of God from that of irrational beasts.' [2]

He dissects the charge that the Hebrews were a pack of lepers expelled from the country, and insists upon its absurdity and the lack of consistency in its details.

Ostensibly his book is a refutation of Apion, who had in particular attacked the Alexandrian Jews, so Josephus takes the opportunity of enlarging on the privileged position of his people not only in the Egyptian capital, but in the other Hellenistic cities where they had been settled.[3] We have already seen the importance of his statements in regard to the question of the Jewish citizenship at Alexandria. He elaborates and amplifies what he had stated on the privileges of the Jews in the *Antiquities*, and adds a short account of

[1] Joseph. *Cont. Ap.* i. 6 seq.　　[2] Joseph. ibid. 223.
[3] Joseph. ibid. ii. 33 seq.

the miraculous delivery of the Egyptian Jews during the short-lived persecution of Ptolemy Physcon.[1]

Apion had invented a detailed story of ritual murder to justify Antiochus Epiphanes for his spoliation of the Temple, but Josephus brings proof of the emptiness of the charges.[2]

The rest of Josephus' book comprises a defence of the Jewish legislation—his broad aim is to show that the Law inculcates humanity and piety. He then gives a summary of the principles of Judaism, which is unlike anything else he wrote, in its masterly grasp of the spirit of the religion and in its philosophic outlook.[3]

He denounces, in a peroration, the pagan idolatry in the manner of the Greek rationalists, who had made play with the Olympian hierarchy. The greatest of the Greek philosophers (Plato), indeed, agreed with the Jews as to the true notions about God.[4] ' In two points, in particular, Plato followed the example of our legislator (Moses). He prescribed, as the primary duty of the citizens, a study of their laws, which they must learn by heart. Again he took precautions to prevent foreigners from mixing with them at random, and to keep the State pure and confined to law-abiding citizens.'[5]

He compares with the Jewish separateness the national exclusiveness of the Spartans, and claims that the Jews show a greater humanity in that they admit converts from other peoples[6] : in fact the Mosaic law is being spread over the civilized world.[7]

It is interesting to note that the Apology of Josephus became the guide, in its turn, of the early Church fathers in their replies to heathen calumniators who repeated against them the charges that had been invented against the Jews. It is still more interesting to notice that the Christians themselves in the Middle Ages took over the charge of ritual murder, amongst many of the other accusations that Alexandrian hostility had invented against the Jews.[8]

Anti-Semitism, as such, and the doctrines cited to support it evidently originated in Alexandria, as did the first pogroms. The Protocols of Zion in the modern world and the false belief that had been fostered that the Jews aim at a supremacy over the Gentile nations are simply nothing else but grandiose repetitions of Alexandrian anti-Semitism composed by many a modern Apion. What the modern world has now done, actually, is to attempt to put anti-Semitism on a scientific basis.

The problem the ancient world tried to solve once the idea of the unity of mankind came to fruition in the Roman world, after having been anticipated in some ways by Alexander, was the same as confronts the modern world to-day. In the case of kindred or un-

[1] Joseph. Cont. Ap. ii. 52 seq.; cf. III Maccabees, chs. v.–vi.
[2] Ibid. 89 seq.   [3] Ibid. 145 seq.
[4] Ibid. 255 seq.; cf. Plato, Rep. iii. 398 A.
[5] Ibid. 257; cf. Plato, Legg., esp. xii. 949 E. seq.
[6] Ibid. 258 seq.   [7] Ibid. 279–80.
[8] Cf. A. H. Jonker, The Scapegoat of History, Central News Agency, South Africa, 1941, pp. 88 ff.

developed races a world-empire like that of Rome finds a large measure of success.

But where many of the subject races of such an empire are of a different race, have an older culture and civilization, and often a different religion incapable of assimilation to the general religion in vogue, what measure of success is possible ?   Even in the case of the Greek Orient, Rome had some difficulty in finding co-operation as Alexandria is witness.   Yet here, as Rome herself had long adapted the culture and civilization of Greece and transmuted them and her own into a common Graeco-Roman heritage, the question was only one of time.   In the case of the Jews, apart from the political aspects of the situation, which were the more important issue, the factor of a people with a much older culture and civilization, and a religion which, though superior to the polytheistic cults of the ancient world, was unassimilable (except later in the form of a world religion—Christianity), presented a more difficult problem.

If we desire a parallel in the modern world, we need only think of the many alien and subject races in the British Empire to-day. Where these are European the problem of assimilation causes some difficulty, but not as much as where they are heirs of a totally different civilization and possess religions which have little or nothing in common with Christianity—the dominant religion of the European rulers.   In India alone, to take an excellent example, it has always been difficult to reconcile people whose ideals, culture, civilization, and religion vary so much from European standards, with the rule of a European race.   In a sense this was to some extent Rome's difficulty with the Greek Orient, but to an even greater extent with the Jews.

BIBLIOGRAPHY

I. ANCIENT AUTHORS

Greek and Latin (Loeb editions unless otherwise stated).

Aelius Aristides (Teubner).
Aeschylus.
Appian.
Aristeas (Teubner).
Aristotle.
Arrian.
Augustine.
Cicero.
Demosthenes.
Dio Cassius.
Diodorus Siculus (Teubner).
Diogenes Laertius.
Euphorion (F. H. G. vol. iii, p. 71).
Euripides.
Eusebius (Teubner).
Herodotus.
Homer.
Horace.
Isocrates.
Jerome.
Josephus (Teubner, and Loeb vols. i–vi, containing ' The Jewish War ',
   ' The Life ', ' Against Apion ', and Books i–xi of the ' Antiquities ').
Justin (Teubner).
Juvenal.
Livy.
Marcus Aurelius.
Martial.
Menander.
Nepos.
Oracula Sibyllina (Teubner).
Ovid.
Pausanias.
Philo (Cohn & Wendland, Berlin, 1866 ; Teubner ; and Loeb, vols. i–ix
   have already appeared).
Philostratus.
Plato.
Pliny (Teubner).
Plutarch.
Polybius.
Porphyrius (Teubner).
Pseudo-Callisthenes (ed. C. Müller, *Scriptores Rerum Alexandri Magni,*
   Paris, 1846 ; also ed. W. Kroll, i., Berlin 1926).
Seneca.
Sophocles.
Stephanus Byzantius, ed. A. Meineke, Berlin, 1849.
Strabo.
Suetonius.
Tacitus.

Terence.
Theocritus.
Thucydides.
Varro.
Velleius Paterculus.
C.A.F. T. Kock, *Comicorum Atticorum Fragmenta*, 3 vols., Leipzig, 1880–8.
F.H.G. C. Müller, *Fragmenta Historicorum Graecorum*, 5 vols., Paris, 1841–84.
Sel. Frag. *Select Fragments of the Greek Comic Poets*, A. W. Pickard, Cambridge, Oxford, 1900.
S.H.A. *Scriptores Historiae Augustae*, 3 vols., Loeb Library.
Tab. Lug. *Tabula Lugdunensis* (in Furneaux's edition of Tacitus, vol. ii., pp. 210–14).
Hebrew.
The Bible (revised version).
I–III Maccabees. (See *Vetus Testamentum Graece redditum* (LXX), ed. H. B. Swete, ed. 3, Cambridge, 1901). Books i–ii are translated in Everyman's Library (J. M. Dent, *Ancient Hebrew Literature*, vol. ii).
The Mishnah. (Trans. by H. I. Danby, Oxford, 1933.)
The Babylonian Talmud. (Trans. by the Soncino Press, London, 1935).

II. EPIGRAPHICAL PUBLICATIONS

C.I.G. A. Boeckh, *Corpus Inscriptionum Graecarum*, Berlin, 1828–77.
C.I.L. *Corpus Inscriptionum Latinarum*, Berlin, 1862.
C.I.S. *Corpus Inscriptionum Semiticarum*, Paris, 1881.
I.L.S. *Inscriptiones Latinae Selectae*, H. Dessau, Berlin, 1892–1916.
O.G.I. *Orientis Graeci Inscriptiones Selectae*, W. Oittenberger, Leipzig, 1903.
O.G.I. *Orientis Graeci Inscriptiones Selectae*, W. Dittenberger, Leipzig, 1903–5.

III. PAPYROLOGICAL PUBLICATIONS

B.G.U. *Berliner, griechische Urkunden* (Ägyptische Urkunden aus den Königlichen Museen zu Berlin), 1895.
Mitteis Chr. L. Mitteis and U. Wilcken, *Grundzüge und Chrestomathie der Papyruskunde*, Leipzig and Berlin, 1912.
P. Amh. *Amherst Papyri*, ed. B. P. Grenfell and A. S. Hunt, 2 vols., London, 1900–1.
P. Cair. Preis. F. Preisigke, *Griechische Urkunden des ägyptischen Museums zu Kairo* (Schriften der Wissenschaftlichen Gesellschaft zu Strassburg, Heft 8), Strassburg, 1911.
P. Cair. Zen. C. C. Edgar, *Zenon Papyri*, 4 vols. (*Catal. gen des Antiq. égypt du Musée du Caire*, p. 79), 1925–31.
P. Eleph. *Elephantine Papyri*, ed. O. Rubensohn, Ägyptische Urkunden aus den Kgl. Museem zu Berlin. Griechische Urkunden : Sonderheft, Berlin, 1907.
P. Frankf. H. Lewald, *Griechische Papyri aus dem Besitz des rechtswissenschaftlichen Seminars der Universität Frankfurt.* (Sitzungsberichte der Heidelberger Akademie der Wissenschaften, Phil.-hist. Kl. 1920, 14, Abh.)
P. Gies. *Griechische Papyri im Museum des oberhessischen Geschichts—vereins zu Giessen*, Bd. 1, Hefte 1–3, ed. O. Eger, E. Kornemann, P. M. Meyer, Leipzig, etc., 1910–12.
P. Grenf. Series 1. B. P. Grenfell, *An Alexandrian Erotic Fragment and other Greek Papyri chiefly Ptolemaic*, Oxford, 1896, Series 2, B. P. Grenfell and A. S. Hunt, *New Classical Fragments and other Greek and Latin Papyri*, 1897.

P. Gurob.   *Greek Papyri from Gurob*, ed. J. G. Smyly (Royal Irish Academy, Cunningham Memoirs, No. 12, Dublin–London, 1921).

P. Hal.   Halle Papyri—Dikaiomata : *Auszüge aus Alexandrinischen Gesetzen und Verordnungen* in *einem Papyrus des Philologischen Seminars der Universität Halle, mit einem Anhang . . . herausgegeben von der Graeca Halensis . . .* , Berlin, 1913.

P. Hib.   Hibeh, *Papyri*, Part I, ed. B. P. Grenfell and A. S. Hunt, London, 1906.

P. Lille.   Institut papyrologique de l'université de Lille : *Papyrus grecs publiés sous la direction de Pierre Jouguet . . .* , Paris, 1907–28.

P. Lond.   Greek Papyri in the British Museum, vols. i and ii, ed. F. G. Kenyon, vol. iii, ed. F. G. Kenyon and H. I. Bell, vols. iv. and v. ed. H. I. Bell, London, 1893–.

P. Lond. 1912–29.   H. I. Bell, *Jews and Christians in Egypt*, London, 1924.

P. Louvre.   Brunet de Presle, *Notices et Extraits des Manuscrits de la Bibliothéque imperiale, Notices et textes das papyrus grecs.*

P. Oxy.   Oxyrhynchus Papyri, ed. B. P. Grenfell and A. S. Hunt, vols. i–xvii., London, 1898–.

P. Petrie.   The Flinders Petrie Papyri, Pt. 1, ed. J. P. Mahaffy (Royal Irish Academy, Cunningham Memoirs, No. 8), Pt. 2, ed. J. P. Mahaffy (ibid. No. 9) ; Pt. 3, ed. J. P. Mahaffy and J. G. Smyly (ibid. No. 11), Dublin, 1891–1905.

P. Rev. Laws.   B. P. Grenfell, *Revenue Laws of Ptolemy Philadelphus*, Oxford, 1896.

P. Ryl.   Catalogue of the Greek Papyri in the John Rylands Library at Manchester, vol. i., 1911, ed. A. S. Hunt ; vol. ii., 1915, ed. A. S. Hunt, J. de M. Johnson, V. Martin ; vol. iii., 1938, ed. C. H. Roberts.

P.S.I.   Papiri greci e latini (Pubblicazioni della Societa italiana per la ricera dei papiri greci e latini in Egitto). Firenze, 1912–. Vols. i–ix. by S. Vitelli and others.

P. Tebt.   Tebtunis Papyri, ed. B. P. Grenfell, A. S. Hunt, H. G. Smyly, E. J. Goodspeed, London and New York, vol. i, 1902 ; vol ii, 1907 ; vol. iii, pt. i, 1933, pt. 2 (ed. A. S. Hunt, J. G. Smyly, C. C. Edgar ; London and Univ. of California Press), 1938.

Sel. Pap.   Select Papyri, Loeb Library : *Non-Literary Selections*, by A. S. Hunt and C. C. Edgar, vol. i, Private Affairs ; vol. ii, Official Documents. *Literary Selections*, by D. L. Page, vol. i, Poetry.

Wilcken *Chr.*, v. Mitteis *Chr.*

IV. PERIODICALS

Abhandlungen der Sächs Gesellschaft de Wiss., Phil.-hist. Kl. xxvii. (1909).

Aegyptus, Milan 1920–.

Ann. du Service.   Annales du Service des Antiquités de l'Égypte, 1899–.

Archiv. Pap.   Archiv für Papyrusforschung, 1900–.

B.C.H.   Bulletin de Correspondance Hellénique, 1877–.

B.S.A.   Annual of the British School at Athens, 1895–.

B.S.A.A.   Bulletin de la Société Archéologique de Alexandrie, Alexandria, First Series 1898–1902 (Nos. 1–5) ; Nouv. Série (vol. i, No. 6), 1904–.

Class. Phil.   Classical Philology, Chicago, 1906–.

Greece and Rome, Oxford, 1931–.

Hermes.   1866–.

J.E.A.   Journal of Egyptian Archaeology, 1914–.

J.H.S.   Journal of Hellenic Studies, 1880–.

J.R.S.   Journal of Roman Studies, 1811–.

Journal des Savants.

Klio.   Klio, Beiträge, zur alten Geschichte, 1901–.

Philol. *Philologus,* 1841–.
Proceedings of the Society of Biblical Archaeology, 1878–.
Recueil de Travaux. *Recueil de Travaux relatifs à l'archéologie égyptiennes et assyriennes,* 1870–.
Rev. Eq. *Revue égyptologique.*
Rev. Phil. *Revue de Philologie,* Nouv. Série, 1877–1926 ; Troisième Sér., 1927–.
Riv. Fil. *Rivista di Filologia,* 1873–.
Z. Aeg. *Zeitschrift für aegyptische Sprache und Altertumskunde.*

V. WORKS OF REFERENCE

C.A.H. *Cambridge Ancient History,* vols. i–xii.
Ency. Brit. *Encyclopaedia Britannica,* 14th edition, 1937.
How and Wells. *A Commentary to Herodotus,* Oxford, 1912.
Liddell and Scott. Liddell and Scott, *Greek Dictionary,* 8th edition, and the New, 1940 edition.
Pauly-Wissowa. Pauly-Wissowa, *Real-Encyclopädie der Classischen Altertumswissenschaft,* Stuttgart, 1893.

VI. MODERN WORKS

Bailey, C. *Epicurus,* Oxford, 1926 ; *The Greek Atomists and Epicurus,* Oxford, 1928.
Bell, H. I. *Jews and Christians in Egypt,* London, 1924 ; *Juden en Griechen in Römischen Alexandria* (Beihefte zum Alten Orient, 9) Leipzig, 1926.
Bentwich, N. *Hellenism,* Jewish Publication Society of America, Philadelphia, 1920.
Bevan, E. *A History of Egypt under the Ptolemaic Dynasty,* Methuen, London, 1927.
Bickerman, E. *Das Edikt des Kaisers Caracalla,* Berlin, 1926.
Bouché-Leclercq, A. *Histoire des Lagides,* 4 vols., Paris, 1903–6.
Breasted, J. H. *Ancient Times, A History of the Early World,* Ginn & Co., 1916 ; *A History of Egypt,* Hodder & Stoughton, London, 1924.
Budge, Sir E. A. W. *The History of Alexander the Great,* Cambridge, 1889.
Bury, J. B. *History of Greece,* 2 vols., Macmillan, London, 1902 ; *History of Greece to the Death of Alexander the Great,* Macmillan, London, 1912.
Caiger, S. L. *Bible and Spade,* Oxford, 1936.
Cary, M. *A History of Rome,* Macmillan, London, 1935.
Casson, S. *Macedonia, Thrace, and Illyria,* Oxford, 1926.
Chapot, V. *The Roman World,* Kegan Paul, Trench, Trubner, London, 1928 (Eng. trans.).
Charlesworth, M. P. *Five Men : Martin Classical Lectures,* Harvard Univ. Press, 1936.
Coudenhove-Kalergi, H. *Anti-Semitism throughout the Ages,* Hutchinson, London, 1935.
Cowley, A. E. *Aramaic Papyri of Fifth Century B.C.,* Oxford, 1923.
Evans, Sir A. *Palace of Minos,* i–iv and Index, Macmillan, London, 1922–37.
Eyre, E. *European Civilization : its Origin and Development,* Oxford, 1935.
Garry, T. G. *African Doctor,* Trinity Press, Worcester and London, 1939.
Glotz. *Histoire Grecque,* Paris, 1925.
Glover, T. R. *Herodotus, Sather Classical Lectures,* Univ. of California Press, 1924.
Goodenough, E. B. *Jewish Courts in Egypt,* Yale Univ. Press, 1929.
Haarhoff, T. J. *The Stranger at the Gate,* Longmans, Green, 1938.

Hellenistic Age, The (J. B. Bury and others).   Cambridge, 1923.
Hicks, R. D.   *Stoic and Epicurean*, London, 1910.
Hogarth, D. G.   *Philip and Alexander*, Murray, London, 1897.
Holm, A.   *The History of Greece from its Commencement to the close of the
        Independence of the Greek Nation.*   4 vols., 1894–98.   Macmillan (Eng.
        trans.).
Jardé, A.   *The Formation of the Greek People*, Kegan Paul, etc., London,
        1926 (Eng. trans.).
Jones, A. H. M.   *The Cities of the Eastern Roman Provinces*, Oxford, 1937 ;
        The Greek City from Alexander to Justinian, Oxford, 1940.
Jonker, A. H.   *The Scapegoat of History*, Central News Agency, S. Africa,
        1941.
Jouguet, P.   *Macedonian Imperialism and the Hellenization of the East*,
        Kegan Paul, etc., London 1928 (Eng. trans.) ;   *La Vie municipale dans
        l'Égypte romaine*, Paris, 1911.
Juster, J.   *Les Juifs dans l'Empire romain*, Paris, 1914.
Knight, C. A. F.   *Nile and Jordan*, J. Clarke & Co., London, 1921.
Laistner, M. L. W.   *A History of the Greek World*, 479–323 B.C., Methuen,
        London, 1936.
Legacy of Greece, Essays.   Edited by R. W. Livingstone, Oxford, 1928.
Legacy of Israel, Essays.   Edited by A. D. Lindsay, Oxford, 1928.
Lesquier, J.   *L'Armée romaine d'Égypte d'Auguste à Dioclétien*, Cairo, 1918.
Mackail, J. W.   *Lectures on Greek Poetry*, Longmans, Green, 1926.
McEwan, C. W.   *The Oriental Origin of Hellenistic Kingship*, Univ. of
        Chicago Press, 1934.
Meyer, E.   *Geschichte des Altertums*, Stuttgart, 1893.
Milne, J. G.   *A History of Egypt under Roman Rule*, Methuen, London,
        1924.
Momigliano, A.   *Claudius : The Emperor and his Achievement*, London,
        Oxford, 1934.
Mommsen, Th.   *Römische Geschichte*, i–v, Berlin, 1912.
Moret, A.   *The Nile and Egyptian Civilization*, Kegan Paul, etc., London,
        1927 (Eng. trans.).
Morton, H. V.   *Middle East*, Methuen, London, 1941.
Otto, W.   *Priester and Tempel in hellenistischen Aegypten*, Leipzig and
        Berlin, 1905–8.
Pearson, L.   *Early Ionian Historians*, Oxford, 1939.
Peet, E. T.   *Egypt and the Old Testament*, Liverpool Univ. Press, Liverpool,
        1922.
Pendlebury, J.D.S.   *The Archaeology of Crete*, Methuen, 1939.
Prescott, W. H.   *History of the Conquest of Mexico*, Routledge, London,
        1899.
Radin, M.   *The Jews among the Greeks and Romans*, Philadelphia, 1915.
Reinach, Th.   *Un Code fiscal del' Égypte romaine.*   Le Gnomon de l'Idiologue,
        Nouv. Rev. Hist. de Droit fr. et etr. (xliii, 1919 ; xliv, 1920).
Robinson, Th.   *History of Israel*, vol. i, Oxford, 1932.
Rostovtzeff, M.   *The Social and Economic History of the Roman Empire*,
        Oxford, 1926 ;   *The Social and Economic History of the Hellenistic
        World*, 3 vols., Oxford, 1941.
Sayce, A. H.   *The Egypt of the Hebrews and Herodotus*, Rivington, London,
        1896.
Schürer, E.   *Geschichte des jüdischen volks im Zeitalter Jesu Christi*, 4th ed.,
        1898–1909.
Seltman, C. I.   *Greek Coins*, Methuen, 1933.
Sherwin-White, A. N.   The Roman Citizenship, Oxford, 1939.
Spence, L.   *The Civilization of Ancient Mexico*, Cam. Univ. Press, 1912.
Spiegelberg, W.   *The Credibility of Herodotus' Account of Egypt*, Blackwell,
        Oxford, 1927 (Eng. trans.).
Strack, M. L.   *Die Dynastie der Ptolemäer*, Berlin, 1897.

Stuart Jones, H. *The Roman Empire*, Fisher Unwin, London, 1908.

Tarn, W. W. *Hellenistic Civilization*, Arnold, London, 1927 ; ' Alexander the Great and the Unity of Mankind ', Raleigh Lecture, 1933. (*Proceedings of the British Academy*, vol. xix.)

Wilcken, U. ' Alexander der Grosse und die hellenistische Wirtschaft.' *Schmoller's Jahrbuch*, xlv, 1921 ; *Alexander the Great*, Chatto & Windus, London, 1932 (Eng. trans. of *Alexander der Grosse*, Quelle, Meyer, Leipzig) ; *Griechische Ostraka aus Aegypten und Nubien*, Leipzig and Berlin, 1899.

Wonders of the Past. Edited by J. A. Hammerton, Amalgamated Press, 1934.

Woolley, C. *The Sumerians*, Oxford, 1930 ; *Ur of the Chaldees*, Benn, 1931.

Yahuda, A. S. *The Accuracy of the Bible*, Heinemann, London, 1934 ; *Die Sprache des Pentateuch in ihren Beziehungen zum Aegyptischen*, Erstes Buch, Berlin and Leipzig, 1929.

Zeller, E. *Outlines of the History of Greek Philosophy* (Eng. trans.), Kegan Paul, etc., London, 1931.

INDEX

ABRAHAM, 60, 76
Absolutism, 46–9
Achaeans, 1
Acta Alexandrinorum, 118
Actium, 153
Acts of the Heathen Martyrs, 121
Acts of Hermaiscus, 123
Aelius Aristides, 144, 151
Agrippa I, King of Judea, 99, 118–20, 154
Agrippa II, King of Chalcis, 122
Akhnaton (Amenhotep IV), 80
Alexander I, King of Macedon, 4, 5
Alexander the Great, effects of his conquest of the East, 8; political ideals of, 91; political development and constitutional position of, 11; apostle of Hellenism, 12; in favour of democracies in Greek cities, 13; his racial policy too rapid, 14; his idea of unity of mankind, 17; Alex. Romance, 35; as son of Ammon, 35, 45; organizes government of Egypt, 36; founds Alexandria, 66
Alexandria, mixed population of, 10; one of only three or four Greek cities in Egypt, 48; focus of disturbance under later Ptolemies and under Romans, 61, 62; founding of, 66 ff.; population of, 69; constitution and senate of, 70; outbreaks of violence between Greeks and Jews, 71, 118; laws of, 71; hybrid position of, 71; literature of, 72; Jews of, 90; their quarter and synagogues, 92; citizenship at, under the Ptolemies, 94–5, and under the Romans, 96; second city of Roman Empire, 151
Alexandrines, 69 ff., 96
Allegorical Interpretation of Scripture, 129
Amasis, Saite (XXVIth Dynasty), King of Egypt, 6, 24, 25, 28, 29, 31
Amenhotep II, 81
Amenhotep III, 80, 86
America, effect of discovery of, 8; result of Spanish Conquest on native population of Central and South America, 52–3
Ammon (Amun), 14, 27, 35, 48
Amorites, 74
Amphicytonic Council, 7, 11
Anaxagoras, 26
Antinoopolis, 62, 146, 150
Antioch, 99, 102, 111, 156
Antiochus III, King of Syria, 58

Antiochus IV (Epiphanes), 115, 124, 157, 164
Antipater, 153
Anti-Semitism, Introd.; 91, 113 ff.; in literature, 115 ff.; 117, 156 ff., 164
Apion, 116, 119, 132, 163 ff.
Apocolocyntosis, 142–3
Apollonius Molon, 116
Apries (Hophra), 23
Arab Conquest of Egypt, effects of, 53, 56, 60, 65
Aramaic, 89, 91, 125, 126
Arameans, 76
Archelaus, ethnarch of Judea, 154
Archelaus, King of Macedon, 6
Argos, 3, 7
Aristobulus, 153
Aristotle, 2, 9
Arrian, 14
Aryans, Introd.
Assembly (Ecclesia), 71, 94, 102
Assimilation, 52 ff., 55, 60
Assyrians, 20, 86
Athenians, 30
Athens, 7, 11, 16
Augustus, 97, 100, 101, 116–18, 140, 150–4, 157, 161
Aurelius Marcus, 17, 149
Avillius Flaccus, 101, 118, 119

Babylon, 23, 86
Bar Kochba, 115
Barbarians, 1, 2, 9, 144
Bell, H. I., 65, 68, 100, 102, 105, 107–8, 117, 120, 122, 148
Bevan, E., 52, 97, 125, 127
Bickerman, E., 149, 150
Breasted, J. H., 33
Britons, 143, 144
Brotherhood of Man, 10, 16
Bury, J. B., 7

Caesar, Julius, 14, 99, 115, 140–1, 152, 153
Caiger, 82
Caligula (see Gaius).
Cambyses, 29
Canaanites, 74, 80, 86
Caracalla, 17, 64, 146, 147
Caria, 36
Carians, 23, 28
Cary, 147
Cassius, 153
Chapot, 152
Chora, 47 ff., 146

PRINTED IN GREAT BRITAIN BY RICHARD CLAY AND COMPANY, LTD.,
BUNGAY, SUFFOLK.